FORMING THE PATHFINDERS

THE CAREER OF AIR VICE-MARSHAL SYDNEY BUFTON

HUGH MELINSKY

The History Press

Never, never, never believe any war will be smooth and easy, or that anyone who embarks on that strange voyage can measure the tides and hurricanes he will encounter. The statesman who yields to war fever must realise that, once the signal is given, he is no longer the master of policy but the slave of unforeseeable and uncontrollable events. Antiquated war officers, weak, incompetent or arrogant commanders, untrustworthy allies, hostile neutrals, malignant fortune, ugly surprises, awful miscalculations – all take their seat at the Council Board on the morrow of a declaration of war.

Attributed to Winston Churchill

Sydney Bufton. (Dr Downer)

Cover captions
Front: A post-war image of Bufton beside a Lincoln bomber.
Back: Bufton being awarded the Commander Legion of Merit on behalf of the President of the USA. (Dr Downer)

First published 2010

The History Press
The Mill, Brimscombe Port
Stroud, Gloucestershire, GL5 2QG
www.thehistorypress.co.uk

British Library Cataloguing in Publication Data.
A catalogue record for this book is available from the British Library.

ISBN 978 0 7524 5453 5
Typesetting and origination by The History Press
Printed in Great Britain

Contents

PREFACE

A word of explanation is perhaps due about this biography, having been written by one who has not served in the RAF – though it was not for want of trying. While still at school in 1942, the author of this book was interviewed by a selection board consisting of one fairly senior RAF officer and was recommended for aircrew duties (as a pilot). Being underage for conscription, he went up to Cambridge for a year and was there diverted into learning Japanese due to a desperate shortage of translators in the Far East. So it was that he found himself in Australia in early 1944 in the British Army; attached to the Australian Army; detached to the Royal Australian Air Force (to a Wireless Unit); under the operational command of a captain in the Royal Navy; in a unit commanded by an American General. His task was the decoding and translating of messages intercepted from Japanese naval aircraft. So his interest in the air war was rewarded in an unexpected fashion. That interest has continued to the present.

The suggestion of writing the life and work of Air Vice-Marshal Bufton came from Anthony Furse, who had recently published his life of Air Chief Marshal Sir Wilfrid Freeman, one of the most important officers in the history of the RAF. He had hoped to write a comparable work on Bufton, but was exhausted, and suggested that the present author take over the task. He has given him very generous help.

The work has been made easier by a full collection of Bufton's papers preserved at the Churchill Archives at Churchill College, Cambridge, and the archivists there have given the author every consideration in his use of them, and in his use of the library attached. Much use has also been made of the National Archives at Kew (formerly the Public Record Office) and the author is happy to record his gratitude to the staff there for helping him find his way around their labyrinth. Another useful source of information has been the library of the RAF Museum at Hendon.

A more personal contribution has come from Bufton's daughter, Dr Carol Downer, who holds a large collection of his private letters and photographs and has graciously made them available. The author is happy to record his appreciation for the time and effort she has given to him.

Special thanks are due to Mrs Marilyn Evans who, in the midst of a busy working life, found the time, and had the patience, to decipher the author's handwriting and transfer it immaculately to the computer. She also spotted some mistakes, as, for example, mention of the birth of Bufton's first daughter, though there had been no record of his marriage!

I am happy to acknowledge copyright permission from the following for many photographs: *Aeroplane* and *Air Britain*; Mr E. Creek;the Archive of Wuppertal, Germany; the Imperial War Museum's Photo Archive; and The Random House Group Ltd for the quotation from *Portal of Hungerford* by Denis Richards published by William Heinemann. While efforts have been made to trace all permissions relevant to the book, unreserved apologies are offered to anyone who may have been inadvertently omitted.

The reader may wonder at the general lack of rank given to the officers who figure in the narrative. This implies no disrespect, but is done simply to avoid tedious repetition. Where the rank is important, it is given.

CHAPTER 1

Early Years

O f the writing of many books extolling the gallantry of RAF aircrews there is no end, and rightly so, but fewer have appeared praising the work of staff officers, much of it done behind unromantic desks. It has often been maligned, yet without it no war could be waged. These officers had their battles to fight too, the outcomes of which were just as important as that of the bravest bombing raid.

One such was Sydney Bufton who served from 1941 to 1945 as Deputy Director and then Director of Bomber Operations in the Air Ministry. He was a keen pilot who loved flying and was awarded the Distinguished Flying Cross for bravery in a series of bombing raids; he was also a first-rate squadron commander who reckoned that to be the best job of all. So when he was posted to the Air Ministry at the age of thirty-three, he brought with him a gust of fresh operational air which enabled him to speak and write with authority, and his decisions affected the lives of many airmen.

Buf, as he was universally known, was a Welshman, and a Presbyterian one at that, who entered the world on 12 January 1908, a world that was noticeably different in many ways from that of the previous century. A little more than four years before, on 17 December 1903, the Wright brothers in America had made the first controlled aeroplane flight, and in the year after Buf's birth, Henri Farman in France won a contest to fly a kilometre round a closed circuit. When Buf was eighteen months old, on 25 July 1909, Louis Blériot flew in his rickety monoplane from a field near Calais to a slope near Dover. Meanwhile, in Germany, Count Ferdinand Zeppelin had been making strides in airship design, which the Admiralty in this country took seriously. In 1912 the Royal Flying Corps was established, consisting of a naval and a military wing, but inter-service rivalry did not allow this partnership to continue, despite the efforts of the then First Sea Lord, Mr Winston Churchill. A month before the war broke out, General Haig pronounced to a military gathering:

I hope none of you gentlemen is so foolish as to think that aeroplanes will be able to be usefully employed for reconnaissance purposes in the air. There is only one way for a Commander to get information by reconnaissance, and that is by the use of cavalry.

When Britain's 'contemptible little army' landed in France in August 1914 it was accompanied by an equally contemptible little air force, amounting to four squadrons with sixty-three aircraft, leaving behind a motley collection of machines clearly incapable of home defence. The anti-aircraft defences for London amounted to twelve three-inch guns and some converted pom-poms. 1915 was the year of the Zeppelin, much vaunted by the Germans, and on the night of 31 May, LZ38 reached

London and scattered thirty explosive and ninety incendiary bombs from Stepney to Leytonstone, killing seven people. The first British victory came on the night of 6 June when Flight Sub-Lieutenant R. Warneford, RN, became the first pilot to shoot down an enemy airship.

Airships proving too vulnerable, the Germans turned their attention to long-range aeroplanes, and the bomber that won the contract was the huge AEG Gotha, with its Mark IV version being ready by February 1917. On 25 May twenty-three Gotha IVs, fully laden, took off from their Belgium base and flew in formation towards London. They flew over Canvey Island and Tilbury, but London was blanketed by heavy cloud. The formation passed over Ashford, Lympne and Hythe towards Folkestone and here they released most of their bombs, killing more than seventy people, mostly civilians. One Gotha was shot down over the Channel.

On 13 June the Germans achieved their objective, 'fortress London'. Bombs fell on Fenchurch Street and Liverpool Street stations, on the Dockland, on Limehouse and Poplar, including a direct hit on a school which killed eighteen children. The final casualty list numbered 170 dead and 432 wounded.

All this was happening a long way from Llandrindod Wells in the county of Radnorshire in central Wales, where Sydney started his education at the town's primary school and went on to Dean Close School at Cheltenham from 1922 to 1926. During the war years, when he was between six and ten, he could hardly have missed the news of this 'blitz' that had shocked the whole country. When he had finished his secondary education the school suggested a career in the Royal Navy, but Buf rejected this idea because it would restrict the sports activities – soccer, swimming and hockey – which he greatly enjoyed. He also declined the army because he disliked its serge uniform, high collars and puttees. Eventually his father organised a high-powered conference with the Chief Constable, the Chairman of the County Education Committee – a post that his father had held – and his former headmaster. Buf had already shown an interest in radio, even constructing a one-valve set which could receive an American station in Boston, and so the final selection came down to either Marconi or Vickers for an engineering course. In 1926 he was selected to be an engineering pupil at Vickers and an evening student at Erith Technical College, where he passed his intermediate BSc in June 1927.

While he was home on holiday a friend suggested the Royal Air Force, pointing out that, with his qualifications, selection would be almost certain. Buf applied, was accepted, and was appointed on 16 December 1927 for a Short Service Commission as a Pilot Officer on probation in the General Duties (that is to say flying) Branch. His first training was a fortnight's square-bashing at the Uxbridge Depot, though he did have the services of a batman to clean his kit and tidy his room. He was nineteen. This over, he embarked at Liverpool with the other Pilot Officers and ten airmen for pilot training in Egypt at No. 3 Flying Training School at Abu Sueir.

This Training School is a saga in itself. It was the creation of one man, Lieutenant Colonel, acting Brigadier W.G.H. Salmond (later Air Chief Marshal) who moulded the shape of the Air Service in the Middle East during the First World War. He wrote a letter to his wife on 17 July 1916:

The school I have made at Aboukir and the Aircraft Depot is a regular city, all to my design. I have only to say, and it is done. Whereas in May there was nothing but a blank space, it now has buildings, office quarters, workshops, power stations, enormous sheds, electric light plant, railway sidings, men's barracks, bomb stores, petrol stores all mostly erected. Roads all over the place, just where I want them, altogether now when I go to see it, it is wonderful. I shall never get the chance again. I have just seen one of my squadrons off. The Australian Squadron is trained and is now doing its work. On 23 April they arrived with just 200 men and no stores, training, aeroplanes or transport. They have all been trained out here – and are jolly good.

This school remained active until after the Second World War. The main argument in favour of a training base in Egypt was the weather, particularly in the early morning. Unlike England, where days and weeks could go by with impossible weather for novice pilots, at Abu Sueir flying almost every day was possible. The main bugbear was the dust storm that obliterated everything, but on most days flying could start at six in the morning, with much of it completed before breakfast. The rest of the morning was devoted to lectures and the afternoon to sports and the odd siesta.

Buf's first flight was on 23 January 1928 as a passenger in a DH 9A on a 'reconnaissance' to Ismailia, followed two days later by a similar trip to Cairo. On 30 January he flew dual in an Avro 504K, a gallant veteran biplane from the First World War which, together with its later variant 504N, was remembered with affection by most pilots who learned to fly before 1933. 6 March was the great day when he first flew solo, and soon he was doing loops, half-rolls, stall turns and sideslips. In June he progressed to the Ninak (DH 9A), a famous wartime bomber which continued in service throughout the 1920s.

It did not take Buf long to master this, and on 26 July he flew his first solo in this machine. In September he did two triangular cross-country flights, and on 1 October he flew to Heliopolis in fifty minutes, and back in sixty-five. In the same month he took his first passenger, dropped his first 112lb practise bombs, and suffered a minor landing collision, though this did not stop his Commanding Officer grading his proficiency 'Above Average'. He completed his course in December.

In a leave period in May he went on holiday to Cyprus with a companion, Maurice Carroll, known as 'Maori', doubtless because he was a New Zealander. They spent a 'disappointing weekend' in Alexandria, swam at Port Said, arrived at Limasol on the south coast of Cyprus, and travelled the next day to Kyrenia, a small port

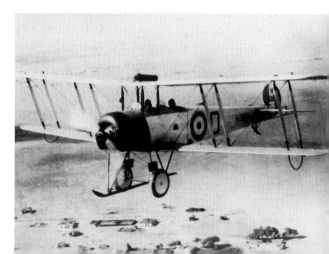

Avro 504k of the Flying Training School. These were mainly Great War survivors. (Dr Downer)

A Westland Wapiti of 55 Squadron at Hinaidi. (Air Britain)

A Rangoon of 203 Squadron at Basra. (Air Britain)

on the north coast, where they booked into the Sea View Hotel at seven shillings a day full board. They swam, sunbathed and explored the local sights, the Crusader Castle, the ruins of St Hilarion Castle, and Bellapaix Abbey, but this was not enough. Some forty miles north they saw in hazy outline the mountains of Turkey and decided to sail there. They booked an eighteen-foot felucca for a day's fishing and the owner promised to have it ready by 4.00a.m. the next morning.

They equipped themselves with a compass, two watches, swimming costumes, a torch, two cameras and pistols, just in case; also water, a box full of sandwiches and a basket of apricots to ward off scurvy. Up at 2.30a.m., they stowed their baggage and set off. With a gentle offshore breeze filling their triangular sail they left the small harbour. They calculated that at five knots they should reach the Turkish coast at about midday, but by 5.00p.m., after a day of fluctuating breezes, the coast of Cyprus still appeared closer than that of Turkey. The sun sank in a mixture of red, gold and violet glory but they continued northward, guided by Polaris. At last they came close enough to the rugged coast to see a light, but this moved with them and they wondered whether it belonged to coastguards watching their course or a band of cut-throat brigands about whom they had been warned. So, at about 4.00a.m., they turned south and arrived back in Kyrenia shortly before midnight. They were greeted with a beaming smile by the boat owner, who was duly compensated for his anxiety.

Left: Pyramids. (Dr Downer)

Opposite: Well, well! A Siskin come to grief at the Central Flying School. (Dr Downer)

Most of the newly qualified pilots were posted to squadrons in the Middle East, but Buf put in a special application for a posting to England so that he could complete his degree. The Personnel Department clearly thought that this would be of benefit to the Royal Air Force, and in December 1928 he joined No.100 Bomber Squadron at Bicester, some twelve miles north of Oxford. It was equipped with the Hawker Horsley, a clumsy looking biplane which was first built of wood throughout, then of metal and wood and finally all of metal. Its purpose was day bombing, carrying up to 1,500lb, or with the later models, a single eighteen-inch torpedo, with a maximum speed of 126mph, one of four such regular squadrons.

For the first six months, Buf was busy (when the weather permitted) with cross-country flights using photography, radio communication with bases and other aircraft, bombing practice on ranges and rear-gun and front-gun exercises. Again his proficiency was rated 'Above Average'. He moved on to formation bombing, affiliation with fighter squadrons (whose aircraft were about 30mph faster than his), exercises with the Observer Corps, further radio practice, and mock forced landings. In November 1929 he took part in a formation flight for the benefit of a photographer from *The Aeroplane*. Little could he have imagined that in fifteen years' time he would be directing the biggest fleet of night bombers that the world had ever seen – or would ever see again.

Clearly the authorities had an eye on Buf with his consistent rating of 'Above Average', and in May 1930 he was posted to the Central Flying School for the 32nd Flying Instructors Course, of nine weeks' duration at Wittering, three miles south of Stamford. Here he met the Avro Lynx, which was in fact the faithful old 504 with a new engine, the Brisfit or Bristol Fighter, a formidable machine which first went into action on the Western Front in April 1917 and remained the backbone of the Royal Air Force until the early 1930s, and the Armstrong Whitworth Siskin III, a fighter, both single and two-seat, with a top speed of 134mph. Life here was not only a succession of circuits and bumps, and in July he flew to Northolt to take part in the Royal Air Force Athletics Championships. There is no record of first prizes there, but the same month he won the Clarkson Trophy Cup for aerobatics. Little wonder that his proficiency was graded 'Above Average'.

In August 1930 he was posted as an instructor to No.5 Flying Training School and the following January, as a Flying Officer, he took charge of No.8 Flight. Again his proficiency was recorded as 'Exceptional', and he was chosen to take part in the Hendon Air Display that summer. He worked hard; during October he put in forty-nine hours of flying and on one day he was airborne ten times giving instruction on the Bristol Fighter. In July 1931 he was rated an 'Exceptional' pilot and an 'A1' instructor.

Even so, his future was by no means assured. He held only a Short Service Commission, which meant five years' service and then four years on the Reserve List, and only fifty per cent of such officers were appointed as regulars. Buf began looking elsewhere and sounded out three aeronautical firms in Canada, but their response was not encouraging. The outlook in England was no better, and so he concluded that the best path to a permanent commission was to gain a specialist qualification. To that end he applied and was accepted for a two-year course in aeronautical engineering at the Home Aircraft Depot at Harlow, Bedfordshire. Another student there at the same time, though one year ahead, was Frank Whittle, who was experimenting on his new invention, the turbo-jet, on which he had written a thesis, and he was persuaded to take out a patent. Nobody was interested and Whittle almost forgot about it, but a former Cranwell friend put him in touch with a prominent industrialist, one J.C.B. Tingling, and together they formed a company called Power Jets on £2,000. After 1937 the Air Ministry began to take an interest and dribbled in a little money at the instigation of Wilfrid Freeman. In Germany, however, his patent had been noticed and, by 1935, a young scientist, Hans-Joachim Pabst von Ohain, had constructed a turbo-jet, and was referred to Prof. Dr Ernst Heinkel who was impressed and placed the facilities of his company at von Ohain's disposal, omitting to inform the German Air Ministry. His first jet aeroplane flew on 24 August 1939, and by the end of 1940 more than 9,000 people were working on it, compared to about sixty in England. The consequences for the Royal Air Force were grave.

That, however, is to diverge. Buf was clearly doing well, and in September 1932, before he had even completed his course, he was appointed to a Permanent Commission as a Flying Officer; in April he was promoted to Flight Lieutenant. He finished in July 1933 with a final mark of eighty-two per cent, with distinctions in pure mathematics, applied mathematics, internal combustion engines, aeronautics, electricity and mechanical drawing. The final assessment on his certificate was 'Exceptionally capable both in practical and theoretical work'.

Life, however, was not all work, and Buf had a notable sporting record, particularly in hockey. He not only represented the Royal Air Force in this on many occasions up to 1937, but he also played for Wales in seven internationals between 1931 and 1937, against Scotland twice, Ireland three times and England twice. Even in the Middle East amid the heat and the sand he maintained his enthusiasm to keep fit.

In October 1933 Buf was posted as an engineering officer to the Aircraft Depot at Hinaidi in Iraq. He decided with a friend to proceed overland by car, and looked for a reliable second-hand one. Their first choice was a Buick, but none were available. The car dealer then suggested a Rolls-Royce Silver Ghost, in good condition and with only one owner, the Marquis of Exeter. The price? Eight pounds! After further investigation they found a passage for the car from Liverpool to Basra for fifteen pounds, where the car was unloaded and driven in state to Baghdad. Hinaidi was close by and on their arrival there they were immediately offered a hundred pounds for it, but they declined. It served them well for three years without any mechanical failures despite, on shooting expeditions, having to carry up to twenty-five occupants. One reason for choosing the Rolls was that the Royal Air Force armoured cars in Iraq were of the same make, and Buf reckoned that the supply of spare parts would be easier.

The Air Force station was just south of the capital on the banks of the Tigris, and its buildings were mainly relics of Turkish domination, built of *mutty*, the equivalent of wattle and daub. Rooms were ample in size, with fly screens and adequate fans for ventilation. Playing fields were provided, but only of rolled mud: grass was an English luxury. Operations were governed by the weather, for the average summer temperature was 42°C (108°F), occasionally reaching 53°C (128°F). So work began at 6.00a.m., with a break for breakfast, and finished at noon. Afternoons were given over to sleep and evenings allowed a game of tennis. Summer produced sandstorms that could rise to 8,000 feet, when prudent flyers landed as quickly as possible and picketed down their aircraft. Winters were short and mild, providing the best working environment. The rainy season from November to March quickly converted mud paths and roads into quagmires, and aerodrome runways soon became unserviceable with persistent haze limiting visibility. Flights over a generally featureless and poorly mapped terrain demanded care and precision in navigation. As at Henlow, Buf retained his flying skills, now mainly on that reliable old warhorse the Westland Wapiti. As an engineering officer he flew test flights, but also mail runs and local trips.

In July 1934 he visited England on leave, which was odd because he had only been in the Middle East for eight months. One day in August, he visited the Royal Air Force Club in London and was presented with a cable from Lady Lucy Joan Hoare, the wife of Sir Reginald Harvey Hoare, the British Minister in Teheran, Iran (not to be confused with Sir Samuel Hoare, the Secretary of State for Air). No doubt he had met her in the Middle East because she knew him well enough to ask if he would be prepared to fly a de Havilland Gipsy (Major) Moth from England to Teheran. Assuming his acceptance, she had also cabled de Havilland naming him as the pilot for the delivery flight. He replied immediately that he was keen to do so. Without delay he visited the de Havilland factory to examine the machine and discuss possible modifications. The endurance of a Moth was three hours at a cruising speed of 90mph, which dictated a flight of many short legs. An extra fuel tank appeared necessary, but nothing was available at the factory, so Buf re-planned his route via France, Italy, Sardinia and the North African coast. The Automobile Association provided maps

The Rolls-Royce Silver Ghost in Iraq. (Dr Downer)

and guides for the route, and the aviation department in Shell House provided a Shell Carnet, an authority Buf described as 'one of the world's most useful items possessing all the outstanding characteristics of Aladdin's lamp'.

On returning to the Club, he was surprised and pleased to meet a pilot named Larking from No.55 Squadron, also based at Hinaidi, who was similarly enjoying a spell of home leave. He was about to depart for the South of France to continue his leave before returning to his unit at Hinaidi, when Buf suggested that he could meet him at Cannes whence they could continue the delivery flight together, a plan that met with an immediate welcome. On 19 August de Havilland informed him that the aeroplane was ready and so he travelled to Hatfield the next day accompanied by his sister, Mary, who was hoping to make her first flight. In fact the plane was not ready and the weather deteriorated. They were able to start the next day, but only after a further delay, and so they decided to drop Mary at Lympne and Buf would fly on to Paris that evening. It had been a very bumpy flight, but Mary put on a brave face and stoutly maintained that she had enjoyed the experience.

Buf set off again over a lone stretch of water in a new machine with an unproved engine in a strong wind. Once over the Channel his confidence increased, though he wondered if he would reach Le Bourget before nightfall. He did, and finally found the floodlights which marked the landing area. He identified himself with his navigation lights and proceeded to carry out his first night landing, which he completed successfully. It was only after he had taxied onto the tarmac that he realised it was still twilight: he had been wearing his tinted goggles! The flight to Cannes was uneventful, and here he met up with Larking. They both found it very hard to leave the South of France, but they tore themselves away on 24 August, heading for Pisa.

The first part of this leg along the coastline in warm sunlight provided lovely scenery for the tourist, but was less appealing to the airman as there was absolutely no place for an emergency landing. In that event, they decided that they would put down in the sea and try to swim ashore. Fortunately, this was not necessary. With themselves and the Moth refuelled they set off for Rome, making Littoria airport in two hours. Here they discovered that the refuelling point was up a large ramp on top of the main hangar. For aircraft with wheel brakes this would provide no difficulty, but their Moth had no such refinements. On the way down, the attendants let go halfway and the plane made an unduly speedy descent.

From here they travelled on to Naples, where they spent the night and sampled the wine, continuing down the length of Italy via Catania to Palermo in Sicily. Since the next leg to Tunis in North Africa involved a sea crossing of 100 miles, they gave the Moth a careful check and found trouble with one magneto. They thought they had put this right, but before leaving the coast of Sicily they decided to carry out a further check: the port magneto was fine, but with the starboard one the engine cut dead, and so it was back to Palermo for further adjustments. They set off again and Buf found consolation in reciting poetry and singing to himself. Eventually the coast of Africa appeared in a hazy blur and they landed at Tunis after a flight of three hours and five minutes – with very little petrol left.

The next day they made a leisurely flight along the coast to Idris airport, some eleven miles south of Tripoli, which later changed its name to Castel Benito (as a due

Lady Hoare and the Moth. (Dr Downer)

acknowledgement to Signor Mussolini). They spent a comfortable night in a Tripoli hotel and prepared for a long day, 28 August, flying to Tobruk via Sirte, El Agheila and Benghazi, names to become familiar from the campaigns in the Western Desert ten years later. They were airborne for over nine hours, but the next day was easier with just five hours to reach Almaza airport at Cairo, with a stop at Mersa Matruh.

It was early to bed that night, setting off before dawn for Gaza the next morning, following the coastal railway. A hurried breakfast and they were off again to Amman. The next refuelling point was Rutbah, a lone fort 270 miles out in the empty Saudi Arabian desert. Fortunately, an oil pipeline with a road next to it ran directly to Rutbah, and refuelling there presented no problems. The next stage to Baghdad was over familiar territory, and after nearly nine and a half hours' flying time, they arrived. They were now only 550 miles from their destination, but owing to their hurried departure from England they had omitted to obtain permission to fly over Persia (now Iran). The next day, Friday, was the Muslim day of rest and the authorities assured the restless couple that all would be ready by Sunday.

As many documents had to be signed and photographs attached, it was just after noon before they were in the air and so there was no hope of making Teheran that day. They refuelled at Kermanshah, a city in the mountains 4,500 feet above sea level, and struggled for height to take-off. They planned to land and spend the night at some reasonably flat spot beyond the ranges around Hamadan. They had forgotten to re-set their watches and suddenly realised that sunset would be at 6.00a.m. and not 6.30a.m., and so an early landing was necessary. They spotted a village with apparently suitable flat ground nearby, put down, and awaited developments. A large crowd quickly gathered, but their attempts at conversational Arabic to find the name of the place did not succeed. Eventually sign language revealed the name as Saveh, and they found it on the map. Shortly afterwards uniformed officials arrived, and in a mixture of Arabic, French and English the situation was explained to everyone's satisfaction, and the flyers were invited to the police house to enjoy its hospitality. The price for this was that the next morning the Moth had to be inspected by the wives of the police chief and a demonstration given of take-off and landing. With handshakes all round and the gift of some tasty melons they were away, and ninety minutes later arrived at Teheran where they were met by Lady Hoare and the de Havilland area representative. The delivery was accomplished.

In 1936, Lady Hoare wrote a long article for *The Aeroplane* about her flying experiences in Iran. She paid a handsome tribute to Buf and Larking for the difficulties they had to overcome on the delivery of the first flight and admitted her total unawareness of the problems involved. She had no idea that flying was 'much more complicated than having a Magic Carpet to transport one at any time to any place'.

But that was not the end of Buf's association with Lady Hoare. His logbook records that he was flying her from 3–7 September 1934, and again on the 20 October in a Moth with the comment 'Turns, circuit and landings', which looks remarkably like instruction for a budding aviatrix. There were further entries with her for 14 and 15 November.

Life had other diversions. In January 1935 he was engaged on mail-carrying duties in a Wapiti. A couple of months later (on 1 April) he had his first flight in a flying boat, the Short *Rangoon*, a large three-engined biplane of all-metal structure, with which No.203 Squadron at Basra was equipped. He was clearly intrigued with this because he immediately applied to join a flying boat pilot's course due to start at Calshot, on Southampton Water, in January 1936. However, he was keen to return to a flying post. The next month, his logbook recorded 'Proficiency – Above Average'.

In June 1935 he was approached by the Iraq Petroleum Company to return a de Havilland Dragon, a small twin-engined airliner which they had chartered, to its parent company at Heston in England. He applied for 28 days' annual leave to complete the journey and, approval granted, he made the flight in July, following in reverse his earlier journey. It was uneventful and, by the second week of August, he was back at Hinaidi.

The next year he continued to fly a great variety of aircraft: Wapitis (in January he clocked up 149 hours on those), Moths, Vincents, Valentias, Demons and Hardys. The Vickers Valentia was a mighty twin-engined bomber-transport with a wingspan of eighty-seven feet, and No.70 Squadron had those at Hinaidi. It looks as if Buf borrowed one in March to take his hockey team on a trip to Heliopolis and other bases.

This Middle East tour of duty ended for Buf in July 1936 and he returned home for an extended period of leave. His application for a period with flying boats was not successful and he found himself posted to the Air Ministry Staff in the Directorate of Training.

CHAPTER 2

Directing Training

It was a vital period for the Royal Air Force. At last the country had woken up to the threat of the German Air Force. In 1935 in a speech in the House of Commons, Mr Churchill had warned, 'there is no doubt that the Germans are superior to us in the air at the present time and it is my belief that by the end of the year, unless their rate of construction is arrested by some agreement, they will be possibly three or even four times our strength'. He was right, and there was no international agreement. Between 1934 and 1939, Royal Air Force personnel increased from 31,000 officers and men to some 118,000 with reserves of 45,000. Between 1935 and 1938, the intake of pilots totalled some 4,500. This presented formidable problems for training, and Air Commodore Tedder, then the Director, decided that elementary training would be done at civilian flying schools, to the horror of some traditionalists on the Air Staff. By the time Tedder left that post in 1936 there were eleven civilian training schools in operation. Similar provision was made for other branches of the Service, such as Signals, Equipment and Engineering – a heavy burden for the newly constituted Training Command.

Bufton was concerned with the practicalities of training, for the Air Ministry paid a fee to the school for each pilot who graduated successfully, and with matters like the acquisition of accommodation in town centres. He sometimes flew on visits, keeping his hand in on nothing more exciting than Tiger Moths, Harts and Audaxes. On 18 December 1936 he flew in a Hart from Hendon to Perth (with stops) in three hours. His second year was spent mainly overseeing the establishment of training schools for wireless operators and technicians, for which his own engineering qualifications made him entirely suitable. In 1937 he was promoted to Squadron Leader.

He also renewed his association with Lady Hoare, taking her in October 1936 on a lightning week's European tour (in the same plane that he had helped to deliver to her in Teheran) including Brussels, Frankfurt, Nuremberg, Lenz, Vienna, Budapest, Belgrade and Bucharest. They cannot have had much time for sightseeing. He recorded that for two sessions they flew dual, so clearly his protégée was making progress. He flew again with her in November 1938.

In January 1939, he was posted to a course at the Royal Air Force Staff College at Andover, one of Trenchard's masterly foundations. It was designed to shape the senior operational commanders of the future, and its first intake in 1922 included Sholto Douglas, Keith Park and Charles Portal. The syllabus covered the principles of war, imperial strategy, the tactics and organisation of air, ground and naval forces, intelligence, supply and communications, domestic and foreign policy and the relationship of economics, commerce and science to Royal Air Force affairs, together with basic staff duties including letter and report writing and organising formal receptions.

By way of preparation for this course, Buf was attached for a fortnight each to two operational squadrons, one bomber and one fighter, since it was over ten years since he had flown operational aircraft. The first was No.110 Bomber Squadron equipped with Bristol Blenheim I (the short-nosed one), which had come into service in 1937, marking a tremendous advance on the Hind biplane. It was a twin-engined mid-wing monoplane, and was actually a development of the 'Britain First' civil plane presented to the nation by Lord Rothermore the previous year. With a crew of three, it had a top speed of 260mph, cruised at 200mph, with a range of 920 miles and a bomb load of 1,000lb. This compared with the biplane Hind's 430 miles, a top speed of 186mph and a bomb load of 500lb. Buf first flew it dual before taking it over and practising landings.

His second attachment was even more exciting: to No.19 Fighter Squadron, the first squadron to be equipped with the new eight-gun Supermarine Spitfire powered by the Rolls-Royce Merlin engine of undying fame. It had a maximum speed of 355mph and a range of 500 miles, compared with the biplane Gloster Gladiator with four guns, which came into service in 1937 with a top speed of 253mph and a cruising speed of 210mph. After being taken through the cockpit drill and warned of the enormous torque provided by the Merlin engine, he took off and flew it successfully. Over the

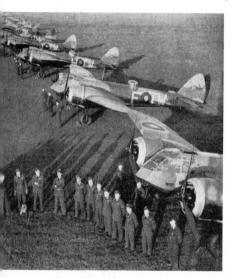

three days he flew five times, an exhilarating experience. He was initiated into the oxygen mask for battle climbs and the use of radiotelephony for position finding and homing, not to mention the retractable undercarriage. At the Staff College he had to revert to Hinds, Harts, Magisters, and their rather rare cousin, the Miles Mentor.

During the summer vacation, all students were required to do an attachment to one of the other Services, and Buf and a friend opted for submarines. They joined the submarine depot ship HMS *Forth* at Dartmouth and sailed with her to Rosyth. This shakedown cruise ended spectacularly when the vessel thumped the jetty and sent some of the timbers flying. The next week provided great enjoyment on a small 'S'-class submarine with what they described as a marvellous crew who made them feel very much at home.

Having successfully completed the course, Buf graduated from the College – just in time for the Second World War. He was thirty-one and a Staff Officer.

Bleinheims and crews of 90 Squadron at Bicester, November 1938, and Spitfires of 19 Squadron at Duxford in 1938 (with wooden propellers). (*Aeroplane*)

CHAPTER 3

War in France

On 1 September 1939, Hitler invaded Poland and full mobilisation was proclaimed in Britain. In April 1940 Germany overran Norway, and the next month the country was ready to launch her *blitzkrieg* through neutral Holland, Belgium and Luxembourg on the way to France. The French had put their trust in a massive fortification line along the frontier from Switzerland to the Ardennes, the Maginot Line, envisaging a largely static war. That left a suitable gap to the northwest, blocked by Holland and Belgium. Staff conversations had been going on between Britain and France since March 1939, and detailed plans had been worked out to fill this gap with thirty-three French Divisions, seventeen Belgian Divisions and the nine Divisions of the British Expeditionary Force. Facing them were fifty-five German Divisions, of which ten were Panzer Divisions armed with heavy, fast and well-armed tanks. We British could not produce one tank division. The Dutch and Belgians, anxious to protect their neutrality, would not join in with staff talks before the war. Once the war began on 10 May they fought gallantly, but the Germans swept through and drove the last nail into their coffin by launching some forty *Stuka* dive-bombers on to Rotterdam, destroying 20,000 buildings and killing nearly 1,000 of its inhabitants.

The other gap was through the forests of the Ardennes, which the French held to be impenetrable by armoured vehicles. The Germans drove their way through and then swept westwards to meet up with the other thrust and attempt to flush their enemies into the Channel.

German children were brought up to hate. The writing on the wall reads: 'All calamities come from the Jews.' (Stadtarchiv Wuppertal)

The RAF contribution was also divided into two forces: in the north-west was the RAF component of the Expeditionary Force, with five squadrons of Lysanders for tactical reconnaissance, four Blenheim squadrons for longer-distance reconnaissance as far as the Rhine, and four (later six) Hurricane squadrons for protecting troops, bases and other aircraft. To the south-east, centred on Rheims and right opposite Sedan on the River Meuse, was the Advanced Air Striking Force, to serve the needs of the whole Allied Front with ten squadrons of Blenheims and Battles and two (later four) squadrons of Hurricanes to support the bombers and defend their bases. Their commanders, however, had great doubts about their ability to carry out tactical bombing against advancing columns well supported by anti-aircraft guns and a large fighter force. A sharp lesson had been learned early in the war when five Battles had been sent on a reconnaissance some twenty miles over the Franco-German border, four of which were shot down by Me 109s and the fifth damaged beyond repair.

Nevertheless, Battles were sent into action on 10 May against well-armed German columns and, out of thirty-two, thirteen were destroyed and the rest damaged. The next day, eight Battles were ordered to make a low-level attack on a German column moving towards the Luxembourg border and one returned. On 14 May the whole strength of the Allies in France was hurled against the vital bridgehead at Sedan, and out of seventy-one RAF bombers, Battles and Blenheims, forty did not return. It was the highest rate of loss ever sustained by the RAF. M. Reynaud, the French Premier, phoned Mr Churchill in despar begging for ten more fighter squadrons. The Prime Minister put the matter to the War Cabinet and Dowding, head of Fighter Command, asked to be present at their meeting on 15 May. He maintained that the decisive struggle was not in France but in Britain, and while Fighter Command survived, Britain might also. He won over the meeting, though the decision was over-ruled by the War Cabinet the next day and four of the ten squadrons requested were sent.

Buf had gone out with the Advanced Air Striking Force (AASF) centred on Rheims. At first there were two headquarters, one for the AASF and one for the Air Component to the north-west, but these were amalgamated in January 1940 at Chauny under Barratt as Commander-in-Chief, at the Headquarters of British Air Forces in France. Its tasks were: to coordinate with the French Army and Air Force; to act as an information centre (the French gathering of intelligence was very sketchy); to organise cooperation exercises with the army; and to develop new aerodromes out of grassy fields. Much time and energy had to be given to 'domestic' matters as, for example, with a squadron moving to the Rheims area where only thirty-five airmen had been expected by the French authorities and 225 officers and airmen arrived. For accommodation two tents had been provided, of which one was occupied by the French Guard unit. There were no feeding arrangements, no slit trenches had been dug and the bomb dump was only partly constructed. Matters were not improved by the bitterly cold weather of that winter when most of the aircraft had to be serviced in snow and frost.

The staff had to arrange coordination not only with the French Army but also between the two RAF Headquarters, that of the Air Component of the Expeditionary Force in the north and that of the Advanced Air Striking Force in the south-east. During this 'quiet' period, cooperation exercises were also organised with the army.

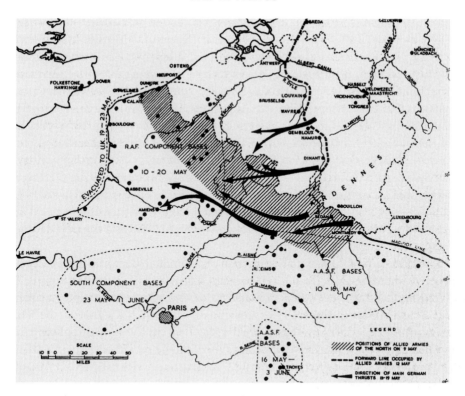

The German advance through France, May 1940.

As a result of the débacle that was to follow, in which all our forces had to abandon almost all of their equipment, very few records have survived. Once the real war had started Buf decided (against orders) to keep a personal diary, but he was careful not to make any detailed reference to the fighting taking place. On 10 May he was woken by the sound of French anti-aircraft guns and learned that Germany had invaded Holland, Belgium and Luxembourg. At 10.30a.m. the Commander-in-Chief, Air Marshal Barratt, arrived, followed by a long wait for information, including permission from General Gamelin to let loose his bombers against the advancing German columns. The French Generalissimo, however, was reluctant to start a 'bombing war' and so eventually Barratt took matters into his own hands and ordered Playfair, in Command in the north, to send out the first waves of Battles. Of the thirty-two despatched that day, thirteen were lost for negligible results.

The next day the French detected a southerly German advance towards the Luxembourg border and eight Battles were ordered to carry out a low-level attack on this column. One Battle returned. On 12 May, the Belgians appealed to the Allies for help against a column heading from Maastricht to Tongres, and volunteers were called for from No.12 Squadron to bomb the bridges over the Albert Canal. Six Battles set off for a low-level attack and all succumbed to heavy ground fire. Slight damage was done and Flying Officer Garland and his Sergeant Gray were posthumously awarded the Victoria Cross.

By the evening of 12 May, the Striking Force had been reduced from 135 serviceable bombers to seventy-two, and so on 13 May these were rested. The Germans used the opportunity to force a crossing of the River Meuse just north of Dinant, with the terrifying appearance of 200 Ju 87 dive-bombers which overwhelmed the French at the junction of their First and Ninth Armies, and so began the German sweep westwards to the sea. Before midnight, Barratt warned Playfair that the full strength of the Striking Force would be needed the next day, and also that he should prepare plans for retirement. Between 3.00p.m. and 4.00p.m. on 14 May, the entire force of the Battles and Blenheims was hurled against pontoon bridges and columns of troops at the Sedan bridgehead, but now the Me 109s were on guard. From the seventy-one bombers that took off, forty did not return. The Germans paused for a few hours and then set off on their 'joy-ride' westward through France to join up with the northern thrust at the Channel. Buf wrote that he was 'thrilled by the courage, audacity, and cheerful sacrifice of the RAF'.

By 14 May, Buf's office was at Chauny, with a large military camp nearby at Tergnier. This was bombed on the 12th with 400 soldiers killed. He was on duty all night of the 13/14th, and at dawn at the open window he saw the bombers come across the sky again. There was no anti-aircraft fire, no fighters. He heard the whine of bombs and saw them burst near Tergnier again. On 15 May he went to bed to the sound of the ammunition dump at Laon being blown up: the bombing raid occurred about 8.00p.m. and the detonations carried on until about 3.00a.m. the next morning.

Some extracts from his diary portray the scene:

At 11.30 p.m. I was ordered by B. who said we were moving at once ... All maps and equipment were rapidly taken from the Ops room and Intelligence Section ... All the work of the past nine months was undone ... The drive to Coulommiers was not very pleasant. After the heat and haste of packing it was warm to start with, but by 0430 jolly chilly. Passed lots of refugees on the way in all sorts of vans, wagons, on foot and on bicycles.

Near Meaux we came across tank traps – or rather obstructions – odd guns here and there and an occasional pill-box ... German tanks would have walked through it without batting an eyelid. We arrived at BAFF [British Air Forces in France HQ] at about 0645 hrs and found the organisation there pretty poor; it was a long time before the troops were settled in and one could go to the mess for a shave and breakfast. The watches were re-opened in BAFF Ops Room – the Commander-in-Chief and Group Captain were already installed on our arrival.

17 May 1940
In the morning left ... for a liaison visit to Zoan HQ at Chantilly ... found all our old friends. They were not very happy and the HQ was not very inspiring. Obtained targets for night attack ...

Situation seemed pretty black. Break-through between 7th Army and BEF, and enemy armoured vehicles pushing on towards Arras and Cambrai etc. Enemy dive-bombers were the basis of their success.

18 May
Left in the morning for AMLU to see suitability for alternative HQ ... Left after dinner at Café de la Rocher and arrived back at about 1.15 a.m. What a beautiful place!

19 May
Left for Zoan at 1900 with Group Captain Strafford to discuss move to new HQ with General d'Astier in Chantilly ... Then to Zoan. All lights out. General d'Astier not in ... operations unimpressive ... Dirty little map on table, couple of candles ... left quickly. Morane [a French fighter] in hedge in main road. Exciting journey back. Shot at by sentry. Bombing in Senlis – terrific shambles. Eventually arrived back 0115; then took over night duty.

20 May
Left for new HQ site at 1600 hours. Saw house burned out by Heinkel which crashed into it. Arrived at _____s at about 1740 ... Arranged layout of basement – started off signallers – got myself installed in Trianon – marvellous hotel ... Had a wonderful dinner and went to bed.

21 May
Got wood for partitions ... Gave lecture to the troops on security ... Made 'em suspicious. Shopped. Met woman who said 'RAF? Bien ça!' Dinner in hotel with the Baron and Baronne. They were most depressed. I tried to cheer them up.

22 May
News getting worse. Irritation at the French for doing nothing with their Army. Isolation of BEF. Why not a French counter-attack?

[Here a gap of five days.]

27 May
Coulommiers aerodrome bombed ... One bomb dead in the middle of the hangar. Hangar like a chicken going backwards upwind. Of our aircraft two Rapides and one Percival Gull written off by machine guns ... Curious thing was French knew at 1030 in the morning that an attack would be made at lunch time, but all the pilots went into town for lunch. They're not trying.

29 May
0300 in Ops Room. On duty. It's not a pretty picture. The news of the Belgian King's capitulation without warning to the Allies, 24 hours ago, shocked the world and treacherously betrayed the BEF and the French forces in the north ... now fighting for their lives ...

I feel this war will be won in the air. Our pilots are magnificent. We must build up our superiority, and bomb their war machine out of existence.

The big fear is that the French will capitulate. They've shown no guts or spirit yet. There seems to be no sign of it anywhere.

These are fateful days. The BEF is fighting its way to the sea, gradually contracting onto its position on the coast near and around Dunkirk. Three Panzer divisions are at present trying to cut them off ...

And so, should they capitulate, what of us? I am confident that we can fight our own battle – in the air! It will be a stand-up knocking match between us and the Huns.

Air War

First we must have control of the air – complete control ... Any major blow against the enemy air power would do two things. First, reduce the enemy's power of hitting us; second, increase our actual power of hitting him

First steps. Perfect RDF [radar] and observer systems; buy all American fighters; buy all American bombers available. All AA defences.

30 May

We are expecting an air attack on Coulommiers today. Don't know whether that means the aerodrome or the HQ. Have arranged for 73 Squadron to be available, as attack will, like the last one, probably be made at lunch time when the French pilots are having lunch in town.

Sunday pm, 2 June

By this time the evacuation of the BEF and the French and Belgian forces with them must be completed. What an epic! What a Combined operation! What a lesson!

[...]

Our raids on the Ruhr have done enormous damage and have lowered the moral of the people ... If we can go on and on now we may achieve our aim. If our attacks would only force them to retaliate – probably by day, then, we will have a chance to shoot them out of the sky.

I am attracted by the idea of air war. It's the same thing as sea-faring. An adventurous, hazardous, individual game, calling for resources, initiative and unwitnessed courage.

The time is coming when I must play a more active part in this air war.

3 June

Was getting up at lunch time, after a night on duty, when the first raid on Paris passed overhead at about 1315 hours ... The raid took about 10 minutes to pass; wave after wave of sections of three in line ahead ... about 18,000 feet. The strange thing was that there were no French fighters and no AA fire.

... the cool evening and the trees framed against the pale sky; and overhead the deep blue sky studded and palely lit with stars.

I thought of Ann and the poems we'd known and the foolishness we'd perpetrated. And then of a new [?] – the beautiful Sandra, deep blue eyes, and the kindest mouth I've ever seen. How I hated the thought of being killed before I had achieved.

9 June

Once more on the road. The Huns make a rapid advance over the Somme – Aisne position which from the beginning was obviously untenable ... We left at 0045 and re-opened the Operations at Olivet, Orleans, at 0430. Was most impressed with the lack of organisation at BAFF.

10 June

The Huns are on the Seine and are even crossing ... Decide to visit Paris ... Never have I seen such traffic ... It took four hours to reach Paris. There was a calm ... still the open cafés, still apparently hope. Around one unexploded bomb on the pavement was a ring of sandbags and a road sign 'Bombe, Danger du Mort'.

11–14 June

The Watches continue. The bridgeheads across the Seine increase ... Refugees continue to pour south ... At each stage the communication gets worse. The C-in-C wrestles with the telephone, bangs it on the table, bellows at the top of his voice in an endeavour to be heard at the other end ... For an air force in the field an efficient, all-embracing radio system would appear to be ideal – scrambled speech perhaps ... We relied almost entirely – or to a great extent – on the information brought by our special reconnaissance sorties. How right was Ugly when he refused to give them up. [Ugly was Barratt's nickname.]

14 June

At about 1800 hrs the order was given to move to the new location at Angers [some 100 miles] westwards towards our base. We arrived at about 0400 hours and went to the Château which the Polish Embassy was just vacating.

Got up about 0900 and managed to scrounge some tea, biscuits, bully, and a wash and a shave. Felt better. Strafford spoke to me on the steps at about 0800, and said we had to move on immediately to Nantes, that our role as operational HQ was now ended.

15 June

Moved off about 0830 through Angers and out on the road to Nantes, the RAF base ... By about midday the new HQ was functioning, allotting tasks to the fighter squadrons covering the evacuation and also to the bombers operating from England. The Battles had been told to land back in England on completion of their first sortie.

After lunch Strafford called me in to C-in-C's office and said I was to stay behind for a day or two to keep an eye on operations ... I didn't know the C-in-C was staying on. It was an honour in a way to be his sole Ops 1 ... parties being evacuated as rapidly as possible to Brest and St Nazaire.

17 June

Reconnaissance showed enemy west and south of Orleans. Decided to evacuate immediately. Main parties left by 1400. Great hush falls on camp. Fair amount of equipment was abandoned.

After lunch there was little else to do but arrange for the fighter cover for final stages of the embarkation. Transport to sail during night ... St Nazaire was to be closed at 0900 the next morning. Telephone exchanges were broken down from 1500.

Air transport was arranged for the ground parties of the remaining squadrons. Remaining staff of the C-in-C then made up air parties for return in Blenheims and DH 89 ...

We drove around the aerodrome – it was stiff with aircraft. The Huns had done a recce of it at midday. Why it wasn't bombed is difficult to imagine.

However, all went well and at 1750 we took off [in a Blenheim]. We flew north across the Brest peninsula to Jersey, then to Poole, and finally landed at Gatwick at 2000 hours.

We were immediately impressed with the security of our island – calmness, the absence of the [?] of war – and the tidiness. The air felt fresher ... We went up to London and I to the Club.

[...]

The second phase of the war had ended; what the next would be, what the future would mean and hold we could only conjecture. For the present we were tired, and only too pleased to enjoy the luxuries of a still unaltered civilization.

Invasion is upon us. Will enough be done this time?

[...]

I have succeeded at last in getting a flying job. It was difficult to get, and I could easily have got myself a Staff job or an engineering one.

However I have basked so long in the glory earned by the pilots and crews of the RAF – I must earn it for myself. I have lived through these years in the glamour of the service – the reputation for daring and devilry; I have been paid by the nation through all these years and I owe the nation all I can give.

Apart from these considerations I have ability, judgement. I have captained the RAF hockey team – I feel that I could lead a Squadron; and I hope to lead it and inspire it.

Having weighed everything, and taken the decision my mind is at rest. I am happy and look forward to the adventures with anticipation.

Here is the record of a highly intelligent and capable staff officer who would rather have been flying. He had considerable self-knowledge and was certainly sensitive to the finer things of life. His experience had inspired him in how not to wage an air war, though the Allied situation was very different from the German. During the Battle for France the RAF had lost on its bomber side 142 Blenheims, 153 Battles, twenty-four Wellingtons, twenty-four Whitleys and twenty-eight Hampdens, with 526 aircrew killed and a further 201 taken prisoner. In addition, we had expended 432 precious Hurricanes and Spitfires. The Luftwaffe paid heavily for its success, with the loss of 1,284 aircraft.

CHAPTER 4

Flying Again

After a well-earned period of leave Buf had got himself posted to Command No.10 Bomber Squadron at Leeming in Yorkshire. This squadron had a history going back to the beginning of 1915 for army cooperation and reconnaissance duties on the Western Front. In September 1918 it was dropping baskets of pigeons to advanced parties of infantry so that they could report progress of their movement to headquarters.

After disbandment in 1919, No.10 Squadron was re-formed as a heavy-bomber unit in 1928 and flew a variety of mighty twin-engined biplanes, Hyderabads, Hinaidis and Heyfords until March 1937 when Armstrong Whitworth Whitleys arrived, the first 'heavy' monoplanes. The Mark V version came into service in 1939, with the much more powerful Merlin X engines in place of the radial Tigers, providing a top speed of 222mph at 17,000 feet, and a range of 1,650 miles with 4,500lb of bombs. No.10 made the RAF's first visit to Berlin on the night of 1 October 1939 in order to drop not bombs but leaflets.

Buf had never flown anything heavier than a Blenheim and so he paid two swift visits to Operational Training Units to get acclimatised. The first was a week at Kinloss in Scotland, which culminated in a forced landing near Fort Augustus, occasioned by the loss of an aerial through lightning, slight icing and the failure of the starboard engine. Fortunately there was no damage. The second was a fortnight at Abingdon, learning to fly the Whitley for war purposes, during which he had twenty-four hours' day-flying experience, ten hours' night-flying, and nearly six hours' instrument flying.

Thus prepared, he assumed command of his first squadron on 19 July 1940 with the rank of Wing Commander. He was thirty-two, which was old among flying crews, but he was determined to lead from the front and not from his office. There were no bands or ceremonial parades to welcome the new Commanding Officer to Leeming. He checked in at the Guard Room and then proceeded to the Station Headquarters where he was introduced to the Station Commander,

A Whitley of No.78 Squadron in 1941. Night bombers were painted black. (*Aeroplane*)

Group Captain W.E. Staton, a previous Commander of No.10 Squadron. Buf was impressed with his decorations, describing him as an 'enthusiastic, press-on perfectionist'. Staton quickly briefed him on the personalities in the squadron, the nature of its operations, and the high standard it had achieved. A hard lead to follow!

After this introductory conversation, Buf proceeded to the Squadron Headquarters in No.2 hangar where, he was told, he would be met by the Squadron Adjutant. Both its vast sliding doors and the small steel doors at its side were closed, but he found a window insecurely fastened and so he climbed on to the sill and looked around at what was clearly the Commander's office. He was about to leap to the floor when the door opened and an amazed Flight Lieutenant appeared. He recognised the intruder's rank and reacted quickly. 'Welcome to 10 Squadron, Sir,' he said. 'I was expecting you, but I must admit I was a little surprised to find you arriving by the window!' Cohen was the Adjutant and over the next few months Buf was to find him a tower of strength. He was familiar with all the squadron members and also provided a link with the Station staff.

Equipment consisted of sixteen Whitley Mk Vs with another two in reserve. With a crew of five it could carry three tons of bombs to Berlin or North Italy. It carried one .303-inch machine gun in the nose, manned by the second pilot when needed, and a tail turret with four guns. It was powered by two Rolls-Royce Merlin X engines of remarkable reliability. Its principal drawback was its lack of heating which, in winter weather, could all but paralyse the crew.

The Squadron strength was officially twenty crews, but their operational experience was low. Each crew consisted of a captain, second pilot, navigator (who was also bomb aimer), wireless operator and rear gunner. Roughly half the aircrews were officers and half non-commissioned officers, and captaincy of an aeroplane was based not on rank but on the skill and experience of the pilot. Before any pilot could act as captain on a flight he had to carry out two operations as second pilot under the guidance of an experienced captain. Thus, on 22 July 1940 (three days after joining the Squadron) Buf flew as second pilot to Sergeant Pilot Johnson for an attack on oil refineries at Bremen.

Navigational aids were primitive. Forecast winds were given at the briefing and from these and the known ground speed the navigator calculated the time either to the target or to the turning point. Aircraft from 4 Group (in Yorkshire) would normally try to set course for an easily recognised pinpoint. like Spurn Head or Flamborough Head. From this he could check the actual windspeed that had been affecting his flight. From this he should be able to identify the position at which he would cross the Dutch islands.

Frequently, however, bad weather made this impossible. Some radio aids were available but unreliable, as were German beacons. Astronomical observation with the use of a sextant was not possible for the majority of navigators, and in any case it took them twenty minutes or more to plot their findings on a chart.

In the estimated target area the pilot would put down a flare to illuminate the ground and the navigator, now in the bomb aimer's position, would try to identify what he could see with his target map. This achieved, another flare was dropped and the pilot turned down-wind to prepare for the bombing run. He then turned back, hoping that the target was still lit up by the flare. The bomb-sight then in use required straight and level flight at a pre-determined height and airspeed for which the reading on the altimeter and airspeed indicator were not sufficient: they had to be calculated and then the sight could be set. The bomb aimer then took control and would tell the pilot, 'Right, right' for a turn to starboard, 'Left' for one to port, or 'steady' for straight on, until came the call 'Bombs gone', to the great relief of the crew. All this assumed a clear sky and no interference from searchlights, anti-aircraft fire or marauding enemy fighters: a very unlikely set of circumstances.

On Buf's first operational flight (as second pilot), they had a clear sky and met some searchlights and anti-aircraft fire, but returned safely to Leeming after seven hours and twenty minutes in the air. Then followed a thorough debriefing in which the Squadron's Intelligence Officer took full details of the operation, followed by the privileged breakfast of bacon and eggs with mulled beer, and so to bed.

Buf's second flight, again under the supervision of Sergeant Johnson, was against oil installations in the port of Hamburg. They set course visually over Flamborough Head but the North Sea was cloud-covered. Over the island of Heligoland they were greeted with anti-aircraft fire that caused their Whitley to lurch, but they were still seventy minutes from their target. Then they were presented with another problem: the regular beat of the engines suddenly fell out of synchronisation and both engines lost power. The heavy bomber began to glide downwards, and there was a moment of frozen silence. A quick cockpit check, however, showed that the air-intake lever was in the 'Cold' position, the normal position for summer flying, but in cloud there was always a risk of icing. Quickly the 'Hot' position was selected, and the engines reassuringly restarted. The troublesome cloud persisted in the Hamburg area and although searchlights and flak were seen, the target could not be identified. Reluctantly the crew gave up the search and set course for home with their bombs still on board. Landing was a risky business, accompanied by disappointment for the crew at an aborted operation lasting over seven and a half hours.

Buf's first flight as Captain in the pilot's seat was on 5 August against the Dornier aircraft factory at Wismar, east of Lübeck, on the Baltic coast. Again there was thick cloud that obscured the target, and so instead they bombed an aerodrome at Neumünster, south of Kiel. They landed back at Leeming after seven and three-quarter hours of flying, seven hours of which was by instruments.

About this time, Buf wrote in a letter to his father:

The job of Squadron Commander is really grand. It is the finest in the RAF and is the most important one. You are wrong when you say the staff jobs I have held are more important.

We in the Squadrons are the knife-edge of the huge organisation behind us – the Station, the group, Bomber Command, The Air Ministry, The War Cabinet, the Government, the whole aircraft industry with its sub-industries and thousand of workers. We are the knife edge, and mine is the responsibility of keeping it sharp and gleaming, and directing its blow aright,

This is a fascinating and unending task. First the maintenance organisation must run like clockwork, giving us our aircraft in a state of 100% efficiency, so that their engines do not falter in their 10-hour flights across the enemy territory, across 400 miles of sea each way in between, on across the gleaming peaks and the yawning chasms of the Alps. Our guns and turrets must work with battleship precision; our radio must develop no fault for often with it we must feel our way home, and down through the clouds into valleys where our homes lie. Each aircraft is as complicated as a submarine, and each must be perfect.

Then the operational flights must be at all times trained to perfection. Each aircraft crew must be balanced and drilled like a hockey team. The new arrivals must be fitted in and coached along under the care of the captain, older ones must be selected for captaincies when they become capable of bearing the responsibility. Characters must be weighed up; capabilities assessed. Defects or failures must be sifted in minute detail and explained to all crews so that they may avoid the same mistakes.

A Squadron is not an organisation or a unit; it is a living, writhing power which must be groomed, trained, and directed at its objectives with everything done to make it effective, and with its mind filled only with a determination to find it and destroy it. For on these missions, when wireless fails, or motors falter, when ice gets you in its white clutching fingers, or black thunder clouds engulf you and there are still hundreds of miles of empty ocean, and the enemy's defences in front of you, it is determination which governs the Captain's sole decision.

The things that matter most in a squadron are a firm conviction that your squadron is the best there is, and a determination to do all you can to keep it that way.

For all this the squadron commander is responsible, and all this can only be fully achieved by leading, rather than pointing the way.

So you see why this is the most important job in the RAF – and the most interesting job in the world.

Not all Squadron Commanders were leaders. Some allowed themselves to be dominated by administration, others chose targets that were relatively easy, and these actions were reflected in squadron morale, though perhaps the crews chosen for such targets were cheered by the thought that the Squadron Commander considered them a low risk.

Buf's next target on the night of 13/14 August was not a low risk one. It was the Fiat aircraft factory at Turin in Northern Italy. To shorten the journey by over 100 miles each way, the Squadron was sent to re-fuel at Abingdon, near Oxford. Buf's observer had calculated that there would be seven hours and twenty minutes of total darkness that night and that the total flight time and return would be nine and a half hours, and so take-off time was carefully calculated to provide maximum darkness as protection against German fighters in France. None, however, was encountered. The brightly lit city of Geneva (in neutral Switzerland) provided a useful check-point after which lay the Alps, which they had to cross near their loftiest point, Mont Blanc, nearly 16,000-feet high. Fortunately the observer could see its snow-capped peak forty miles ahead, and as they approached the icy peak gleaming brightly in the moonlight its sheer bulk seemed to dwarf their aircraft. Eventually it slid slowly past their port wing tip and they began their descent to the Po Valley. The weather now changed to cloud so that they continued their descent on instruments. As they flew on, the cloud became broken, the moon reappeared and the sweep of the Po Valley could be seen, from which Pilot Officer Forrest, the observer, advised his captain that they were only four miles from their target.

As they flew over the darkened city, Sergeant Nicholson, the wireless operator, was told to release a flare. Excitedly, the observer advised Buf that the flare was directly over the target. Buf descended to 4,000 feet for the run-in and Forrest gave the pilot alterations necessary for a precise approach. The Whitley gave a slight lurch as the bomb doors were opened and then steadied. Finally, after a long minute, came the call 'Bombs away'. Forrest confirmed that there had been no hang-ups and the Whitley began its long climb back to Abingdon, England. Apart from an unexpected encounter with the balloon barrage over the Thames Estuary, the flight was without incident and they arrived back after spending nine hours and forty-five minutes in the air.

The Squadron Record Book reported that 'the crew attacked the primary taget from a height of 4,000 feet ... Hits were observed on the main part of the target and incendiary bombs started many fires. Two large explosions were also seen after the bomb blast ... AA fire was very much above the aircraft, and no damage or casualties were incurred.' The report did not mention the fact that Italy had no night fighters.

This was not the first raid on Italy. On 10 June, Italy had declared war on France and Britain. Mr Churchill wrote: 'The rush for spoils has begun. But Mussolini was not the only hungry animal seeking prey. To join the Jackal came the Bear' *(Their Finest Hour,* p. 120). On the night of 12 June, our Bomber Squadrons, after a long flight from England, dropped their bombs on Turin and Milan in order to let Mussolini know that we meant business, even at our darkest hour.

On 15 August, the Air Officer Commanding Bomber Command, Sir Charles Portal, received this message from the Secretary of State for Air:

> Congratulations on the success of your raid on Italy. The accounts of it have been read here with immense admiration for the skill and endurance of the pilots and crews of your Squadrons and for the thoroughness of your planning.
> *Archibald Sinclair.*

After two more raids in August, one on an ammunition factory at Rheinfelden and one on an oil installation at Wesseling, without damage to aircraft or casualties, Buf – with a new crew – was briefed for a long-range attack on Berlin on 3 September. The war was one year old. The composition of the crew was interesting: as second pilot he had Squadron Leader MacNair from the Staff of 4 Group Headquarters, Flying Officer Bastin as rear gunner, Sergeant George Bessell as observer and Leading Aircraftsman Cowie as wireless operator. (The decision to grade all operational aircrew as at least Sergeants had taken a long time to fulfil: on his next operation a week later, Cowie had become a Sergeant.) The target in Berlin was the Friedrichseelde Transformer Station, a pious hope in view of Berlin's reputation for a cloudy sky. There was in fact total cloud cover and only one Whitley claimed to have carried out the mission. Bufton dropped a bomb, unsuccessfully, on a Berlin searchlight, and on the way home attacked an airfield south of Bremen, with no observed results. They reported intense flak in the Bremen area, and one fragment of a shell pierced Buf's windscreen resulting in a cold flight home. In September, the Prime Minister sent a signal to 4 Group:

> ... it is very satisfactory that so many tons of British bombs have been discharged with such precision under difficult conditions and at such great distance, and that so many important military objectives in Germany and Italy have been so sharply smitten ...

It was a message clearly designed to raise spirits on the home front.

September was a busy month for Buf and his crews. On the 11th they attacked Bremen and dropped a stick of bombs from 10,000 feet. They reported that immense fires were visible from eighty miles away. On the 17th they dropped seven sticks on an aerodrome at Trier, just east of Luxembourg, where they went down to 1,000 feet amid intense searchlights and AA, and put out four lights and a battery of guns. They went on to a factory near Maastricht in the extreme south of Holland. On the 27th they attacked the German submarine base at Lorient, dropping two sticks from 9,000 feet, later reporting fires and green explosions amid intense AA fire, in a flight lasting nearly nine hours.

On 30 September, Buf and his crew were again briefed for an attack on the centre of Berlin, to be precise the German Air Ministry, the Reichluftfahrtministerium on the Wilhelmstrasse. Failing that there were other offices slightly to the north. Forty-two aircraft had been detailed for this, but again were handicapped by total cloud cover. Only eight were able to report results. Buf was unable to locate any military target but reported heavy flak at 10,000 feet and fairly intense searchlight activity. On the way home they bombed a factory with a blast furnace at Verden, south of Bremen. They landed safely at Marham in north Norfolk as an alternative to their Yorkshire base. At the debriefing in the early hours of 1 October, Bessell, the observer, was asked if he had been able to find the primary target. 'No, sir', he replied with a wry smile, 'but I did manage to find the Chancellery'. 'Good man,' said the intelligence officer. 'Was Hitler at home?' 'I think not,' replied Bessell, 'the lights were out.'

On 24 September Buf was recommended for the award of the Distinguished Flying Cross. In his submission his commanding officer at Leeming, Group Captain Staton, wrote:

> Wing Commander Bufton has commanded No.10 Squadron since 20 July 1940. By his own example he has maintained a very high operational standard. The Squadron has recently passed through a bad time as far as this is concerned owing to the build up of new crews. There is no doubt his own operational efficiency has gone a long way towards inspiring confidence among members of operational crews. Operational efforts have shown a calm and unruffled determination resulting in a high degree of efficiency.
>
> Strongly recommend the award of the DFC.

The Commander of No.4 Group, Arthur Coningham, added that Buf was:

[A] very keen and capable Squadron Commander who has set an excellent example to the members of his Squadron. In spite of his multifarious Squadron duties he has himself, as Captain, recently carried out eight operational flights over enemy country in a period of six weeks. His calm confidence and cheerful demeanour invariably imbue an excellent offensive spirit in his Flight crews.

Strongly recommend for the award of the DFC.

The award of the Distinguished Flying Cross to Wing Commander Sydney Osborne Bufton was announced in the *London Gazette* on 22 November 1940.

In a letter to his father Buf said that he was very pleased with the award, especially as 'four other members or ex-members of the Squadron got one at the same time ... I hope they won't overdo the publicity about it. I'd prefer none myself.' The pride and joy of the Bufton household was overclouded by the news, late in October, that Pilot Officer John Raymond Bufton had been killed in air operations while serving with No.49 Squadron. Born in 1914 he had, like his older brother, had an outstanding record in engineering at Southampton University. He had gained his wings before the war, flying with a university air squadron. On 29 September 1940 he was posted to No.49 Squadron at Scampton, near Lincoln. His fourth operational flight as captain of a Hampden was to bomb an oil refinery at Hamburg. He took off at 5.40p.m., after which nothing more was heard from him, but at four minutes past two the next morning his plane came down in the sea half a mile from Skegness. The local police were unable to salvage it, though they did recover one body. The cause of the crash remained a mystery, but there was a possibility that it had been shot down by an enemy intruder because another Hampden had been attacked. John's body was recovered on 29 October and buried with full military honours at Llandrindod.

Two days before he died he had written to his fiancée:

I'm not pessimistic. I've rarely felt happier and more set on a job in my life, and my chances are as good as anyone else. But I'm not ass enough to assume that I'm going to be OK and everyone else will be unlucky as it's a sheer gamble in the game, but damned good fun while it lasts ... If the chances were very good I wouldn't dream of writing like this, but I'm no dreamer and the facts are, that immediately ahead is the winter, with all the danger that filthy weather invariably brings to flying ... If anything happens to me I'll want you to go and have a perm, do up the face, put the hat on and carry on ... I'm prepared for anything. Over the last three months I've got used to the idea of sudden accidents – they've happened so often to friends and acquaintances that the idea doesn't startle one much now ...

Buf had always felt the need to maintain the highest peak of physical fitness. Whether it was in the desert heat of Hinaidi or the damp cold of a Yorkshire winter, it was an early morning run round the airfield perimeter, followed by a cold shower. Unfortunately, this Spartan regime played havoc with his sciatic nerve. He had to borrow the air cushion from his Riley to ease the pains in his back incurred by long hours at the controls of the Whitley. Entry through the nose hatch – even without a parachute harness and a thick Sidcot flying suit – required gymnastic ability. Finally, in October 1940, he sought the help of the Station Medical Officer who sent him off to the Army hospital at Catterick. From there he was transferred to a hydro spa at Harrogate. Within a fortnight, the combination of massage and hot sulphur baths had effected a complete cure and he returned to his duties at Leeming.

For the Station Commander there was always enough work, even if he had assistance, because for a good deal of it he bore the responsibility. The gaps created by operational losses or training accidents had to be promptly filled, and there were the ongoing requirements for ground training and leave, not to mention absences from injury or sickness. A full record had to be maintained of the operational flights of each individual crew member, because some might be borrowed to make up an operational crew from one not flying that night. Successful bombing was a team effort and changes in crew composition were not welcomed. When a particular target or weather conditions made it appear that the task was not an easy one, a Squadron Commander might well put himself down *pour encourager les autres*. If not, he would normally attend the briefing and join the crews for their pre-flight meal, if only for a coffee and a chat. He would see them again at the crew room as they kitted up and then do a quick run round the dispersals for a final check. Finally, he would go to the control tower for the take-off, and after the last Whitley had left there would be, perhaps, an eight-hour wait for their return. So he had his supper in the Officers' Mess followed by a visit to the Operations Room to see if any aircraft had signalled problems. Then he could snatch a few hours' sleep.

After that, a similar procedure was carried out in reverse: first to the Operations Room for any signals from the aircraft that the mission was completed or that the aircraft was returning damaged; then to the control tower to check on the expected weather conditions for landing, the state of the flare-path and the possibility of enemy intruders. After the landing he would normally attend the debriefing and check on any overdue aircraft, before breakfast and bed. The day's work started at reveille as though a full night's sleep had been enjoyed. Bomber operations were continuous, dangerous and exhausting.

Then there were the aircraft, many of which came home badly damaged, and the task of repairing them as soon as possible for service, or replacing them from store. Often the conditions under which the groundcrews worked were arduous in the extreme, especially in winter. This was the domain of the Squadron Engineering Officer, but Buf being a highly qualified engineer would have taken a particular interest in this.

There was also the aerodrome itself. Like most others in 1940, Leeming had a grass surface with the added disadvantage of a subsoil mainly of clay. After prolonged rain it would often take Buf an hour's car ride to find an area firm enough for the night's operations. Often it was necessary for the Whitleys to depart at minimum take-off weight and fly to Dishforth or some other 4 Group aerodrome with concrete runways and there take up their full fuel and bomb loads before proceeding in their operations.

Towards the end of 1940, with the prospect of new and heavier bombers entering service, concrete runways and taxiways were essential. Work was started at Leeming, but progress was slow because both men and materials were in short supply. About a hundred yards of topsoil had been removed at each end of the new runway and replaced with hard core. At the hangar end this jutted out into the frequent floodwaters like Brighton Pier. To confirm the illusion, hundreds of seagulls would gather on both sides solemnly contemplating the waters. This did not make the choice of a suitable runway any easier.

From mid-November 1940 until 1 March 1941 Buf carried out six more operational flights. On the night of 15/16 November the target was an airfield at Eindhoven in the south of Holland. A total of eighty-two aircraft – Hampdens, Wellingtons and Whitleys – took part and ten were lost, the heaviest night loss up until that point. He also took part in attacks on Gelsenkirchen (a favourite oil refinery target), Frankfurt, Bremen and Hanover.

Buf carried out his last war operation on the night of 1/2 March 1941 in a raid on Cologne, in which 131 aircraft were involved and six were lost either to fighters or to anti-aircraft fire. Those, however, were the only losses because their home bases had been blanketed in fog and the 10 Squadron aircraft were diverted to bases in East Anglia where they all, with one exception, landed successfully. The one exception acknowledged the diversion order and later transmitted three SOS messages. Although its position was advised, nothing further was heard.

In April 1941 it was announced that Buf, together with half of No.10 Squadron's crews, were going to move to Linton-on-Ouse to begin the formation of No.76 Squadron, the second unit to be equipped with the four-engined Handley Page Halifax now entering squadron service. Buf's successor at No.10 Squadron was Wing Commander Bruce Bennett, who had been serving in the Air Ministry's Directorate of Bomber Operations. He was welcomed by a solitary Heinkel 111 sweeping in under a 600-foot cloud base and dropping a stick of bombs right across the camp. Fortunately no major buildings were hit, though many windows were broken and great clods of earth covered many of the flat roofs. One unexploded 500kg bomb came to rest under the power ring-main behind the hangars. There were no casualties. Buf hastily reassured his successor that this was their first assault.

He moved to Linton-on-Ouse (some ten miles north-west of York) on 12 April, where No.35 Squadron under Wing Commander R.W.P. Collings was already well established

Halifax of No.76 Squadron. (Air Britain)

with a limited number of Halifaxes. They had carried out their first operation on the night of 10/11 March when seven aircraft successfully attacked the docks at Le Havre. One suffered flak damage and one was lost by a tragic misidentification when on the return flight it was shot down by a British night fighter. Only two of the seven crew survived.

The Halifax had a troubled career. It started life in 1936 as a design for a twin-engined medium-heavy all-metal bomber powered by two Rolls-Royce Vulture engines, in response to the Air Ministry Specification P 13/36. These engines had not yet flown, and their future looked difficult, and so Wilfred Freeman, then Air Member for Development and Production, took it upon himself – on the advice of his staff – to tell Handley Page to redesign the air frame for four Rolls-Royce Merlins.

By 1941–1942, however, service tests proved that a fully loaded Halifax I climbed slowly, had a very poor performance above 13,000 feet and could only just maintain height at 17,000 feet. After many modifications, the final Mark VI model in 1944 with the Bristol Hercules 100 engine rivalled the performance of the Lancaster. The early Halifaxes also had undercarriage problems, and No. 76 Squadron was grounded for a time because frequent failures of the hydraulics resulted in several wheels-up landings. The tail-wheel tended to be troublesome: instead of retracting forwards it often stayed up or, if it did come down, it would fail to centre itself and produced a severe shimmy throughout the plane. These faults were remedied in time.

Buf, nonetheless, was delighted with the Halifax after the Whitley and likened it to 'going from an old banger of a motor car to the luxury and performance of a Rolls-Royce'. He considered it smooth, powerful and relatively spacious, and the reliability of four Merlins compared with the Whitley's two was reassuring. It did not take him long to learn the ropes. His first flight of just under two hours was spent in learning how to handle the machine, then in circuits and landings. This was followed by ninety minutes of local flying under the guidance of an experienced second pilot. Two days later, Buf and crew did thirty minutes of local flying followed by a four-hour cross-country navigation exercise. To complete his conversion he did thirty minutes of take-offs and landings with half a bomb load. The intention was that crews of No. 10 Squadron would be converted to the Halifax by 35 Squadron instructors and once they had reached operational standard they were to form a third flight within 35 Squadron to gain experience: thus they provided the nucleus of the new No. 76 Squadron. In fact this began operations on the night of 12/13 June 1941, when three Halifaxes were sent to bomb Hüls.

Even when the Halifaxes were not flying, the Luftwaffe was active. On the night of 12 May 1941, Buf was woken by sounds that he eventually identified as an attack. For protection, Linton-on-Ouse had been provided with guns which depended on visual gun-sights, but as no searchlights had been provided to illuminate the target the guns remained silent. The raid lasted half an hour and left the Station Commander, Group Captain Garraway, and three airmen from No. 35 Squadron dead. Damage to the airfield was light.

On 29 May 1941, Buf was promoted to Group Captain (which did not mean captaining a Group) with orders to open up RAF Pocklington and its two satellites, Melbourne and Elvington. (Melbourne did not become a squadron base, but Elvington became home to No.77 Squadron in October 1942 and later to two French Squadrons, 346 and 347 in 1944–1945.) Pocklington is some twenty miles east of York and its two satellites a few miles to its west.

On arrival at his new Station at the beginning of June, Buf found four officers and twelve airmen already in residence. All three Stations were new but with runways completed, and Pocklington was compact and neatly laid out with temporary buildings. Melbourne and Elvington had extremely limited facilities, with most of their buildings, including Control Towers, still to be sited. The buildings at Pocklington proved to be empty shells, with the Control Tower, Operations Room, and the Wireless Telegraphy section totally devoid of service equipment. Following a conference the next morning the Flight Sergeant from the Signals Section said that if he could borrow a three-ton lorry for two days he could obtain all the necessary signals equipment. Three days later it was being put in place. No questions were asked and no explanations given. It was never reclaimed.

On 17 June, Buf recorded the Station's strength as twenty officers and 460 airmen, and most of the fittings, furniture and equipment had been obtained from regular and irregular sources. All that was needed was an Operational Squadron, and that was due to arrive three days later. Just before 4.00p.m. on the 20th a reception committee headed by Buf gathered on the Control Tower roof to greet Pocklington's first squadron. Buf looked at his watch and turned to the Squadron Commander, Wing Commander Gilchrist, saying: 'Gilchrist, there's half a minute to go to 1600 hours and there's no sign of your blasted Squadron, not even a sound. Are you sure they're due at 1600?' He reassured the Station Commander that all was well, and at that moment the roar of twelve Wellingtons was suddenly heard. At treetop height, and using local contours to hide their approach, they had made a punctual and spectacular arrival. Buf kept to himself that he was not greatly pleased with the manner of their arrival, since it involved risks for the aircrews and annoyance to the local population.

The Squadron was the first heavy-bomber Squadron of the Royal Canadian Air Force in this country, No.405. Many Canadian aircrew were already serving in RAF squadrons, but there was a strong feeling that there was a case for entirely Canadian squadrons, though the Air Staff was not at first happy with the idea. The Empire Air Training Scheme, largely based in Canada, produced a steady flow of Canadian aircrew to this country, and by 1944 there were forty-three RCAF squadrons and a new Group, No.6, of Canadians in Bomber Command. On 17 June, Buf had been responsible for twenty officers and 460 airmen, on the 22nd for thirty-five officers and 843 airmen, and on the 27th for fifty-one officers, one WAAF officer and 915 airmen. By the time he left at the end of October, the roll had gone up to fifty-eight officers and 1,406 airmen, of whom twenty-one officers and 504 airmen were Canadian. The Squadron had already flown its first night-bomber mission on 12 June when it was stationed at Driffield.

The move from Driffield to Pocklington was not popular because it meant leaving the comforts of a pre-war RAF aerodrome for the chilly temporary buildings of Pocklington. Of greater concern was the problem of the main runway. Its siting took into account the need to provide 1,200 yards of take-off and landing run into the prevailing wind, but this meant that fully laden aircraft were heading almost straight for the parish's thirteenth-century church. To overcome this problem a new runway

Above: The future Mrs Sue Bufton as a Wren in 1943 wearing the new 'good conduct badge' which carried an increase of pay of two pence a day. (*Sphere*)

Right: Bufton walking out with Sue Browne.

was built inclined at ten degrees to the original, but this new construction created another problem because it passed very close to the Control Tower. To alleviate a disaster in the event of an aeroplane swinging on take-off, the base of the building was protected with extensive sandbagging. How effective this would be against a bomber laden with fuel and high explosives was, fortunately, never put to the test.

With all this on his hands, Buf found little time for flying: just four local flights in a Miles Magister. He never converted to the Wellington. On 1 November 1941 he was posted away from the operational scene to another even more important post as Deputy Director of Bomber Operations at the Air Ministry in London. Buf was thirty-three and a Group Captain, one of the youngest officers on the Air Ministry staff and one of the very few who had flown on operations in the Second World War.

A new star, however, was rising in Buf's firmament, in the person of Petty Officer Susan Browne of the Wrens. He had met her at a *thé dansant* at the Grosvenor House Hotel on 20 December 1940 and they entered into a regular correspondence. She had been modelling uniform for the Wrens, but was working at Bletchley Park, the highly secret Government Code and Cypher School, so secret, in fact, that she could give Buf no indication of the work she was doing. She wished him good luck for his posting to Pocklington, and soon afterwards she was moved to Chelmsford. She was to play a very important part in his life.

CHAPTER 5

High Policy

In 1941, the RAF was not yet twenty-five years old. It had come into being on 1 April 1918. For most of the First World War, aerial reconnaissance and bombing was done by the Army's Royal Flying Corps and the Navy's Royal Naval Air Service, and the power struggle between these two ancient bodies continued for many years. As a result, however, of the German bombing of London on 7 July 1917 and the lack of aerial defence, an immediate public outcry called for drastic action and the Prime Minister, Lloyd George, agreed to set up a committee to examine both the question of home defence and also that of the 'higher direction of aerial operations'.

With remarkable speed, the committee was constituted with two members, the Prime Minister and the South African General, Jan Smuts, who was a member of the War Cabinet. Since the Prime Minister was already fully occupied, Smuts busied himself and produced his first report in eight days. This recommended a unified command for the air defence of London, including fighter squadrons not only over London but to meet bombers before they reached London. This put paid to daylight German raids. A month later, on 17 August, Smuts submitted his second report, which recommended that the RFC and the RNAS should be amalgamated into a single air service, and that the Air Board should be expanded into a full Air Ministry under an Air Minister. This was approved by the Cabinet on 24 August. Smuts' report remains one of the most important documents in the history of the RAF and of British air policy. It pointed out that the air arm was treated by the Army and the Navy as a subordinate arm, like artillery, but went on:

> Essentially the position of an Air Service is quite different from that of the artillery arm, to pursue our comparison; artillery could never be used in war except as a weapon in military or naval or air operations. It is a weapon, an instrument ancillary to a service, but could not be an independent service itself. Air service on the contrary can be used as an independent means of war operations. Nobody who witnessed the attack on London on 7th July could have any doubt on the point.
>
> Unlike artillery an air fleet can conduct extensive operations far from, and independently of, both Army and Navy. As far as at present can be foreseen there is absolutely no limit to the scale of its future independent war use. And the day may not be far off when aerial operations with their devastations of enemy lands and destruction of industrial and populous centres on a vast scale may become the principal operations of war, to which the older forms of military and naval operations may become secondary and subordinate.

It argued that an Air Staff was necessary for the planning and directing of independent air operations and the strategic purpose to which the new machines were going to be put. (The new heavy bomber, the Handley Page 0/400, originally designed to an Admiralty requirement, equipped seven squadrons by the end of the war, and a total of 549 of this type were produced.) With remarkable foresight the report stated:

> It requires some imagination to realize that next summer, while our Western front may still be moving forward at a snail's pace in Belgium and France, the air battle-front will be far behind on the Rhine, and that its continuous and intense pressure against the chief industrial centres of the enemy as well as on his lines of communications may form an important factor in bringing about peace. The enemy is no doubt making vast plans to deal with us in London if we do not succeed in beating him in the air and carrying the war into the heart of his country. The questions of machines, aerodromes, routes and distances, as well as nature and scope of operations require thinking out in advance, and in proportions to our foresight and preparations will our success be in these new and far-reaching developments.

This doctrine was not entirely new. General Trenchard wrote to Douglas Haig in September 1916 when the RFC, under Trenchard's command, was trying hard to overcome the 'Fokker scourge'. He argued that the aeroplane was not an effective defence against the aeroplane. The answer to air attack was to increase our own offensive, to fight the enemy behind his own lines and compel him to divert his aircraft from offence to defence.

When the Germans began to re-arm after the First World War their policy was the opposite. The Luftwaffe was an arm of the army and was seen, and equipped, as a highly mobile form of artillery, of which the *Stuka* was the familiar example. They failed, significantly, to produce a single successful long-distance bomber, since the Heinkel He 177 and the Junkers Ju 288 were technical failures, not least because Hitler demanded that the former should be capable of dive-bombing.

After 1918, the new RAF underwent a drastic reduction of personnel and finance: in 1920 the Air Estimates were nearly £23,000, in 1921 £18,400 and by 1922 rather less than £11,000. It also had to contend with a vigorous attempt by admirals and generals to regain their former control. Largely under the determined leadership of Trenchard, these were repulsed, and he was to lay the permanent foundations for future growth. Permanently commissioned officers (only half of the total) would enter through the RAF Cadet College, to be opened in 1920 at Cranwell in Lincolnshire. Five thousand boys were enlisted for three years' apprenticeship in trades before being passed into the ranks (to become famous as 'Trenchard's brats') at Halton, with the retention of the experimental establishments at Farnborough, Biggin Hill and Martlesham Heath. For the future, an Air Force Staff College was envisaged which began in 1922. 'I have laid the foundations for a castle,' said Trenchard. 'If nobody builds anything bigger than a cottage on them, it will at least be a very good cottage.' The Secretary of State for Air from 1919–1921 was Winston Churchill, and the Chief of Air Staff (CAS) from 1919–1930 was Trenchard.

By the time of the Second World War or rather, to be precise, from 25 October 1940 the task of Chief of Air Staff fell to Charles Portal who had for six months commanded Bomber Command. The best account of what that involved is his own description in an address he gave to the boys of Winchester College in 1945:

A Chief of Staff in war has two jobs rolled into one, though of course he only gets paid for one and only has the normal 24 hours a day for both.

The first has to do with his own Service on such matters of policy as the higher appointments, the selection of the types of aircraft to have, general methods of using them, the numbers provided for each kind of job in each different area and so on. He keeps an eye on the running of the Service as a whole but, of course, he cannot direct actual operations, so the idea one sometimes sees presented in war films that the Chief of Staff sits in his office surrounded by Staff Officers holding maps and spends his time deciding what shall be blown up that night in Germany, where the secret agents are to be dropped, or at what moment the night fighters shall leave the ground, is all nonsense. One of my first war experiences as a Chief of Staff has a bearing on this point. Very soon after I was appointed I went to stay at a house where there was a small boy of eight who was the kind of boy who knew every aeroplane by its sound without having to look at it. He greeted me with a demand to know what my job was. Did I send the bombers out? No, that was the job of the C-in-C Bomber Command. Then did I send out the fighters? No that was for the C-in-C Fighter Command. Then what *do* you do? 'Well', I said, 'I sat up till 2 o'clock this morning arguing with the Prime Minister.' That boy's face was a wonderful mixture of disappointment and disillusionment. 'Oh!', he said, 'my mother told me you were somebody quite important.'

My other job as Chief of Staff is to be one of the four members of the Chiefs of Staff Committee, the other three being the Chief of the Imperial General Staff (Field Marshal Brooke), the First Sea Lord (Admiral Sir Andrew Cunningham) and General Ismay. General Ismay forms the link between the Chiefs of Staff and the Prime Minister, when the Prime Minister himself does not preside at our meetings (which he quite often does). The work of the Chiefs of Staff Committee is to advise the Government through the Prime Minister on all questions of British military policy and strategy and we also combine with the American Chiefs of Staff (General Marshall, Admiral King and General Arnold) to form the Combined Chiefs of Staff who advise the President and the Prime Minister together on matters affecting American and British forces jointly.

In the Chiefs of Staff and the Combined Chiefs of Staff each one of us deals not just with his own Service but with the other Services as well. I don't know if Field Marshal Brooke knows more about the Air Force by now than Sir Andrew Cunningham knows about the Army, but we are all well able to understand each other's problems and it may be of interest to you to know that we are all entitled to the same old school tie, namely the tie of the Imperial Defence College where all of us and most of the other senior Commanders of this war studied for a year between the last war and this one.

In case anyone here is thinking of becoming Chief of Staff I would like to warn you that it is quite hard work. I have now had to attend nearly 2,000 meetings, each taking 1½–2 hours or more, needing perhaps 3 or 4 reading beforehand ...

This at least makes the point that waging war is not simply a military or aeronautical matter. It is in the first place a political one, with the final responsibility lying with the Minister of Defence, as Churchill described himself (or to be more precise with the sovereign whose minister he is). It is also a cooperative one, because the Air Force is not the only service, and after the USA became an ally, the matter became even more complex.

The manner of Portal's appointment as Chief of Air Staff is not altogether clear, as most of the official papers are missing, but he had a distinguished record. On 6 August 1914 he was enrolled in the Royal Engineers and eight days later spent a highly dangerous time as a despatch rider as the British Expeditionary Force advanced into Belgium and then retreated to the Marne. He became so tired that, once, he fell asleep on his motor-bike and rode into the back of Haig's staff car. Within eight weeks he was commissioned. In 1915 he asked for a transfer to the RFC as an observer and in July 1915 he joined No. 3 Squadron. After six months he qualified as a pilot and became an expert in artillery spotting and tactical reconnaissance. In the eleven months following the start of the Somme offensive he had made more than 300 operational sorties and received the immediate award of the MC. By mid-1917 he was a Major in Command of No. 16 Squadron, which was suddenly required to undertake night bombing for which his RE 8s were not designed. On one night in January 1918 he made five raids over enemy lines. He finished the war as a Lieutenant Colonel with a DSO and bar, and had quickly come to the notice of Trenchard.

After the war, Portal became the Chief Flying Instructor at Cranwell, a student at the new RAF Staff College and a pupil of Wilfrid Freeman, then Squadron Leader on Trenchard's Staff. In 1927, he was posted to command No. 7 Bomber Squadron with Virginias, and

from 1933–1937 he was on the Air Staff as deputy Director of Plans, Director of Organisation and Air Member for Personnel, playing a key part in the creation of the WAAF and the Commonwealth Air Training Scheme. He was also responsible for adding some thirty new main RAF stations. In April 1940, he became Air Officer Commanding-in-Chief of Bomber Command. In November of that year, as soon as he became Chief of Air Staff, he summoned 'Bert' Harris from the command of No. 5 Group to the Air Ministry to be his Deputy Chief, and when Bomber Command was at the nadir of its life, he appointed Harris to command it.

Portal needed powerful assistance in carrying out his appalling responsibilities, not least in the matter of appointing officers to senior posts. He appealed to his former instructor, Wilfrid Freeman, who was actually

Freeman (left) and Portal. (IWM)   senior to him (they were both Air Chief Marshals), to join him as Vice-Chief of Air Staff. He had been offered the post twice but had turned it down. He was devoted to his task of procuring the best aeroplanes for the RAF and had a shining record both as Air Member for Research and Development and as Air Member for Development and Production. The fact that the RAF came to be equipped with Spitfires, Lancasters, Mosquitos and Mustangs was largely his achievement. (For the first two years of its life, the Mosquito was known in the Air Ministry as Freeman's Folly: who had ever heard of a wooden bomber without any defences?) Why was he not chosen for the top post? The answer, it seems, is that he had been divorced and remarried, and certainly in peacetime this ruled out top appointments. In May 1940, Churchill formed a new coalition government and set up a new Ministry of Aircraft Production (MAP), giving control of it to one of his oldest friends, Lord Beaverbrook, the newspaper magnate.

In the early months of 1940, Freeman took three of his most decisive steps, despite his difficulties with Beaverbrook. He ordered 320 new fighters from a small and little known American firm, North American. The first flight of the prototype of what later became famous as the Mustang took place on 26 October 1940, 178 days after the order was placed. Second, he won the award of a contract for the American motor firm Packard to make the Rolls-Royce Merlin engine. (The combination later of the Mustang and the Merlin proved to be almost a war-winner.) His third decision concerned the twin-engined Avro Manchester, the last survivor of the 1936 specification. By August 1940 there were great problems with its engines, the Rolls-Royce Vulture, supplies of which in any case were going to be inadequate. Chadwick at Avro convinced Freeman that the Manchester could be adapted to accept four of the now highly reputable Merlins, and thus the Lancaster came into being, the most successful heavy bomber of the war. The first prototype flew on 25 July 1939 and the second, more radically redesigned, on 26 May 1940, and deliveries started in the summer of 1940.

Despite the problems with MAP, Freeman finally gave in to Portal's pressure, even though it meant taking a step down the ladder, and he began work as Vice-Chief of Air Staff in November 1940, a post which he hated but in which he served with distinction for two years. His knowledge of senior officers of the RAF, his familiarity with the aircraft industry, both in Britain and in the USA, and his insight into the needs of the air war were of incalculable value to Portal and the Air Ministry.

This rather long diversion about the two officers at the head of the Air Staff at the beginning of the Second World War – men of very different temperaments – sets the scene, to some extent, of Bufton's service. The working out in detail of the policies that the Chiefs planned had to be left to subordinates in the various departments, and these key appointments had to be held by highly competent officers. A first-class pilot did not necessarily make a good administrator, and there was also the problem (which Bufton emphasised soon after his arrival) of ageing officers, many of whom had not flown for years, and very few of whom had had any experience of recent operational flying. Alan Brooke, Chief of the Imperial General Staff, Portal's opposite number in the Army, wrote that his most unpleasant duty was relieving senior officers of their command. The diagram overleaf illustrates, in very abbreviated form, that part of the Air Ministry with which this book is concerned.

In 1941, the Air Ministry was housed in a fine Victorian building in King Charles Street opposite the Home and Foreign Office, known familiarly in the Service as 'the

House of Shame'. The second floor (with superior carpeting) contained the quarters for the Chiefs and their Deputies, the Directors and the Secretary of State for Air (Sir Archibald Sinclair). The office of the Director of Bombing Operations was opposite that of the Chief of Air Staff. A canteen in the basement provided meals round the clock. In the sub-basement was the War Room, which collected and collated statistics relating to Air Force operations worldwide. Further underground were passages leading to the Prime Minister's War Room beneath No.10 Downing Street and the Defence Committee Conference Room. As it was not unknown for senior staff to have to work halfway through the night, beds were provided in their offices.

Each day, except Sunday, began with the Air Staff Conference at 9.00a.m., attended by all the Operational Directors and associated Assistant Chiefs, and chaired by Norman Bottomley, the Deputy Chief, who had the reputation of 'playing the Air Ministry organ with more skill than anyone had ever achieved before'. (He had followed Harris as Commander of No.5 Group of Bomber Command in November 1940 and served there until May 1941.) The various Directors would brief the meeting on the previous day's activities leading into a discussion of the problems, shortages and requirements disclosed, and steer towards the appropriate Director for action. The rest of the day would be taken up with the mountain of correspondence from other meetings, messages from the Prime Minister, the Secretary of State and other Directorates and dealing with numerous visitors.

The Directorate of Bombing Operations was responsible for drafting the Directives to Bomber Command guiding their operations, and preparing briefs for Portal's meetings with his Chiefs of Staff Committee. In November 1941, the Director of Bomber Operations was Air Commodore J.W. Baker who was responsible through the Vice-Chief (Freeman) to the Chief himself.

The Director and his Deputy were responsible for the operational policy and the direction of the air striking forces, the composition, organisation, armament and equipment of Bomber Command, and for dealing with issues affecting air striking forces generally, both at home and overseas. The Directorate had three sub-divisions, each

Secretary of State for Air and
President of the Air Council
(Sir Archibald Sinclair)

|

Parliamentary Under-Secretary
of State for Air
(Captain Harold Balfour)

|

Chief of Air Staff
(ACM Sir Charles Portal)

|

Vice-Chief of Air Staff
(ACM Sir Wilfrid Freeman;
AVM Charles Medhurst
[Acting VCAS], from
19 October 1942;
AM Sir Douglas Evill,
from 21 March 1943)

|

Deputy Chief of Air Staff
(AVM Arthur Harris,
25 November 1940–20 May 1941;
AVM N.H. [later AM Sir Norman]
Bottomley,
21 May 1941–3 May 1942 and
31 July 1943–14 September 1945)

|

Assistant Chief of Air Staff
(Operations)
(AVM N.H. Bottomley,
5 April 1942–30 July 1943;
AVM W.A. Coryton, 16 August 1943;
AVM T.M. Williams, from 1 August 1944)

|

Up to eight Directorates, including
Directorate of Bomber Operations
(Air Cdre J.W. Baker, to 9 March 1943;
Air Cdre S.O. Bufton, from 10 March 1943
[previously Group Captain,
DD Bomber Ops,
from 14 November 1941])

Air Ministry chain of command.

headed by a Wing Commander: Bomber Operations 1 (B Ops 1), responsible for bomber operational planning, the selection of targets and for liaison with Air Intelligence and the Ministry of Economic Warfare; B Ops 2 (a), for operational analyses and returns, the composition, organisation and expansion of Bomber Command, navigational aids, blind approach and night-flying requirements; and B Ops 2 (b), for the development and provisioning of offensive bombing weapons including incendiary and gas weapons, mines and depth charges.

The Directorate did not issue orders; that was for commanders in the field. It did, however, issue 'Directives' containing broad lines of actions within which orders had to be issued. They came with the authority, if not the name, of the Chief of Air Staff. When Harris was head of Bomber Command and had himself set up the Directorate, he was violently critical of this process, even though he had served for six months as Deputy Chief of Air Staff until May 1941. But then Harris never took kindly to receiving orders from anyone. In his usual jocund manner he referred to Bottomley, Baker and Bufton as 'the three Bs'.

The 'strategic air offensive', that is to say the long-range bombing of the enemy's industrial towns and cities, in 1940 had shown the weakness of Bomber Command and its Whitleys, Wellingtons and Hampdens. Daylight photographic reconnaissance revealed that none of the oil installations had been seriously damaged and that many of the attacks on towns had been very inaccurate and the damage exaggerated. The long-range Spitfires with improved cameras producing large-scale photographs showed, for example, that in the mass raid on the industrial town of Mannheim on 16 December 1940 the damage, though considerable, was widely dispersed and much of it was outside the target area: all the air crews had reported that most bombs had fallen in the target area and that the centre of the town had been left in flames.

In April 1941, after a detailed study of large-scale daylight reconnaissance photographs of further raids, the Directorate of Bomber Operations recognised that the estimate of 300 yards for bombing accuracy at night in good conditions was unattainable. This figure had been taken, without justification, from a pre-war estimate for daylight bombing, whereas the correct figure was 1,000 yards. In June 1941, a further advance in bomb-damage assessment showed that Bomber Command had neither sufficient accuracy in target location nor adequate bomb-aiming equipment even to produce the results expected from area bombing. Two months later, Lord Cherwell (or Professor Lindemann, as he then was), the Prime Minister's scientific adviser, instituted the first thorough investigation of the Command's operational reports in light of the night photographs taken by bombers during their raids. (About one in five of the aircraft were fitted with night flash cameras to record, as far as possible, the explosion of their bombs.)

The task was given to Cherwell's secretary, Mr D.M.B. Butt, who began his report, dated 18 August 1941, with a summary of his findings:

Statistical Conclusions

An examination of night photographs taken during night bombing in June and
July points to the following conclusions:

Of those aircraft recorded as attacking their target, only one in three got within
   five miles.

Over the French ports, the proportion was two in three; over Germany as a whole,
   the proportion was one in four; over the Ruhr, it was only one in ten.

In the Full Moon, the proportion was two in five; in the new moon it was only one
   in fifteen.

In the absence of haze, the proportion is over half, whereas over thick haze it is
   only one in fifteen.

An increase in the intensity of AA fire reduces the number of aircraft getting
   within five miles of their target in the ratio three to two.

All these figures relate only to aircraft recorded as attacking the target; the
   proportion of the total sorties which reached within five miles is less by one
   third.

Thus, for example, of the total sorties only one in five get within five miles of the
   target, i.e. with[in] the 75 square miles surrounding the target.

The particulars were collected from about 650 photographs taken during night-
bombing operations between 2 June and 25 July. They relate to twenty-eight targets,
forty-eight nights and 100 separate raids.

This kind of analysis was not new. Bernard Babington Smith (Pilot Officer) had
arrived at Oakington on 1 December 1940 for the task of photographic interpretation,
at first to assess the damage caused in raids. When the statistics for three months had
been sent to Bomber Command it proved that, of the 151 flashlight photographs, not
more than twenty-one showed the target area. In one case, a crew had estimated its
position as within fifty miles of a certain pinpoint when in fact it was 100 miles further
east. It became clear that the crews were being asked to do the impossible. During
the spring of 1941, some of the crews who were told of their errors disbelieved the
photographs, while others who took them seriously became worried and depressed. At
one Group Headquarters the intelligence officers found it best to keep quiet about the
photographs that did not show the target area, and at another, an officer who passed to
his chief an interpretation showing that an attack had missed its mark found it later on
his desk with scrawled across it in red: 'I do not accept this report.'

For Churchill, the matter was clear. He wrote:

The air photographs showed how little damage was being done. It also appeared
that the crews knew this, and were discouraged by the poor results of so much
hazard. Unless we could improve on this there did not seem much use in
continuing night bombing.

A copy of the report went to Portal with a minute from Churchill:

This is a very serious paper and seems to require your most urgent attention. I
await your proposals for action.

CHAPTER 6

Illumination and Marking

As soon as Buf moved into the Directorate of Bomber Operations as Deputy Director in November 1941 with the rank of Group Captain (the Director was Air Commodore John Baker whom he had known at the Staff College), it was clear to him that two things had to be done to improve bombing performance: one was to provide more effective means of illuminating targets so that crews could actually see where they were on a dark night; and the other was to provide them with a means of improving their navigational performance, though a new method of guidance by radar (an American abbreviation of the earlier British term 'radio direction finding') was soon to come into effect. It came to acquire the name 'Gee', apparently from the grid-lines on the map used. There was, of course, the matter of better aircraft, but the Lancaster was to come into service in March 1942.

One other matter, however, lay in a file on his desk, concerning emergency aerodromes for crippled aircraft (and often wounded crews) near the east coast. Three sites had been chosen: Carnaby in north-east Yorkshire; Woodbridge in east Suffolk, near Ipswich; and Manston at the north-eastern tip of Kent. Only Manston had been an existing aerodrome, but it had to be greatly enlarged. This plan was likely to cost £250,000 (roughly £5 million in present-day value) and the Treasury was not happy. Since a Lancaster cost about £80,000, three of those saved would pay for the work, not to mention the lives of the crew. The work went forward with runways seventy-five yards wide and 3,000 yards long with huge grass extensions at either end. Each aerodrome had three parallel hard runways running almost east–west. At night, the southern strip had green lighting and aircraft in distress could land on it without authorisation from Flying Control. The centre strip had white lighting, while the northern strip had yellow.

One of the three aerodromes was equipped with Fog Investigation and Dispersal Operation (FIDO), a wartime invention that helped to save the lives of hundreds of aircrew. It consisted of lines of burners fuelled by petrol along the edges of the runways. The heat generated would actually burn off the surrounding fog and so enable aircraft to land and take-off. The Carnaby piping consumed 120,000 gallons of petrol each hour, but they proved their worth. The airfield could be located by a plume of black smoke above the fog and then, on final approach, by the rapidly approaching red glow. Donald Bennett, the future leader of the Pathfinder Force, and the first to land at a fog-shrouded – but FIDO-equipped – aerodrome, said that it reminded him of lions jumping through a hoop of flames at the circus. Woodbridge became operational in November 1943, and both Carnaby and Manston in April 1944. By the end of the war, 2,694 aircraft, mainly heavy bombers, had made forced landings on them.

The major issue, however, was the improvement of flare dropping to illuminate the target. Flares were not a new invention: they had been used in the First World War, mainly to help with night landings. This was still the case until 1932. In June of that year, the Air Ministry had given approval for selected night-bomber squadrons to drop six flares per squadron in the following year, but Air Commodore Gossage wrote to the Air Ministry to explain that, 'owing to the limited amount of weather suitable for night bombing, it was not found convenient to drop the flares.' He also suggested that investigations should be carried out to assess their usefulness as an aid to night bombing.

His first question concerned the amount of illumination provided by the four-inch (actually 4.125-inch) reconnaissance flare then under trial: would it be sufficient to enable the bomber crew to locate the target and then carry out an accurate attack? How many attacks could be carried out using only one flare? At what altitude should the flares operate? What of the possibility of using specially selected crews as target-finders to release relays of flares to assist in target identification? The matter was clearly not considered urgent, because in December 1933 his headquarters reported to the Air Ministry that, 'owing to the severity of the safety precautions imposed and to the fact that the wind direction was generally unfavourable, only three flares were dropped during the Armament Training Camp season of 1933'. Flares were rationed! No.7 Squadron had requested eight-inch flares for trial purposes, but this was turned down because all those particular flares were required in the Far East. The Squadron was told to use the four-inch flare, but to remember that, as each cost £10, 'reasonable economy should be observed in their use'. Trials were held in October 1934 with favourable weather conditions, and the CO reported that the target could be seen only if the flare was within 400 yards of it and lower than 1,400 feet.

In the light of this adverse report, the Air Ministry decided to investigate the possibility of using a five-and-a-half-inch parachute flare, which was expected to become available in July 1935. The trials of this, carried out by No.99 Squadron, were largely inconclusive: they showed distinct possibilities, but required modification to improve the steadiness of burn. The report highlighted the difficulties experienced over several years with trials of parachute flares. It had been intended that numbers of flares would be dropped at the annual Armament Training Camps so as to gather sufficient data to measure their efficiency and also to develop techniques for their use. Unfortunately, the regulations governing the use of bombing ranges in Great Britain, usually located on the coast, had meant that flare trials were very infrequent. The fuse employed, as well as parts of the flare itself, were considered dangerous missiles, and so they could only be dropped when an off-shore wind was blowing. In March 1937 the head of the Armament Group, Air Commodore Garrod, reported (in four pages) that 'this Headquarters has had no recent contact with service trials of parachute flares'.

In September 1939, aware of the urgent need and shortage of time, Saundby (then Director of Operational Requirements at the Air Ministry) wrote to Ludlow-Hewitt (then head of Bomber Command) advising him of the greater capacity of the five-inch flare, but received the reply that the increases did not justify production. All of which illuminated the unspoken and unwritten assumption that the RAF only seriously considered a campaign of day bombing and not of night bombing.

Buf, on the other hand, had witnessed at first hand the disastrous campaign of day bombing in France in 1940 and had himself flown on night operations with No.10 Squadron. He knew the unreadiness of Bomber Command for night bombing and was determined to do all he could to raise Bomber Command from the sad state into which it had fallen. With No.10 Squadron, he had developed techniques to increase the efficiency of night attacks by raising the standard load of flares to be carried from six to ten per plane, and had added a Verey-light signal by the leader to provide a homing beacon for other aircraft of the squadron – but this was only for one squadron. While in command at Pocklington, he had regularly attended post-raid debriefings and learned that the 405 Squadron crews placed little reliance on flares. For them the visual evidence of searchlights, flak, or the presence of sea or river or lake in the vicinity of the target was sufficient confirmation that they had reached the target area. 'Only by constant persuasion,' he wrote, 'could the crews be induced to use their flares at all.'

On his arrival at the Air Staff in November 1941, Buf wrote a long paper on future policy as he saw it, no doubt for the Director of Bombing Operations, Air Commodore J.W. Baker. He asserted that 'any plan which relies on a full moon is unsound ... At the moment possibly fifty per cent of aircraft arrive at the target area'. An important feature of proper flare dropping would therefore be as a 'homing beacon', visible from fifty miles away. A hundred flares must burn continuously, a task for ten to twelve Stirlings. The height of the flares must be no more than 2,500 feet. Haze is not as bad as imagined; it is only bad when flares are fused for 8,000 to 10,000 feet. Flares and incendiary bombs will do better with Gee and will enable unequipped aircraft to perform as well as those with Gee. In ten-tenths cloud, Gee aircraft could drop coloured flares above the cloud to indicate bombing position. They could also drop coloured flares on the way to mark the route. He finished with a stirring challenge: 'If not successful let us think of other schemes. But above all, let us think and let us try.' He noted that:

> Reports on the American Hooded Flare were so promising that we would have been justified in producing our own equivalent immediately. I doubt very much, however, whether we are likely to get one for a year. We really need them now. The American flares which we had in this country for test were unfortunately destroyed owing to failure of the fusing system during dropping trials, and presumably no more progress will be made until a further batch has been received from America.

The purpose of a hood over the flare (the Americans made one of asbestos) was twofold: to stop the aircrew being blinded by their own flares; and to stop the aircraft being illuminated for the benefit of anti-aircraft gunners. Buf also suggested that the armament development organisation should be modified so that immediate operational requirements could be met in phase with developments of tactical importance, and proposed a Development Unit working directly under Bomber Command. He commented that the flare problem was being tackled independently by Bomber Command, but he doubted whether they would organise the scheme on a sufficiently large scale to make it fully effective in view of their extraordinarily heavy commitments at that time.

He then went on to sow the seeds of a Pathfinder Force. 'I suggest therefore that we take the bull by the horns and induce them to allocate certain squadrons to the role of a target-finding and fire-raising force on KG 100 principles.' (KG 100 was a basic operational bomber unit of the Luftwaffe, more or less equivalent to a Group in the RAF, a *Kampfgeschwader*. It was made up, usually, of three operational *Gruppen* with a fourth training or reserve *Gruppe* (KGr). *Kampfgruppe 100* (KGr 100) became operational on 18 November 1939, amid great secrecy, as a beam-bombing unit. But more of that in the next chapter.)

It was clear, Buf argued, that the target-finding force should have every available navigation aid, and so the squadrons selected should be those that would first have Gee, although they would have to be withdrawn from operations for equipping and training. Nevertheless, they should start training and thinking and developing tactics with a view to acting in a target-finding role. Bufton thought that the chosen squadrons should be based in the same area so that they could confer together, and so nominated six squadrons:

115 Squadron	Wellington IIIs	Marham
218 Squadron	Stirlings	Marham
57 Squadron	Wellington IIIs	Feltwell
75 Squadron	Wellington IIIs	Feltwell
419 Squadron	Wellington IIIs	Mildenhall
149 Squadron	Stirlings	Mildenhall

He went on to suggest that their first operation should be carried out against the Renault factory as a full-scale experiment within the next fortnight: 'The target is easy to locate, even on a dark night. We ought, I think, to write the plan for this, even if it is sent to Bomber Command only as a guide.' A copy of this paper was sent to Bomber Command and its receipt was acknowledged with thanks.

The attack on the Renault factory at Billancourt, near Paris, took place on the night of 3–4 March when Harris, the newly arrived Commander, despatched 235 bombers in good weather and clear visibility. (The Cabinet only a month before had given permission for the bombing of targets outside the *Reich* in the hope that it might deter French civilians from working for Germany.) The attack was mounted in three stages. The vanguard was of 'heavies' with fully trained crews, then the main force of medium bombers, and finally all the aircraft equipped to carry 4,000lb bombs. The first wave was to light up the target with flares and bomb with a large percentage of incendiary bombs, then drop its remaining flares to windward. The second wave was to repeat this procedure so that the target would be well illuminated the whole time. The third wave was to do the real damage with high explosive, for most of the factory's machines were only destroyed by a direct hit.

The attack went according to plan. Only twelve bombers failed to reach the target and 461 tons of bombs were dropped; the rate of concentration saturated the defences. Photographs taken during the raid, daylight reconnaissance the next day and reports from secret sources all pronounced the raid a great success. Monsieur Renault himself reported to the Germans that it was buildings that had suffered most, but materials, tools and completed products had also been destroyed. Of the 3,000 workmen on duty, only five had been killed. Nevertheless, within four months of the attack the previous level of production had been regained, and this despite the fact that during the following year the number on the evening shift shrank by nearly a half. It was ironic, as Harris himself wrote in his book, that he, the apostle of area-attack, should have scored his first success against a precision target in France. At any rate, this and two other similar attacks a few days later, served to raise the spirits of Bomber Command.

Buf pressed on with the testing and production of 'marker' bombs. In April 1942, he recommended a test with two Stirlings each carrying twenty-four 250lb coloured marker bombs, half with the new barometric fuse and half with the existing flare fuse. (The former calculated height from the ground; the latter from the aircraft.) He maintained that everyone concerned was satisfied that these bombs would provide an unmistakeable mark, distinguishable from at least twelve miles away, and recommended their immediate employment. He added that a Mark II version would increase the time of burning.

B Ops 1 under Wing Commander Morley was the department responsible for the equipment of bombers, and on 23 June Morley reported to Buf that there could be a monthly production of 500 250lb marker bombs with pressure fuses per week, and a new lethal 4lb incendiary bomb with an explosive charge – a strong deterrent to fire-watchers.

On the night of 2 July, Morley attended a trial of this 250lb bomb: first, dropped from between 11,000 and 3,000 feet and burning on the ground as a coloured pattern; second, as a single bomb at 11,000 feet releasing a stream of coloured flares, providing a most distinctive marker of short duration; and third, as green and red bombs at 3,000 feet streaming to the ground, which continued to burn for about three minutes. He gave a full account of this successful trial to Buf.

It was not, however, until October 1942 that he learned that this marker bomb was actually in production and would be available in a few weeks. Each was filled with sixty 'candles' of red, green or yellow flare composition that were ejected by a barometric fuse at 2–3,000 feet above ground. The candles were lit on ejection and continued burning on the ground for three to five minutes. Each bomb was of 500,000 candle power, and a Stirling could carry twenty-four of them. The hooded flare did not arrive until the following month.

In September 1942, Buf wrote a long paper entitled 'Night Bombing – Tactics and Tactical Development'. He ended it by lambasting 'a totally inadequate development staff and the persistence of a peace-time organisation'. He concluded:

A special tactical development section is essential, with a staff large enough to deal with a number of projects simultaneously. It must work on 'fire-brigade' lines. It should be able not only to meet, but to anticipate requirements. Until this is provided we cannot hope to keep our tactics in phase with enemy developments.

It is clear that we cannot afford to go through the long process of development by which, as in peace-time, we hope to achieve the perfect article. We must work to a rough and ready policy of 'something is better than nothing', and improve as we go along. It may mean subsequent redesign; it may mean re-tooling; it is not economical; but it *is* war.

A special development unit such as that envisaged above must necessarily work in the closest liaison with the users of the equipment who should state requirements, advise during development, and authorise modification in the interest of speed when development difficulties arise.

These problems are now fully appreciated by the Air Staff and steps have already been taken which should improve the situation.

Improvement did take place, but not as quickly as Buf would have liked.

CHAPTER 7

Navigation

Accurate bombing was, for Bufton, essential, but it did presuppose accurate location of the target to be bombed, and the Butt Report had vividly shown how imperfect the navigation of many crews had been. This was not altogether surprising, because the RAF had never taken navigation very seriously, certainly not before the war, and the navigator did not rate highly in general estimation. The exception was Coastal Command, whose crews did not have many landmarks to guide them.

In a talk to the RAF Historical Society, Air Vice-Marshal Oulton recalled his work as Chief Instructor at the School of Navigation in 1938, when he was sent twelve squadron commanders to teach them navigation.

> All claimed to be competent. I set each of them to navigate an Anson flown by a staff pilot to the Terschelling light. Most had never flown over the sea before, and none found his way there or back to Manston. Until 1938 navigation was only taken seriously in the flying boat world, and when the expansion came we did not have enough to provide the instructors. It took several years before we could remedy the situation and initially many of the instructors were little better than the students.

The RAF Manual of Navigation, AP1234 of 1937, devoted half a page to night navigation, 'which will be performed by the light of towns,' and so it is hardly surprising that in the air exercise of 1938, two-thirds of the attacking force failed to find an illuminated Birmingham, a failure noted by the Chief of Air Staff. The Operational Requirement of 1936 for heavy bombers made no provision for a navigator, not even a table, and it was not until 1941 that 'navigator' became a specialised aircrew function.

Until the arrival of radar aids, the navigational equipment in an RAF bomber consisted of a compass, a sextant, an auto-compass and a few other minor instruments with which the navigator would carry out 'dead reckoning' (DR). This involved the calculation of two vectors, the course and airspeed of the aircraft (according to the pilot) and the direction and speed of the wind, the combination of which would produce the third vector, the track and groundspeed of the aircraft.

Unfortunately none of this was foolproof. The pilot's instruments did not always give true readings, especially if he was having to take evasive action, and the wind would certainly alter with the changing height and changing weather. The navigator therefore had to take a 'fix' if he could. This might be by astro-navigation if the stars were visible and if the aircraft was steady enough to allow the navigator to manipulate the sextant, to be followed by some twenty minutes of difficult calculation by poor light and on a vibrating table. Map reading was another possibility, no easy task in the dark, often with cloud, rain or ice, amid the searchlights and flak. In addition, the aircraft were flying to a strict time schedule. There was also direction finding from existing radio transmissions, but this was a lengthy, skilled and generally inaccurate business.

The arrival of radar and other electronic aids in 1942 made all the difference. (Strictly speaking, Gee was not radar.) The business of flying along a radio beam was not a wartime invention, nor was it a British one. In 1933, the German radio industry was working on radio beams to give track guidance, and in the USA by 1935 there was a network of inter-city routes known as Radio Range. This produced four directional beams that could be arranged as required, each giving an audio 'on course' signal, a steady note in the pilot's headphones telling him that he was 'on beam', with deviation to the left producing dots, to the right producing dashes, and a steady note indicating that he was on course. In a similar way, the Lorenz Company in Germany produced a short-range airfield approach to facilitate landings in fog which was adopted by, amongst others, the German airline Deutsche Lufthansa, the Luftwaffe and the RAF. This was based on Very High Frequency (VHF) transmission which only had a short range, but the Germans discovered that a powerful VHF transmitter could be received up to 250 miles away, provided that the aircraft was flying above 20,000 feet.

It did not take them long to produce a blind-bombing system using two such narrow beams sited to give a good intersection and in turn a very accurate fix. No additional equipment was needed in the plane because the beam approach receiver, fitted to most German bombers, was adequate to receive it. Like the Lorenz landing system, dots and dashes indicated an off-centre course and a steady note a correct one. The width of the beam was 0.33° and the frequency 30.0 to 33.3 megacycles per second (mc/s). This system was given the odd name of *Knickebein*, meaning 'Bent Leg'. Its main disadvantage, again, was its limited range, since for a distance of 200 miles the plane had to fly at or above 20,000 feet, which was beyond the capacity of most bombers, especially if they were laden with bombs and full petrol tanks. It had, however, several advantages: many aircraft could use it at the same time; no special training was needed; and signals could not be heard on the ground more than thirty miles away.

The Lorenz Company were now working on another secret VHF bombing aid known as *X-Verfahren* (X-system), a highly complex multi-beam system working in the frequency range 66.0 to 77.0 mc/s. One transmitter provided the approach beam, while three other transmitters provided crossbeams to create intersections at fixed distances from the target, plus an automatic bomb release. The first tests were carried out in 1934, and it was found that good signals could be received at a distance of 220 miles at 20,000 feet. This system required pilots with good instrument-flying ability as height, heading and airspeed had to be maintained accurately, especially in the final phase. No evasive action could be taken in the final twenty to thirty miles.

By March 1939, regular practice flights were being made by selected crews to a height of 30,000 feet. One wireless operator recalled:

We quickly learned that it was important for the pilot to fly the aircraft accurately, but equally important was the co-operation between the observer and the wireless operator especially during the last 30 minutes or so of the flight to the target.

The *X-Gerät* was simple to use ... Morale in the unit was high and our conditions of service and pay were good. Until the outbreak of war we received double flying pay ...

Later, the observer was replaced by the navigator-bomb aimer (*Bombenschütze*). The unit operated successfully during the invasion of Poland.

On 18 November 1939, the unit's role was formally recognised when it was re-titled *Kampfgruppe* 100 (KGr 100) with the full status of an operational wing with two squadrons of Heinkel He 111s, but the utmost secrecy was maintained. The Luftwaffe now turned its attention to Britain, and in December three experimental flights over London were made; further action was curtailed by particularly severe weather. On 13 February the *Gruppe* suffered a severe loss when its commanding officer was shot down by two Spitfires of No. 54 Squadron over the Thames Estuary. Within days the *X-Gerät* was removed from all operational aircraft.

On 9 April 1940, the Germans invaded Norway and the *Gruppe* succeeded in sinking two ships, a British light cruiser and a Polish destroyer. On its last operation in Norway the *Gruppe*'s Commander was shot down by two Hurricanes of No. 46 Squadron, and he and the Staff Technical Officer were captured by the Norwegians and handed over to the British. The importance of the catch, however, was totally missed by British intelligence, and it was only in November, with the capture of another crew, that the RAF learned that the *Gruppe* was using a beam-bombing system. There was no other air force in the world so equipped, and in August, Germany turned its attention to Britain. The *Gruppe* was moved to Vannes in Britanny, midway between Lorient and St Nazaire, and a chain of radio beacons was set up along the coast of continental Europe from north-west France to Norway.

And so the Battle of Britain began. Its aim was to destroy Fighter Command, to starve Britain out with a U-boat blockade and to eradicate her ports and industrial centres by a bomber offensive, indeed the first 'strategic bombing offensive'. Vannes was not an impressive air base. It was a small pre-war civil airfield used by a flying club with no hard runways and one small hangar, without any living quarters. The unit was satisfied with its Heinkels: they were reliable, fairly comfortable and handled well. Their low approach speed was well suited to landings at night. They also found that they had little to fear at night from British night fighters and night bombing was to be their future function.

While the Luftwaffe undoubtedly led the way in precision bombing, the RAF certainly led in the gathering of intelligence. Since early 1941, that department of the Air Staff (AI) had been headed by the Assistant Chief of Staff (Intelligence), whose responsibility it was to keep the Chief informed of all important developments. Beneath him AI 1 (k) was concerned with drawing information from captured German airmen. This was done at the Joint Interrogation Centre by a variety of cunning methods (not involving pain) including hidden microphones and 'stool-pigeons', mainly German refugees carefully briefed. AI 1 (g) had technical officers to examine and report on crashed German aircraft. Another branch specialised in documents of all sorts found in crashed aircraft. But above all was 'Y' intelligence gained from intercepted radio messages at RAF Cheadle which, if encoded, were sent to the Government Code and Cypher School at Bletchley Park for breaking. The Directorate of Signals 'Y' rapidly expanded to become No.80 Wing, working closely with the Wireless Intelligence Development Unit (WIDU), which it eventually controlled.

By the end of 1939, the RAF knew that KGr 100 was using a precision-bombing system and every effort was made to discover its secrets. *Knickebein* was known, and in June 1940 Professor Frederick Lindemann, Churchill's scientific advisor, informed him that 'the Germans had the capability of bombing accurately by day or night, regardless of weather conditions; while they might not be able to hit a particular factory, they could certainly hit a city or town.' The RAF was using both aircraft and weather stations along the south coast that could measure the direction in which the beams were laid, indicating likely targets, but British night defences posed little threat. *Knickebein* was given the code name *Headache* and a jamming system was known as *Aspirin*. However, a better method than jamming was devised, named *Meaconing*, which consisted of picking up the German signals and then re-transmitting them by Meacons so that German aircrews found their needles wandering haphazardly, often pointing to a Meacon site. They were often unsure of their position and sometimes were completely lost. This method, combined with decoy fires, was used in the four German raids on Liverpool and Birkenhead in August 1940. So widely scattered was the bombing in the first raid that the Ministry of Home Security believed the Midlands to be the main target area. On the second night the British reported that, 'the areas attacked were the Tyne and Hartlepool, South Wales, Liverpool and Manchester.' Only a few bombs hit the docks, which were the main objective.

In addition, the RAF's 'Y' Service, with the help of GC and CS at Bletchley Park, was able to gather much information about the strength and organisation of the Luftwaffe, and the call-signs of individual aircraft. Communication between KGr 100's Operations Room and its beam stations was by wireless, as landlines apparently were not adequate, and much of this was intercepted, decoded, and carefully collated at 'BP'.

KGr 100 was given the task of attacking British aircraft factories, and in its first raid on 13–14 August it despatched twenty-one He 111s against the Dunlop works at Birmingham and the Nuffield Spitfire factory at Castle Bromwich. Eleven bombs fell on the latter but did little damage. The fourth raid, on 22–23 August, was by twenty-three aircraft on the Bristol Aeroplane Company's factory at Filton, near Bristol, and No.4 factory and No.11 Test Bed were badly damaged. This attack, lasting two hours, was probably the unit's most successful of the period.

At the same time, the RAF monitors picked up the new *X-Verfahren* transmissions, but at first their purpose was not clear and the assumption was made, wrongly, that this was the same as *Knickebein*, although it fell into the 66–77 mc/s range and the width of its beam was approximately 0.5°

A week after the Liverpool raids, beginning on 5 September 1940, the Luftwaffe turned its attention to London and now they had the benefit of a new bombing system called *Y-Verfahren*. This used a single beam to provide track guidance and a second transmitter-receiver that measured the bomber's distance along the beam.

The standard He 111 autopilot was modified to accept electronic inputs for coupled beam tracking and aircraft remained coupled to the beam until either the autopilot was disconnected or the beam signal faded. Such auto-coupling was about twenty years ahead of any similar system.

The unit selected to operate with *Y-Verfahren* was III/KG 26, equipped with the Heinkel 111 H5 adapted to carry bombs of the largest size and additional fuel tanks. The night of 7/8 September saw the first of many large air raids, the beginning of the Blitz, in which 247 German bombers took part. Among the early arrivals were eight Heinkels of KGr 100, whose crews reported satisfactory results with the explosion of two gasholders on the south bank of the Thames.

Britain had somewhat asked for this, because after the first German raid on 5–6 September, which killed many civilians, Churchill ordered a return attack on Berlin. This was not a success: only about a quarter of the RAF's eighty-one bombers found the city on account of thick cloud and navigational errors, but it so infuriated Hitler that he sanctioned the campaign of heavy night raids which lasted for two months with little effective opposition. The Germans discovered, however, that even London was difficult to find on moonless or cloudy nights without the aid of *Knickebein*. KGr 100, however, with its *X-Verfahren*, was now well practised in more precise bombing and so it was to be used for target-marking as an Illuminator (*Beleuchter*) or Fire-lighter (*Anzünder*) Gruppe. Little did the Germans realise the disastrous repercussions this system was to have in due course on fifty or so of their largest towns and cities. Their methods, however, were not the same as the future Pathfinder Force of the RAF. They did not drop flares or other pyrotechnics, but used mainly incendiary bombs to start fires. They were not always the first over the target and they were allowed two to five minutes for each plane to attack. This unit's aiming was usually precise, but other aircraft bombed on the glow of fires that they saw through clouds and neighbouring residential districts frequently suffered.

On 14 November 1940, the Blitz was widened to include attacks on industrial centres, as the inhabitants of Coventry were soon to discover,

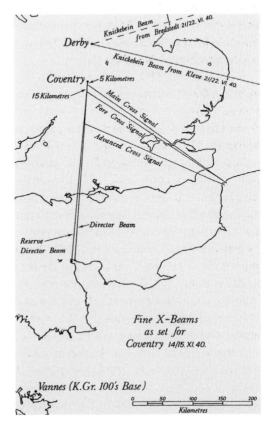

Map showing X-beams for the bombing of Coventry 14/15 November 1940. Bufton and Mackie's *Knickebein* beams are also shown. (F.E. Jones)

despite information from a prisoner shot down five days before about large-scale attacks planned for the next full-moon period on Coventry and Birmingham and decrypts including the word *Korn* – the code-name for Coventry. By early afternoon it was known that Coventry was the target, but little could be done apart from the addition of some barrage balloons.

A very heavy attack was mounted from 7.20p.m. to 5.35a.m., opened by thirteen Heinkels of KGr 100 who dropped forty-eight high explosives and over 10,000 incendiary bombs on the eastern part of the city centre. This was followed by the dropping of sixteen of the heaviest bombs available and another 2,000 incendiaries. Specific targets were clear in the moonlight, and after an hour the inner city was a mass of flames and dense smoke began to shroud the area. The bombing was accurate. Twelve important aircraft plants and nine other major industrial works were hit, all railway lines were blocked, nearly 200 gas mains were fractured and some 500 shops destroyed. Two days later, arrangements had been made to transport 10,000 people out of the centre of the city, but only 300 used them. The raid caused a decline, briefly, of twenty per cent of our aircraft output and cost us many hundreds of machines before production was restored. The Germans lost only one bomber out of 449.

Radio countermeasures were busily at work, especially by R.V. Jones of Scientific Intelligence at the Air Ministry, who had first tracked down *Knickebein*. When the Germans introduced *Y-Verfahren* he had already deduced its principles and it was jammed from the start. On the night of 8/9 May 1941, towards the end of the German offensive, two forces were sent out to attack Derby and Nottingham. The attack on Derby was led by KGr 100 with its *X-Verfahren* beams directed to the Rolls-Royce works, but these were jammed so that the effort was spent on the moors to the north-east. A decoy fire had been lit outside Nottingham, and the pilots detailed to attack Nottingham took this to be Derby in flames, moved to a corresponding distance east of Nottingham, and dropped 230 high explosive bombs on the Vale of Belvoir with a total casualty roll of two cows and two chickens.

In May 1941, the German army began to mass eastwards in preparation for its invasion of Russia on 22 June, but the Luftwaffe had a final fling with savage raids on London, Portsmouth, Plymouth, Merseyside, Clydeside and Belfast. By the end of June, two-thirds of the German Air Force had moved east and south and so Britain's long ordeal was over. Serious damage had been done to aircraft factories, steel and shipbuilding industries, stocks of food and oil, public activities, and some 40,000 civilians had been killed, for the loss of some 600 German aircraft, one and a half per cent of those sent out. The total effect, however, was far from decisive. From now on Britain and Russia were allies, and this was a major factor in shaping air policy, for our air offensive was all we could offer to reduce the pressure on Germany's Eastern Front.

Up to September 1941, the scientists and engineers of the Telecommunications Research Establishment had not been approached for help in direction finding – in any case their main energies had been devoted to the defence of the UK. In October, however, a meeting was held to discuss means of helping Bomber Command and from it emerged three devices that were to transform the pattern of bombing.

The first system, later known as Gee (from 'grid') had roots going back to 1937 in an idea of R.J. Dippy to aid landing in bad weather. An operational requirement was

Gee lattice chart of part of the south-western Chain. 1-7 = AB time differences; 41-47 AD. (J. Clements)

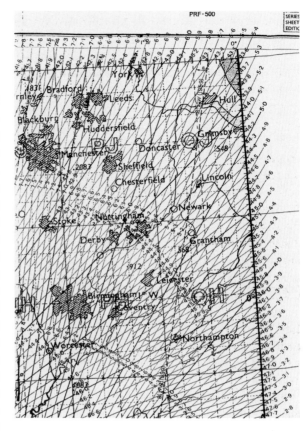

formulated in May 1941 and service trials on twelve hand-made sets began in August 1941 – sufficient for it to go into service on 8 March 1942. It required the aeroplane to measure the time difference between synchronised pulses from three ground stations, a 'master' and two 'slaves'. The placing of all points at which the same time difference is reserved between the arrival of the pulses of the master and one of the slaves is a hyperbola (curve), and so the range of all such time differences produces a group of such curves. The fine differences between pulses from the master and the other slave set up a second group of curves, intersecting the first to form a diamond-shaped lattice or grid (hence the name). The navigator had to overlay this on a plotting chart to convert the grid references to latitude and longitude.

The system had two drawbacks: its accuracy lessened with distance, and in any case was limited by the earth's curvature to about 250–300 miles (though on one occasion an exact reading was made over north Italy at a distance of 700 miles); and it would, in time, be jammed by the enemy, though it continued in use after this. It was certainly useful as far as the northern coastline of Europe and was a great help to returning aircraft in finding their home base.

The other systems were developed later. 'Oboe' went into action in December 1942, and H2S in January 1943, but these will be described as the course of the bomber offensive develops. Such were the main weapons provided (or to be provided) for Bomber Command at the end of 1941. But how were they to be used?

CHAPTER 8

Tactics

When Buf took up his duties on the Air Staff as Deputy Director of Bomber Operations in November 1941, Bomber Command was in poor shape. It had an average force of 250 medium and fifty heavy bombers (the latest being Stirlings with a maximum operational height of about 12,000 feet). The Halifax did not come into service until December 1941, and the Lancaster, developed from the unsuccessful Manchester and enlarged to take four engines, began to replace the Hampdens of No.44 Squadron in the same month, flying its first operation in March 1942. These aircraft had no radar aids and their crews were disheartened by their obvious lack of success and by more than 3,000 casualties suffered in the previous twelve months. They had not been adequately trained and this threw an additional burden on operational squadrons.

Buf was quite clear from his recent experience that two things were necessary for Bomber Command: better means of finding the target and better means of bombing it, taking into account all the opposition the Germans could devise. He was also clear that some navigators were better than others and some bomb aimers were better than others. Several squadrons had already picked out certain crews to lead the rest, as No.10 Squadron did when Buf was in command, but at this time it was a matter of each squadron for itself. The idea of a target-finding force was not new, as Coventry was well aware; it had support in many squadrons and in the Air Staff. One of the first letters to be written in support of the idea was by Squadron Leader (Honorary) D.A.C. Durdney, an oil expert, who made a personal visit to several bomber squadrons. After talking with many aircrews he wrote on 1 February 1941 to Peirse, the Air Officer Commanding Bomber Command, advocating the establishment of a target-finding force. In September 1941, Cherwell, greatly disturbed by the findings of the Butt Report, wrote to Churchill suggesting that Bomber Command should 're-examine most carefully the possibilities of making specially expert navigators or bombers equipped with special navigational aids to fly ahead of the main body to light fires in the right region for the rest to home on, as the Germans do.'

Within Bomber Command Headquarters itself, the navigation section wrote a paper dated 1 November 1941 entitled 'The Problem of Navigating, to Locating and Bombing of a Target by Night'. After pointing out the difficulties of existing methods of navigation, it called for the formation of 'squadrons specially trained and equipped for the task of target location', and emphasised that the selected squadrons should be provided with the latest of navigational and radio equipment on a priority basis. This paper was distributed to the heads of Nos 1, 3, 4 and 5 Groups and their comment invited. Oxland, the head of No.1 Group, argued for improvements in training, but such changes were not the final answer. There was, he wrote,

[a] strong case for the formation of target-locating squadrons. The possibility that the target locators will make a mistake and lead the 'followers' astray is admitted, but it is considered that occasional, perhaps frequent, successes might easily counter-balance the failures ... Only crews considered to be above average should be selected ... they should be required to undergo an intensive training course despite their previous operational experience.

Baldwin, of No.2, Group was opposed to special target-locating squadrons, with a consequent loss of experience in front-line squadrons, a lowering of the general *ésprit de corps*, and the difficulty of providing replacement crews from the Operational Training Units. Torch-bearing, he suggested, should be the responsibility of selected crews in the normal front-line squadrons. Carr of No.4 Group believed that the proposal to form special target-locating squadrons contained the elements of success, but also that the pilots and navigators in the selected squadrons should be expert at their jobs, though they too would need to receive special training. Slessor, of No.5 Group, strongly opposed the idea. He thought all crews should be trained and he foresaw administrative difficulties. His recommendation was 'not to have special target-locating squadrons, but to have locating crews in all squadrons, the proportion of which would increase as our general standard of training improves'. Peirse was not persuaded.

Portal himself was well aware of the need for Bomber Command to improve its performance. In a letter to Tizard of 17 August 1941 relating to the future use of Gee, he suggested that, despite the fact that only a small number of Gee sets would become available before the end of the year, the quicker they were introduced, operationally the better:

It is therefore thought that the best plan would be to emulate the methods of KG 100 and fit the equipment to a small number of aircraft, manned by specially trained crews, to lead the main bulk of the bomber force by raising fires on the target. The number of sets available should enable this to be done on a sufficiently large scale for this method of attack to be really effective.

By the end of 1941, Bomber Command's fortunes had reached a low ebb and serious questions were being asked in high quarters, including the Chiefs of Staff Committee, about the continuance of a strategic-bomber offensive which had little to show either in lowering German war production or affecting the enemy's will to fight. Was the building up of Bomber Command a misuse of scarce resources that would have been better employed in strengthening the Army and the Navy? The question was not a purely military one because on 7 July 1941 Germany invaded Russia, and so overnight Russia became an ally. Churchill immediately sent a message of encouragement to Stalin:

We shall do everything to help you that time, geography, and our growing resources allow ... We are making very heavy attacks both by day and night with our Air Force upon all German-occupied territory and all Germany within our reach ... On Saturday night over 200 heavy bombers attacked German towns, some carrying three tons apiece, and last night nearly 250 heavy bombers were operating. This will go on. Thus we hope to force Hitler to bring back some of his air power to the West and gradually take some of the strain off you ...

The 'heavy bombers' in question were mostly twin-engined Hampdens, Whitleys and Wellingtons. The Stirlings, the first of the four-engined real 'heavies' first went into action in February, and the Stirlings of No. 3 Group were the only heavy bombers to operate by day and night for the remainder of 1941.

Then, on 7 December 1941, came Pear Harbour and the news that much of the American Pacific Fleet had been destroyed by bombers and torpedo-bombers from Japanese aircraft-carriers. Fortunately for the Americans, two of their aircraft carriers were out on an exercise and so avoided destruction. There had been no declaration of war by Japan, but within twenty-four hours Britain had done so, and Churchill wrote: 'No American will think wrong of me if I proclaim that to have the United States at our side was to me the greatest joy.'

This enlarged the sphere of operations enormously and Peirse was promoted to Air Chief Marshal and posted to India to command and re-organise the RAF there, increasing its strength from five to twenty-six squadrons between March, when he arrived, and June. In November 1943, the South-East Asia Command was created with Mountbatten in charge and the air forces, both British and American, placed under Peirse with Major General George Stratemeyer as his Second in Command. The latter published an Order of the Day saying: 'We must merge into one unified force ... neither English nor American, with the faults of neither and virtues of both ...'

So who was to be the new head of Bomber Command? Early in January 1942 Portal had taken Harris aside in Washington and told him that he would be speaking to the Prime Minister about it. Churchill agreed and Portal told Harris the next day. Harris had been in the USA since May 1941 as head of a covert RAF Delegation and as part of a secret exchange of military missions. He soon became aware of pressure to reduce the supply of aircraft that had been agreed by Slessor under the Lend-Lease Act, but was unable to counter this. He did, however, succeed in setting up a training scheme, first with the US Army air force and then with their navy, whereby each offered a third of their capacity for primary, basic and advanced pilot training, with the first batch of 550 pupils arriving in June.

For all his qualities, Harris was no diplomat. He did not mince his words in reports back to his Chief at the Air Ministry and some of these had to be given a strictly limited circulation:

We have been living in a fool's paradise where expectations of quality and quantity in American production and releases are concerned ... The best of them, however, now appreciate that we are getting not only nothing like enough American production for our vital minimum requirements, but not even our money's worth by any standards of business honesty ... They will come in [into the war] when they think we have won it ... but if they come in in any other circumstances short of being kicked in, I'll stand you a dinner and eat, as my share, a pink elephant, trunk, tail and toenails – and raw at that ...

He did actually manage to negotiate the release of nearly all the Kittyhawk fighters that had been arranged (these were to play a vital part in the Middle East fighting), and established excellent relations with Roosevelt, Hopkins, Harriman and Marshall, as with the senior airmen. He had been in the USA before, in 1938, when he arranged the purchase of Hudsons, which proved to be vital for naval reconnaissance and Harvards for initial training. He sailed home in February 1942 with his wife and young daughter.

Harris had also done a short spell in the wartime Air Ministry as Deputy Chief of Air Staff, responsible to Portal and Freeman, Portal's alter ego, from November 1940 to May 1941, but he had no taste for Civil Service methods and little time for the scientists who were trying to help, including the influential Dr R.V. Jones who was working on the Luftwaffe's beams for bombing. Harris was sceptical about the use of such beams: 'We use no beams ourselves, but we bomb just as effectively as the German bomb, deep into Germany.' He claimed that their beams were of more use to us than to the Germans. 'Long may the Boche beam upon us.'

On Sunday 29 December 1940, Harris was working at the Air Ministry when the Luftwaffe carried out its great incendiary attack on the City of London. Climbing to the roof he saw the dome of St Paul's Cathedral silhouetted against a sea of burning buildings, and called Portal to view 'a sight that shouldn't be missed'. By March 1941, when there were prospects of Hitler attacking the Balkans, Harris suggested a series of concentrated attacks on Berlin as a 'demonstration of ruthless force'. He also exaggerated his claims for the success of raids against German oil plants and collided with the Ministry of Economic Warfare with whom he waged a steady war. He organised a full air/sea rescue service to be placed under Coastal Command and sought the right man to run it, and he maintained that many military jobs could as well (or better) be carried out by women, like flying balloons, 'wiggling searchlights', or ferrying aeroplanes. He helped to set up a better transatlantic organisation for flying American-made aircraft to the UK using pilots trained in America and under RAF command. He recommended Donald Bennett, whom he knew well, to run it. As Deputy Chief of Air Staff he met General Arnold again, this time in the Air Ministry. As they walked along a corridor to meet Portal, Arnold commented, 'It's extraordinary, Bert. Nobody seems to be moving. Don't you people realise that you've lost the war?' 'Good God no,' replied Harris, 'we haven't started the bloody war yet'.

One other innovation recommended by Harris was the setting up of a separate Directorate of Bomber Operations. Up till then the Directorate of Home Operations had dealt with both defensive and offensive operations, with most of the emphasis on the former. If the policy and operations of the bomber force were to be adequately analysed, directed and controlled, a separate Directorate, he told Freeman, was needed. His proposal was approved, and Air Commodore J.W. Baker was appointed the first Director of Bomber Operations, with his own staff. Little did Harris know what he had let himself in for!

Harris – 'Bert' to his friends, 'Butch' to his aircrews, and 'Bomber' to the press: 'Bert' was probably a naval term he acquired when commanding No.210 flying-boat Squadron at Pembroke Dock in 1933; 'Butch' was an affectionate soubriquet of his airmen, though it is not clear whether it referred to their heavy casualties or to the deaths inflicted by their bombs – was a complex character. Many of his judgements were manifestly wrong but, as the official historians Webster and Frankland have well summed it up, 'It was his power of command and unshakeable determination which distinguished him as a giant among his contemporaries', and it was this fighting spirit with which he mysteriously imbued the whole of Bomber Command. This was the more remarkable because he did not often visit his squadrons, though sometimes his voice was relayed to crews at their briefing with a short message of encouragement.

One of these visits was recorded by a sergeant Flight Engineer of No.103 Squadron at Elsham in June 1943:

One day, we were honoured by a visit from the Commander-in-Chief, Bomber Command. Air Chief Marshal Sir Arthur Harris was given a terrific cheer as he walked on to the platform in the station cinema. 'Butch' – as we called him – wasted no time on formalities and said that he had come to listen to what we had to say. He invited suggestions, criticism and opinions – nothing barred – on anything which we considered might improve the aircraft, squadron or command. As question after question was fired across the room, I studied the man who had earned the title of 'The Hammer of the Reich'. He looked older and kinder than I had imagined, but there was no doubt that he had a cool, calculating brain, and his whole bearing suggested that he would be utterly ruthless when occasion demanded. It was obvious that he was proud of his men and aircraft, and he promised us an extremely busy time in the coming months. The man-to-man

The Commander-in-Chief on one of his rare visits to an operational squadron. He is leaving a Halifax on 8 May 1943 with Air Vice-Marshal C.R. Carr on his left and Air Commodore G.A. Walker on his right. (IWM)

talking revealed the fact that he was no mere figure-head, content to sit at HQ and pull strings, but that he knew most of the answers and could slug it out with the boys in a manner which proved he valued an honest opinion, be it expressed by Group Captain or Sergeant. I felt that his one ambition was to batter the enemy into an early submission and that he believed Bomber Command, given a free hand, was powerful enough to do it.

But Webster and Frankland add that these priceless and rare qualities found their reflections in serious defects:

Sir Arthur Harris made a habit of seeing only one side of a question and then of exaggerating it. He had a tendency to confuse advice with interference, criticism with sabotage and evidence with propaganda. He resisted innovations and he was seldom open to persuasion. He was sceptical of the Air Staff in general, and of many officers who served upon it he was openly contemptuous. Seeing all issues in terms of black and white, he was impatient of any other possibility, and having taken upon himself tremendous responsibilities, he expected similar powers to be conferred. Only while serving under the 'direction' of General Eisenhower did he really subordinate himself. From the British Air Staff he required to receive absolute and unquestioning confidence or dismissal. In the event he received neither, but because of the policy which he advocated and the prestige which he had acquired this was, perhaps, not surprising.

Air Chief Marshal Sir Arthur Harris entered on his post as Air Officer Commanding-in-Chief of Bomber Command with several firm convictions formed from a long involvement with bombers and bombing. He was quite sure that the only way to win the war was by the general destruction of forty or so (later expanded to eighty) of Germany's principal towns and cities. This would need a force of 4,000 bombers, and there was no possibility of Bomber Command ever reaching that size. The outlook changed when the Americans came in, but their policy was to concentrate on industrial targets with 'precision bombing', rather than 'area bombing'. Harris argued that destruction of the homes of industrial workers and public amenities would have the same effect. He seems to have ignored the evidence of British reaction to German bombing and was oblivious of the remarkable Nazi efficiency in repairing buildings (with the aid of slave workers from conquered countries), providing food and clothing for those bombed out, the evacuation of children from big towns (and adults also) after air raids, and the grim efficiency of the Gestapo in sniffing out any signs of dissatisfaction with the regime. One casual remark of doubt about the certainty of victory could land a person in court followed by summary execution. A remarkable step in maintenance of 'morale' was the granting of leave to soldiers on the Eastern Front to return to their families if their homes had been destroyed in a raid.

Throughout the war Harris stuck to his colours, at first taking Portal with him. He resented any claim by the army for squadrons to be released for army cooperation and by the navy for naval cooperation. Part of his argument was that, by night, heavy bombers could not find and bomb small targets with sufficient accuracy, and that his crews were not trained for daytime close-support bombing. When they actually had to do this and succeeded he was surprised. Portal had to argue his case at the Chiefs of Staff meetings (held nearly every morning) and Alan Brooke, the Chief of the Imperial Staff who chaired most of them, recorded in his diary the following:

11 March 1942
Long COS meeting at which we discussed the naval and army calls on the air force. It resulted in rather a heated debate which did not lead us on to much! I expect some pretty stormy passages within the next few weeks.

My expectations were certainly fulfilled! The Air Force was at this time engaged in an all-out air offensive on Germany and were putting every ounce of their strength into this effort. Many of them held the opinion that, given sufficient heavy bombers, Germany could be brought to her knees by air action alone. In these circumstances it is not surprising that the air ministry was anxious to develop its strength in those types of aircraft that were best suited for the attack on Germany. As a result the army was being starved of any types suitable for the direct support of land forces. We had gone to war with the obsolete Lysander machine, and since then nothing had materialized. Everything seemed to be devoted to the production of four-engine bombers which were unsuited for close cooperation with the army. All Air Force eyes were trained on Germany and consequently all the personnel trained for long distance raids, and little interest was displayed in close cooperation with land forces.

Many doubted that land forces would ever be again employed in large land operations on the Continent – why therefore provide for a contingency that would probably never arise? They could always produce the argument that the Air Force was at that time busy hitting the Germans hard – were they to reduce this effort for the problematical benefits to be derived by producing men and machines capable of cooperating with the Army in operations that were unlikely ever to take place! It was uphill work striving to obtain what would be essential in later stages of the war if we were ever to win!

The navy were also fighting for greater air support in the anti-submarine war which they were engaged in, and on which our very existence depended. Then again the Naval operations seemed purely defensive, promised no decisive results of victory – were they therefore to be allowed to detract from the bomber offensive on Germany, which might hold decisive promises of success?

[The italics represent a later reflection]

He wrote again, a month later:

13 April 1942
A bad COS with much loss of time and interruptions trying to frame a reply for Marshall. Then lunch with Portal and Freeman to settle 'off the record' the differences between Army and Air Force. Evidently little hope of arriving at any sort of settlement.

This was still connected with the fact that the Air Force would at that time still make no provision for Army cooperation and air support. Their energies and outlook were entirely absorbed with the air offensive against Germany, and they considered a re-entry by the Army into Europe as an unlikely contingency which should not be allowed to detract from the air offensive against Germany – through which alone success might be achieved. It was a difficult policy to counter in those days.

It followed from this that Harris treated with scorn what he called 'panacea' targets, particularly ball-bearing factories and oil plants, but also aircraft factories, railways and canals. About the first he was partly right, though Albert Speer, Hitler's Minister of Production, wondered (after the war) why we had not gone for the first much earlier and much stronger. About the second, Harris was undoubtedly wrong, as it was finally shortage of fuel that incapacitated both the enemy's army and his air force.

Harris did not trust intelligence sources, even on occasions messages from Ultra, the decrypts from Bletchley Park. These were not normally sent to him, for the Air Council had its own Intelligence Department whose task it was to obtain information from every source, sift it, evaluate it and pass it on for necessary action. In particular, Harris distrusted the figures and forecasts of the Ministry of Economic Warfare, though admittedly these were not always reliable.

He calculated at five per cent the rate of loss that Bomber Command could stand from the point of view of replacement of crews and of aircraft. In the whole of the war Bomber Command lost 8,655 aircraft (not counting those which crashed on their return), and 49,585 aircrew were killed, pronounced missing or captured. These latter could be replaced thanks to the Empire Air Training Scheme which operated largely in the USA, Canada and South Africa (only the German U-boat crews had a higher proportion of casualties), and the aircraft – and in particular the Lancaster, and later the Mosquito – were the result of brilliant planning and development from 1936 onwards, both on the part of the designers and manufacturers and on the part of the Air Council's Department of Research and Development, notably its Air Member, Air Marshal Wilfrid Freeman. It was he who was captivated by the Mosquito that was greeted with suspicion by the Air Ministry and was branded for two years as 'Freeman's Folly'. It later proved to be one of the finest and most versatile military aircraft of the war, enjoying the lowest loss rate of any of Bomber Command's aircraft.

Such was the Commander with whom Buf had principally to deal in the Department which Harris himself had set up.

CHAPTER 9

Confrontation

A s early as June 1941, Buf's predecessor as Deputy Director of Bomber Operations, A.B. Ellwood, had noted under 'Points for Discussion' the 'training of fire-raising squadrons carrying 100 per cent load and manned by experienced crews on the lines of KG 100 and KG 26 ...' Reinforcement came in August in a paper from a colleague in charge of B Ops 1, Wing Commander Morley, concluding that raids must be heavy and continuous. A Coventry-style attack per month for four to six months would produce a crack in German morale. He argued for the proper use of incendiary bombs, with two to three fire-raising squadrons and first-class navigators and a really heavy incendiary load.

Following a disastrous raid on Nuremburg on October 11–12, Morley suggested the adoption of an entirely new policy by the introduction of incendiary bombs as the primary weapon of attack. He listed five salient points: first, the immediate formation of two or three fire-raising squadrons consisting of Stirlings or Halifaxes; second, specially selected first-class navigators with operational experience; third, at least 30,000 4lb incendiary bombs to be dropped within twenty minutes; fourth, every such aircraft ought to carry a camera; and fifth, five to ten per cent of incendiary bombs should be explosive to discourage fire-watchers and fire-fighters. Morley concluded:

> Despite the recent tactical paper on Fire Raising that was sent to Bomber Command about a month ago, they completely failed to carry out the Nuremburg raid on the lines suggested. The result was disastrous and was undoubtedly due to the fact that the first aircraft to get to the target area bombed a small town about 15 miles from Nuremburg by mistake. It now transpires that the pilot of this aircraft was a beginner operationally and had only made 3–4 trips over Germany at night.
>
> A squadron leader in a Stirling aircraft arriving later over the area saw that the main body of aircraft were bombing the wrong target and himself found and bombed the selected target, Nuremburg, thereby showing it was possible to recognize given sufficient knowledge and experience. The above disaster could undoubtedly have been avoided if specially selected first-class navigators had been dispatched in the first 30–40 aircraft.

A very frank letter came to Morley from the Headquarters of No. 3 Group at Exning (not from the Air Officer Commanding) dated 2 January 1942:

> Many thanks for your letter and notes regarding the proposed fire raising operations which we discussed on your recent visit here. As you know I am very

keen to see anything tried that may get us out of our present unsatisfactory state. I personally think it is frightfully important to send out Mosquito or such type aircraft towards the target to see if the weather is reasonably good before we stage any large scale night operations. How often is a big effort wasted as a result of faulty Met, to say nothing of crews. Secondly, we must develop bigger and better flares. It seems almost impossible to get people to realize that one cannot see in the dark. Thirdly, we must improve the standard of crews leaving OTUs [Operational Training Units]. This standard has fallen dangerously low of late.

Given reasonably good crews, favourable weather conditions and flares which will really illuminate the ground and not simply shed a dim yellow light in the encircling gloom, we should be able to find and hit the target but until these difficulties are overcome I am afraid our striking force is one in name only.

There are many arguments for and against the formation of special fire raising squadrons and I do not propose to go into them here, but my AOC does not, I know, consider the formation of special squadrons desirable, one reason being that our squadrons are so very weak in experienced crews so we favour picked crews in squadrons to do the fire raising.

A week later, Buf sent to his Director a slightly revised version of the paper he had written when he first arrived in November, which may well be seen as the initial specification of the Pathfinder Force:

I suggest therefore that we take the bull by the horns [Harris had not arrived yet] and induce them [Bomber Command] to allocate certain squadrons to the role of a target-finding and fire-raising force on KG 100 principles. With the introduction of 'Gee' in the early stages before all aircraft are equipped, and definitely with Oboe, such a force will be essential, and I think the idea should be initiated now on the basis of the flare scheme. It is clear that the target-finding force should have every available navigation aid, and therefore the squadrons selected for it should be those which will first have 'Gee' ... They should start training, thinking and developing tactics with a view to acting in a target-finding role.

He went on to nominate six squadrons for the task.

In the meantime, Buf wrote a short paper for his Director to take to a meeting at Bomber Command concerning the first trials of Gee over Germany. He said:

We do not <u>know</u> the accuracy <u>over Germany</u> and we must therefore check up, either with 2 or 3 aircraft taking photos, say at Aachen, <u>before</u> the full scale is launched, or by using flares at the beginning of operation to make sure everything is O.K. I favour the latter course ...

It is important to establish the blind-bombing accuracy of 'Gee' in target areas as soon as possible ... Suggest three aircraft drop 4000lb of incendiaries on Aachen and that photos are taken to check up on.

On 26 January, Buf sent a draft proposal to his Director for a Bomber Development Unit. He noted the comment of Sir Henry Tizard (a distinguished scientist and Chairman of the Aeronautical Research Committee, and a former pilot in the RFC) that 'we do not yet know the difficulties of the <u>average</u> crew at night.' Bufton argued that 'we cannot do this round a conference table. The only way is to place scientists in immediate and continuous contact with the <u>average</u> crew engaged in ops – not only concerning navigation but also radio aids, armament and pyrotechnics. Flares are 12 months behind requirements.' He proposed a Bomber Development Unit with a body of scientists in day-to-day touch with an operational squadron on an operational station in a position to tackle 'fire-brigade' lines of development. It should become the nucleus of a Target Finding Force of six squadrons, one stationed with the scientists and the other five as close as possible, in the same group. This would lead to a marked increase in the efficiency of the selected squadrons and to the raising of general standards throughout the Command.

Harris was appointed Air Officer Commanding-in-Chief on 22 February 1942, and five days later Buf wrote an urgent appeal to his Director:

At present, there is a great deal of criticism of our strategic bombing offensive not only in Army and Navy circles and in Parliament but also by members of the public. This stems from a failure to exercise tactical direction and control of the bomber force. I urge therefore most strongly and with the utmost urgency that we should immediately form a Target Finding Force, cut out the dead wood from Bomber Command, and so tighten the sinews of control that the bomber force may be wielded and directed as a sharp, flexible, hard-hitting unit.

Three weeks after his installation, Harris summoned a conference of his Group Commanders (he had five Bomber Groups and two Training Groups) and their Senior Air Staff Officers, and Buf and his Director, John Baker, were invited to attend. Here Buf recounts the episode (as recorded in the Proceedings of the RAF Historical Society, September 1989):

We had a talk with the C-in-C before lunch and he went through the *corps d'élite* arguments and so on, and said, amongst other things, that if you collected into a Pathfinder force some of the best crews from various squadrons, they would lose their possible chance of promotion. This shook me, having two brothers who had been shot down and having been pretty well shot down myself, so I banged the table and said, 'Sir, you will never win the war like that; these people don't know if they will be alive tomorrow and they couldn't care less about promotion'. So he looked at his watch and said it was time for lunch, and off he went. We reassembled after lunch and Bert came in and said, 'I called this conference to discuss the very emotive subject of a target-finding force'. He said, 'I was almost assaulted in my office over this matter this morning, but nevertheless, I would like your opinions. I need hardly tell you that I am totally and fundamentally opposed to the idea, but I wouldn't mind hearing your views.' So when a vote was taken it was sort of 100 per cent and we all went back to the Air Ministry with our tails between our legs.

The next morning I was about to go into King Charles Street when a Bentley pulled up in a screech of brakes, and Bert got out and I stood back and saluted, and he said, 'Good morning, Bufton, what are you going to do to me today?' I said, 'Well. I didn't plan to do anything, Sir'. He said, 'Well, walk upstairs with me, I'm going to see the CAS'. And he said, 'Well, if you've got any ideas, write to me, please write to me'. Anyway this gave us a lead, and we very quickly ran downstairs and wrote him a three-page letter about the Pathfinder force, and he kindly replied and there were about three or four of these letters.

Writing from his own experience, Buf argued that Squadron Commanders have, in practice, a very limited outlook, and similarly a Group outlook is inclined to be parochial. Only when the problem can be viewed from a distance does the solution appear. It is for this reason that the idea of the target-finding force had not originated from the operational units themselves. The development of a tactical method of illuminating the target and creating a beacon conflagration, he claimed, was not likely to happen while squadrons were dispersed about the country. If, however, six squadrons stationed in close proximity were given the sole responsibility of this work, they would devise their own methods in an extremely short time, and as a result of discussion among themselves and the great force of enthusiasm that would be released, would quickly achieve results surpassing any we could expect of them.

The urgency of obtaining immediate results, both for strategic and political reasons, was such that one must initially provide the squadrons with some reinforcements of good crews from the rest of the Command. Assuming one-third of the existing crews are good ones, and that two-thirds of the crews in each squadron are required to be of high quality, it is clear that forty good crews would have to be withdrawn from the rest of the Command. Thus, dilution would be small and non-recurring.

Harris professed to dislike the idea of what he called a *corps d'élite*, but he was happy to create a new squadron, No.617, and feed it with the best aircraft and the best crews available to enable it to carry out a particularly demanding task, the bombing of the Mohne Dam, which he knew would result in a very heavy loss. Thereafter he nurtured that squadron as élite in every sense.

To reinforce his case, Buf decided to do a little consultation of his own, even if it meant going behind Harris's back. At the beginning of April he sent his paper on the Target Finding Force, together with questions requiring a 'Yes' or 'No' answer, to a dozen Squadron and Station Commanders all known to him personally, and he received unanimously positive answers. Here are some of them:

Crews in favour of an illuminating force. No faith in the present Target Finding Force. Lack of necessary skills and experience. Lack of sufficient determination in pressing attacks home, the result of inadequate leadership, especially from station commanders. Impossible for *all* crews to be trained to standard necessary. TFF a very urgent requirement; formation at earliest possible moment vital.

Always a certain number of crews who will bring back a photo near target – well known pilots of outstanding determination. Crews are willing to attack to face dangers but they lack experience and often leadership. Have discussed idea of TFF with many senior captains who all entirely agree.

One out of five crews good enough and sufficiently courageous to mix in with flak and searchlights in Ruhr and bomb targets. Lost many from lack of support from remainder. These should be pulled out and put in crack TFF squadrons: a few will be lost but not half as many as if things are left as they are. As for objections I have never seen anything quite so wet. Creaming off the best for a *corps d'élite* will serve as a tremendous impetus throughout our Bomber Command. Lack of discipline, slackness, and lack of pride in themselves of aircrews is, I regret to say it, pretty well general ... The army has never suffered from having Guards Regiments. Promotion? No, they should only come from parallel posts.

To locate target in strongly defended area requires experience, determination, skill, and luck. About ten percent of attacking crews possess the first three essentials, and a proportion will hit target. The night bomber force is leaderless as in no other attacking force.

The comparative ineffectiveness of our bombing is due to lack of navigation ability both in its elementary and in its advanced phases. A *corps d'élite* even if it were unpopular is absolutely essential. A majority of captains and navigators would only be too pleased to have the target found for them ... a reward for proficiency and professional ability. A most refined 'cream of the RAF' must be used, good navigators, and must be organised as a team. Complete first-hand practical experience and thorough basic professional knowledge are essential for the Commander of this Force.

A unit comparable with KG 100 is vital. Only a small percentage of navigators have the necessary determination. The success of the TFF depends upon youth and a vigorous mind. The crocks must be swept from the board.

Being a 'crack unit' is in its favour. That the TFF is regarded as such will be an added incentive and should be encouraged. I should like to see bomber crews brought into the picture so that they can see how they are linking up with the Battle of the Atlantic or helping Russian armies. Added interest and understanding would increase their enthusiasm enormously.

One or two really good crews in an otherwise mediocre unit do not raise the level of the standard of the other crews but are misemployed.

Buf sent these answers and others off to Harris, to be followed soon after by another letter in which he summed up his whole argument. It is dated 8 May 1942 and is headed 'Secret and Personal'. It is so typical of Bufton with his vision, his technical knowledge and his courage that it is worth printing in its entirety:

Secret and Personal

Thank you for returning the documents and for your letter which accompanied them. In it you say that you still have a fairly open mind on the subject of a target finding force but that you are not yet convinced by the arguments which have so far been advanced. I hope you will not mind my accepting this as an invitation to express further arguments or comment.

I drafted this letter while I was on leave but have not had time to complete it until now. On my return the Director said that you had referred to my having spoken to an MP on the subject of a TFF. The subject has not of course been discussed with any MP or outside the Air Ministry so I don't know how this idea arose. I have in fact, in view of your invitation, made a point of putting my arguments to you in full confidence that you would appreciate them, and, if convinced, form a TFF and that this would be the quickest way of accomplishing the step which I know in my heart will immediately treble or quadruple the effective hitting power of the Bomber Force and which is such a vital and urgent matter that I have had it constantly in my mind for some months past. My greatest difficulty is that nobody seems to want to quadruple our hitting power or realize that we can do it now.

In your letter you raise two points about the general success of our bombing. Firstly, that over the last few weeks the progressive development of our TR1335 [Gee] technique has led to the majority of our bombs landing usefully in built up areas in the Ruhr, reasonably close to the intended target and that our present methods are proving reasonably satisfactory. I will quote three recent examples to illustrate how far we are falling short of what we can achieve: Essen, a heavily defended area; Rostock, lightly defended but deep inside Germany; and Gennevilliers, lightly defended and easy to locate at short range.

An analysis of the 122 plotted photographs taken on the eight raids on Essen between 8th March and 12th April shows that two were on the target, two within one mile, eight between one and five miles, 104 between five and twenty-five miles and six between twenty-five miles and 100 miles from the target. 90% of the aircraft bomb points between five and a hundred miles from the target. I think you will agree that such dispersal shows our present methods fail entirely to achieve the aim in a highly defended area, despite the assistance derived from TR1335 which was being employed on its most favourable line of shoot. Subsequent photographic cover confirms this fact.

In the Rostock raids conditions were perfect and defences negligible. Yet on the first night most of the effort was dissipated away from the target because our methods permitted initial fires to be started elsewhere. Of seventy-two successful photos reported to be of Rostock, only sixteen or 22% in fact were. 78% of our effort as far as the aim was concerned was wasted. Correct tactics would have more than quadrupled the effect of this raid.

Gennevilliers represented the ideal operational conditions: short distance; easy to locate; light; unpractised and not fully organised defences and perfect weather with full moon. Here again the same basic defects were noted and fires away from the target were bombed. The eighty-five aircraft claiming to have attacked took ninety successfully plotted photographs of which only eleven, or 12%, were of the works. The actual results achieved confirm that the raid was only about 12% effective as suggested by the photographs. This raid proves that even under ideal conditions when the target can be clearly seen leadership and a focus is essential.

These three examples, embracing weather conditions better than we can normally expect are indicative of the results obtainable with our present tactical methods. I do not think that there can be any progressive development with them apart from the initial improvement conferred by TR1335. The basic need is the initial unmistakable conflagration. This can never be achieved when second class crews are mixed with first class ones in the initial phase of the attack. Even the first class crews will not be successful unless they are co-ordinated in one body and develop a specialized technique. We want not a '*corps d'élite*' as such but a force expert in achieving this essential part of any large scale operation.

Secondly you suggest that in heavily defended areas such as the Ruhr it is physically impossible to see the pinpoint and bomb it in the face of the searchlights. If this is the case we should surely admit defeat and change our aim. Searchlights, however, only affect seriously those aircraft that are focused on. I have no doubt that the most experienced crews can locate these targets if given the opportunity to work together in a co-ordinated and specially organized body, and all those I have come into contact with are enthusiastically anxious to be given this opportunity.

You refer in your letter to the very serious disadvantages of a '*corps d'élite*'. The main ones I believe are possible effects on morale and promotion. With regard to the effect on morale the unanimous opinion of operational personnel with whom I have come into contact is that a TFF would improve morale. Crews would always be assured of a successful show. They would not feel out of the picture because crews chosen from their own squadron would be in the TFF and would thus give them a personal interest in it. Moreover it would be their ambition to be chosen for it themselves. In this connection we should not I think lose sight of the general lowering of morale of the Command as a whole which has resulted from the inability of crews, either singly or collectively, to find and bomb heavily defended targets under average weather conditions with our present methods.

To suggest that the possibility of slower promotion would be an adverse factor is I think to do an injustice to the spirit and idealism of the crews. Promotion means little to them compared with winning or shortening the War. The majority hold temporary commissions and have no RAF career to worry about, but above all during the five or six months of their operational tour crews do not know from one day to the next which will be their last. Promotion does not therefore enter largely into their calculations, only proving themselves to themselves and achieving results.

The system which has now been introduced, while at first sight appearing to be a step towards the establishment of a TFF does, I suggest, miss the basic and all important principles of the scheme. The main points that occur to me are:

1. The selected squadrons may have a few exceptionally good crews, but their efforts in marking the target are likely to by entirely vitiated by the less efficient crews marking places other than the target. This will immediately lead to dispersion of the main force as we know so well from our experience.

2. If the leading squadrons do achieve their aim of starting an unmistakable conflagration the task of the following, and not so good squadrons will be comparatively simple and thus for the ensuing months an inferior squadron is likely to be chosen to lead the raids. This is a fundamental defect in the scheme.

3. As only two or three crews in each of the squadrons will be first class the aggregate of first class crews in the TFF squadrons will be of the order sixteen to twenty, which is barely enough to illuminate the target let alone cause the essential conflagration with heavy concentration of incendiaries.

4. Owing to the lack of cohesion through geographical separation and the frequent change of role, there will be no development and organic growth of tactical method and technique.

5. By reason of the competitive nature of the scheme the raid leaders will not gain the confidence of the following squadrons in their ability to locate and mark the target. Such confidence would, however, be engendered in a co-ordinated force of able and reliable crews supplied from all squadrons provided it had specialized in the work of target location and marking.

6. An outstanding feature of the TFF scheme, the establishment alongside it of a development and scientific unit, will not be possible.

7. When TR1335 is jammed we will be back where we started.

There seems to be some magic inherent in the phrase '*corps d'élite*' which immediately conjures up battalions of vague and nebulous antagonisms. In peace conditions I would admit them; it would be the only way to progress to disperse the best throughout the whole and encourage development by competition. No one however would dream of trying to defeat the rival school by not turning out the best house team, and that is what we are doing now. It is essential to put the best men in the first team and even that is not enough; they must train and co-ordinate their tactics as a team. Until we do this we cannot start to beat the enemy defences.

It is difficult to realize that the groups, in turning down this one solution to the problem, appreciate fully the vital urgency of the present situation; that our efforts against highly defended targets are falling so short of the mark; and that it is within our power to inflict decisive damage on them. In this connection I wonder whether the issue was put to Station Commanders impartially and fully, with all emphasis on our inability to achieve our aim, and in the light of the overwhelming importance of doing decisive damage now if we are to save thousands of lives by shortening the War, and incidentally to prevent the partial disruption of the Bomber Force. In the shadow of such momentous factors the objections which have been raised surely count but little. I wonder further, whether the majority of the operational Station Commanders were opposed to the scheme. I suggest that the real test would be to call these together, explain to them fully and fairly the scheme and the background and accept their verdict on this purely operational issue.

In conclusion I would like to raise one further matter. Since embarking on this discussion it appears that the arguments raised in it are a manifestation of a much wider issue – a conflict of ideas between the older officers of much general experience and the ever growing body of younger ones who have been actively engaged in operations. It has often been said that this is a young man's war, and this is true to the extent that only the young men have the quick reactions needed to fight our modern weapons. To fight these weapons efficiently they must be directed efficiently, and this can only be done by those who have, or who utilize, a complete knowledge of their possibilities and limitations. Only the young men have this knowledge. Here the difficulty arises. The older officers who, through the years have assumed an increasing responsibility, may perhaps be reluctant to share it, or fully to accept and apply the advice of the younger ones whom they often benevolently regard as inexperienced. This attitude is crystallized in the phrase which you have underlined in your letter – 'their own comparatively narrow spheres'. It indicates that through the years administration and organization have become the broad spheres and operational the narrow. Such an attitude is bound to cramp and frustrate imagination and development in the sphere which is after all the be-all and end-all of Bomber Command. It is this attitude, I feel, which now prevents the formation of the Target Finding Force.

This conflict need never arise. If we could marry, at all levels of command, the mature judgement and wide experience of the older officers with the imagination, drive and operational knowledge of the younger, then I think we should achieve the highest possible standard of morale and achievement throughout Bomber Command.

To bring this about I suggest we need at all Stations a Group Captain (Operations) who would be entirely responsible to the AOC for the operational activities of the Station such as the Ops Room, the Ops/Intelligence Staff, aerodrome control, briefing of crews, control of operations, and supervision and development of tactics. The present duties of a Station Commander are such that he cannot give his best to either the administrative or the operational matters, and therefore there should in addition be a Station Commander of wide experience whose duties would be the running of the base from the purely administrative point of view. This is the German system and it is obviously a sound one and one calculated to extract the utmost efficiency from the operational units.

At Groups similarly, there should be a SASO [Senior Air Staff Officer] who has wide experience on operations. Here again he should be relieved of all responsibilities which are not purely operational by an older officer who might fill the post of SASO (Air).

A similar principle should be applied at Command Headquarters.

In this way the officers conducting operations would be relieved of the grievous administrative burdens which now absorb most of their energies and make it almost impossible for them to analyze results and develop and improve our methods. There would be established, too, that which is now lacking in our organization – an unobstructed and receptive channel for the ebb and flow of new operational ideas from the squadrons to yourself.

In contrast, under the present system, a new idea which might be of extreme value reaches Command, possibly through a non-operational Station Commander, a non-operational SASO, and the AOC, and on the way it is possible its real implications or the supporting arguments are lost and, like so many, the idea is still-born. Under the above scheme too, when a Group Commanders conference is called to decide some tactical question, it might well be advantageous for the Group Commanders to be accompanied by their operational advisors, the SASOs (Ops). I was particularly impressed, at the conference which we were invited to attend, by the fact that the basic tactics for the Command were discussed and determined with no reference to any person of operational experience in this War, and I feel the system here might be improved.

I believe that these measures would confer on the Bomber Force an increased hitting power and brilliancy by unleashing the full potentialities of the operational personnel which at the moment tend to be segregated, unappreciated and hence frustrated.

In conclusion and in spite of Lübecks, Augsbergs and Rostocks, I hope you will not take objection to the frankness of these views which are born only of very great concern for the success of the bomber force. They may prove of interest either in confirmation of ideas which you have already formed, or in the light of subsequent events. In either case I believe this letter will have been justified.

Yours sincerely,
S.O. Bufton

That letter was unanswerable, and by 12 June was still unanswered. Buf then was standing in for his Director, and so was Freeman for Portal. Bufton continues the story:

I was standing in for John Baker one Saturday morning, pondering the problem of the Pathfinder force, when the door opened and Sir Wilfred Freeman put his head around the door and said, 'Good morning, Bufton, any problems?'. I said, 'No, Sir, not really, except we are not making a lot of progress with the Pathfinder Force.' He said, 'Have you got any correspondence on it?' and I said, 'Yes, Sir, I have a big folder.' He said, 'Could I borrow that?' So I said, 'Yes, Sir' and he said, 'Well, I'll go and read through it and give you a ring.' About an hour later, the telephone rang, and he said, 'This last letter, have you had a reply to that?' I said, 'No, Sir.' He said, 'Do you know why?', and I said, 'No, Sir', and he said, 'Because there isn't a reply, you've beaten Bert at his own game' [i.e. writing letters] and he said, 'CAS will be in on Monday; we've got to have a Pathfinder force and I'll talk it over with him.'

To reinforce his case, Freeman arranged a meeting the next day between Buf, himself, and Sir Henry Tizard who had been until recently Scientific Advisor to the RAF, and he gave the scheme his full backing. There is a letter in the file dated 14 June 1942 from Portal to Harris, which was actually the day before Portal returned from leave: it may have been drafted by Freeman.

The letter referred to the inadequate and inaccurate results which Bomber Command was achieving by its present 'rule of thumb' tactical methods using unsegregated crews, and baldly stated that 'the problem confronting us is clearly so great that nothing less than the best will do.' The difficulties were appreciated, but none of them were insuperable. The succession of evasive compromises proposed by Harris were then summarily rejected; they all, of course, implied his admission of the need for a specialist target-finding force:

> Over a period of three months your attitude seems to have progressed from the complete rejection of the target finding force proposal, through a target finding squadron phase, to this present 'raid leader' suggestion. I cannot feel it is logical

The wedding on 1 January 1943 at St George's, Hanover Square. Sue's Wren background is clearly visible. (Dr Downer)

that you should now reject the final and essential step of welding selected crews into one closely knit organisation ... In the opinion of the Air Staff, the formation of the special force would open up a new field for improvement, raising the standard of accuracy of bombing, and thus morale, throughout Bomber Command.

Harris came to see Portal the next day (he normally came to see him once a week) and they discussed the matter. It is said that Harris's introductory remark about the TFF was 'Over my dead body'. They must have had a full discussion because Harris was told to go away and think about it and let Portal know his conclusions the next day. The proceedings were not recorded.

On the Monday, Buf was summoned by phone to see the Chief of Air Staff who said he fully agreed that we had to have a special force for target finding, and that Harris was coming the next day with his final decisions. In the meantime, would Buf please let him have an Order of Battle for this force: who was to be in it and who was to command it. The next day, agreement was reached (though Harris insisted on calling it a Pathfinder Force, which was not strictly accurate). Only Portal, with the support of Freeman, could have ordered Harris to take this step, and Harris resented it for the rest of the war. The Pathfinder Force (PFF) came into existence on 18 August 1942.

On 16 June, Buf broke one of his rules and in a letter to Sue referred to his work, but it was exceptional. He wrote:

... the big conference was postponed for a week till next Thursday – but now it won't take place at all, for WE HAVE WON!!!! Bert came to see the Head Man today, and he hadn't a leg to stand on. It's a shattering result, and is rather like the battle in the last war which was required to set up the convoy system. Last Thursday ... I was seeing the Head Man. He read all my letters, or rather our letters, and everything we'd written, and he was great; apologised for not fully understanding the scheme earlier – he'd not really heard the full story – thanked me for all the hard work that had been put into it, and finally said he was fully convinced. So you see, it was worth while after all.

CHAPTER 10

Pathfinders

On 5 July 1942, Donald Bennett was appointed to command the newly created Pathfinder Force. He was summoned to High Wycombe, the Headquarters of Bomber Command, to the presence of the Air Officer Commander-in-Chief himself. The following is Bennett's account of the interview:

Bert Harris was blunt, honest and, as always, to the point. Roughly, the gist of his conversation with me was that he had opposed the idea of a separate Pathfinder Force tooth and nail – that he did not believe it was right to weaken the Command by taking its best crews in order to form a *corps d'élite* as a leading body. He thought it was unfair to other Groups, and he had, therefore, done everything he could to stop the idea of a Pathfinder Force. However, he had been given a direct order from the Prime Minister through the Chief of Air Staff, and since it was forced upon him he insisted that I should command it, in spite of my relatively junior rank. I was to be promoted to acting group captain immediately, and as a group captain could not command such a force, I should do so in his name as a Staff Officer of Headquarters Bomber Command, and I should therefore have a subordinate headquarters to handle the Pathfinders at a station of my choosing convenient to the aerodromes which I also had to choose for the establishment of the Force. He categorically refused to allow it to be called a Target Finding Force, because that was the name which had been put forward by the Directorate of Bomber Operations, and which he, therefore, automatically opposed. He did not put it in quite those words, but that was obviously the implication. He told me that while he was opposed to the Pathfinder Force and would waste no effort on it, he would support me in every way. This assurance was carried out to the letter and in the spirit from then on to the end of the war. He never really gave the Pathfinders a fair chance relative to other special units; but he always supported me personally to the best of his ability, and he did everything he could to help me. He informed me that he was going to issue a special badge to signify a qualified Pathfinder Air Crew member, an idea entirely of his own which I valued greatly then and all through the war as one of the best incentives and one of the best honours which could be granted to those who led. The tour of operations for a Pathfinder crew would be sixty operations instead of the usual thirty. He fully realised that the chances of survival on such a long tour were small, but agreed that it was unavoidable – that if we were to use the best and most experienced people to lead, they should go on doing so for an appreciable time. [This number was later reduced to forty-five.]

Harris received some cold comfort from the fact that later in the war the Luftwaffe borrowed the term from the RAF, and KGr 100 and other units came to be called *Pfadfindergruppe.*

This was not the first meeting of Bennett with Harris. Earlier that month he was summoned to High Wycombe to receive the Distinguished Service Order because Harris made a point of awarding higher decorations to his men personally. In April 1942, Bennett had been given command of No.10 Squadron with its Halifaxes, and soon after his arrival it was given the task of sinking the German battleship the *Tirpitz* in a Norwegian fjord near Trondheim with a special type of spherical mine. Bennett captained one of the bombers and came under very heavy fire over the target that set fire to his starboard wing. He gave the order 'abandon aircraft', which crashed into a snow-covered, well-wooded mountain. He just managed to escape by parachute and set off eastwards towards neutral Sweden. He met up with his wireless operator and together they had an adventurous journey through snow, along icy streams and across stony mountains, until they finally, after three days, stumbled into a Swedish dance hall where they were given a generous dinner and then arrested. After some diplomatic negotiations in Stockholm he managed to get himself flown back to Britain, to Leuchars, as important diplomatic mail, in a slow unarmed Lockheed 14 in broad daylight, which he described as 'one of the most nerve-racking flights I have ever done'. He arrived back in Yorkshire to command his squadron exactly a month after setting out for Trondheim, only sorry that he had missed the first 1,000-bomber raid on Cologne.

Bennett had had a colourful career before then. He was born in Australia in 1910 near Toowoomba where his father ran a cattle station. When he was twenty he managed to join the Royal Australian Air Force – on the condition that, after basic training, he transferred to the RAF! After a year with a fighter squadron, No.29 in England, he applied for a Flying Boat Pilot's Course and completed this after a happy six months, much of which was concerned with navigation in which he excelled. He was then posted to No.210 Squadron, a flying-boat squadron at Pembroke Dock, and soon after he arrived a new CO took over by the name of Harris. (The 'Bert' was no doubt bequeathed by naval connections because in the Navy every Harris is a Bert, as every Murphy is a Spud.) After that he was able at Calshot to specialise in navigation while continuing to fly flying boats. In 1934 he obtained his First-Class Navigators Licence, an extremely rare qualification.

The Short-Mayo Composite aircraft. Donald Bennett flew the upper component, with a navigator, across the Atlantic in 1938.

He left the RAF in 1935 with 1,350 flying hours to his credit on twenty-one different types of aircraft, of which eight were marine. He also managed to acquire a wife, 'a beautiful and wonderful girl', from Switzerland. Inspections had to be carried out by families in Switzerland and Australia, but he was able to use the lengthy sea trip to finish writing a book on navigation – due to be published by Pitman's – in which he was assisted by his new wife. In 1936 he joined Imperial Airways, which was pioneering the Empire routes to Australia and South Africa and was beginning to receive the new Short 'Empire' four-engined monoplane flying boats, and Bennett was given the fourth to captain.

In 1938 he applied to command the Mercury, the top half of the Mayo-Composite aircraft, a small four-engined flying boat perched on top of a large one, Maia, which, after being lifted into the air, would be able to fly non-stop across the Atlantic with half a ton of mail for America. On 20 July 1938, Bennett and his Radio Officer A.J. Coster flew from Foynes direct to Montreal. Later that year, in October, again flying the Mercury, he broke the world long-distance seaplane record, with a flight from Dundee to Alexander Bay, just short of Cape Town. He also inaugurated the two-way regular transatlantic service using in-flight refuelling. The last such flight was on 2 July 1940 and shortly afterwards he was told by the Ministry of Aircraft Production that he was to go to America to ferry American aircraft across the Atlantic to Britain. The first type was the Lockheed Hudson and Bennett had to select the pilots – many were commercial 'rejects', and all, he said, were grossly overpaid – and train them for the task. He himself led the first formation of seven aircraft in mid-November for this long dark crossing. Despite some icing-up as high as 22,000 feet, all seven completed the trip from Gander, Canada, to Aldegrove in Northern Ireland, and from thence to Blackpool.

Surprisingly, a signal arrived from the Air Ministry via Ottawa asking him to call on the Directorate of Bomber Operations on his next visit to London, as they were seriously worried about the inaccuracy of bombing raids on Germany. The Director was John Baker and his deputy Aubry Ellwood. They wanted his advice as a navigator. Bennett asked them what they should expect from aircrews newly trained in peaceful parts of the world but with no practical experience of operational flying. If, however, a force of experienced navigators with better equipment were to lead the attack and then drop some fireworks to direct the main force to the target, better results should be obtained. That was not his last visit to DB Ops, for the seed had been sown and was beginning to germinate.

When America entered the war it was thought that the Atlantic Ferry service should be regularised, that is to say, put under RAF control, and in the first six weeks after Bennett left, three B 24s (later Liberators) and six Hudsons were lost, most of them avoidably. In August 1941 he spent six weeks completely idle, daily attempting to get back into uniform. It was originally proposed that he should have the rank of acting group captain, but this dropped down to acting wing commander and eventually he was offered a job as a squadron leader. This he refused and finally he was sent as an acting wing commander to be second in command of a new initial navigation school. (The RAF's supercilious attitude towards commercial aviators was similar to the Royal Navy's towards merchant seamen.)

Having seen that off the ground he managed a visit to the Personnel Officer at Bomber Command who welcomed him warmly and sent him to No.4 Group. On arriving there he happened by chance to meet the Air Officer Commanding, Roddy Carr, whom he had known as AOC, Northern Ireland. He gave Bennett command of No.77 Squadron equipped with ageing twin-engined Whitleys that were still dropping half their load of bombs on Germany. He was required to fly as second pilot on at least two flights before he did a trip in command, and so he chose the two most junior sergeant pilots. On the second trip, to Wilhelmshaven, he had to rescue the plane from the pilot's hands. Thereafter he flew with a different crew each night to assess their efficiency and give them some instruction in navigation. His time with 77 Squadron shook his faith in the bomber offensive. Only a tiny percentage of the bombs dropped were falling on a worthwhile target. The vast majority of crews were either not finding the target area at all, or if they did they were failing to identify the aiming point. In many cases they were not even bothering to aim. The necessity of a target-finding force became more evident than ever.

Bennett kept in touch with the Directorate of Bomber Operations at the Air Ministry where, in November 1941, Bufton had arrived as Deputy Director and, as a former Squadron Commander, knew the job first hand. In April 1942, Bennett was moved to command No.10 squadron with Halifaxes, and it was there that the operation against the *Tirpitz* took place.

The spring of 1942 marked a low ebb in the fortunes of Bomber Command and Harris devised a master-stroke in improving them by mounting a raid by over a thousand bombers on a single target. After consultation with every unit in his Command, and some outside it, he gathered a force of 1,047 aircraft for the night of 30 May. He was promised the loan of three squadrons from Coastal Command, but this was over-ruled by the First Sea Lord. Fighter Command and Army Cooperation Command put up fifty-four light aircraft to attack airfields on the way to the target. While 302 aircraft came from Operational Training Units, sixty-four others were attached for training purposes. During that month the number of aircraft with crews normally available numbered a little over 400. The target finally selected on the night was Cologne, largely determined by the weather, which obliged with lack of cloud and a full moon over West Germany, upon which nearly 900 aircraft dropped 1,455 tons of bombs (of which two-thirds were incendiaries) over ninety minutes. The loss rate of 3.8 per cent was considerably lower than the average of 4.6 for the previous twelve months, and the loss rate for the 'heavies' in the third wave of the attack was only 1.9 per cent.

Harris tried to repeat this spectacular operation twice more before he had to disband his huge force, first with a raid on Essen by 956 aircraft on 1 June, and secondly on Bremen with 904. The Ruhr was notorious for its haze, largely generated by its factories, and the German radio reported 'widespread raids over Western Germany'. The attack on Bremen did some damage to the Focke-Wulfe aircraft plant at the cost of forty-four aircraft, 4.9 percent of the total. Harris's comment was: 'We are going to scourge the Third Reich from end to end. We are bombing Germany city by city and ever more terribly in order to make it impossible for her to go on with the war.' Such was his vision of 'area bombing'.

At Cologne, in one and three-quarter hours, 45,000 people had lost their homes, 384 civilians and eighty-five soldiers had died, thirty-six factories were totally destroyed and seventy more badly damaged. The docks and railway system had also been savaged. But it was not as simple as that. In the raids on the Hanseatic towns of Lübeck and Rostock of the previous month, so far from losing the six to seven weeks of industrial output predicted by the Ministry of Economic Warfare, Lübeck was operating at eighty to ninety per cent within days, and even the severely damaged Heinkel factory at Rostock made a marvellous recovery within weeks. The official German communiqué issued on the 4 April about Lübeck that came to Buf's notice is illuminating:

> The British raid began shortly after 11 o'clock. A large number of flares were dropped, after which the waves of enemy aircraft dropped thousands of incendiaries on the closely built houses of the Inner Town. It can be said that at least 6 to 8 incendiaries fell on each house and could not all be put out. In a quarter of an hour the first large fires had flared up in various parts of the Inner Town. Thus the districts near the Krähenteich, the Port and the Breite Strasse began to burn. The A.R.P. units could not concentrate their activities in the face of such bombing and had to put out fires individually. The third wave of British bombers dropped heavy HE bombs on to the Inner Town lit up by the fires. Some of the historic buildings that were burnt down are the oldest German Inn, at present known as the Hotel 'Hamburg', the house in which Geibels and Overbeck were born, as well as almost all the Lübeck Hotels. As if this were not enough the Breitte Strasse which is the main street of the town was almost entirely wiped out.
>
> Notwithstanding the fact that almost one third of the town was either destroyed or badly damaged, the spirit of the town has not been broken, and it has already been decided that the whole of the Inner Town which is now destroyed is to be rebuilt according to the old plan. This will, however, only be possible after the war is over: at present the Inner Town and the main business street will be rebuilt with one-story concrete buildings so that after a time business can be re-started. An enormous number of workmen from all parts of the Reich as well as numerous gangs of prisoners-of-war are being employed in clearing up.
>
> On the second day after the raid, 6 trucks arrived with clothing for 4,000 people, men, women and children. One half of a truck was packed with medicaments. On Thursday 5,000 pairs of stockings arrived and several hundred pairs of shoes. Hot food was given out to 12,000 people. The Reich Ministry of Economics sent several thousand sets of clothing and underwear, 25,000 pairs of shoes, 20 tons of enamel ware and 1,000kg of tobacco. Apart from this 300,000 square metres of glass were issued for repairs.

Significantly, no mention was made of casualties. In the four raids made on Rostock in the same month, the total number killed and severely wounded was quoted as some 6,000. The Führer was very angry, particularly about the failure of anti-aircraft fire in which he put his main trust. It was those raids that prompted him to take reprisals in the form of 'Baedeker' raids on cities of historic importance in Britain, the first of which took place on 24–25 April.

It was, however, ironic that the first raid of Harris's command, on 9 March, was on the Renault works at Billancourt in France, when a wave of flare-droppers – followed by a wave of bombers carrying maximum incendiary loads to the centre of the target, followed in turn by the main force with high explosives – scored an exceptional concentration of bombs around the aiming point. The final assessment suggested that the plant had lost less than two months' production. That raid, however, had been planned on target-marking lines by the Directorate of Bombing Operations at the Air Ministry in the absence of a Commander-in-Chief.

Bennett's main concern was the selection and training of crews; second was the procurement of the best possible navigational equipment; third was the means of illuminating or marking the target. A new device known as Gee had just been introduced. It had its limitations, and the hope for Pathfinders lay elsewhere, with 'H2S' and 'Oboe' (code names given for security). H2S was a system, contained in eight large boxes, transmitting a directional beam of high energy impulses down to the ground which were then reflected back to the sender, received by the aerial, and showed their results on a cathode ray tube, painting a map of the area below. It could distinguish particularly well between land and water, with built-up areas giving the best returns (lightest on the screen), open lands the next best, and sea areas and lakes the weakest (darkest). The system depended on its success on a special valve known as a cavity-magnetron, and for some time when it was coming into production its use over enemy territory was forbidden lest the secret should fall into the wrong hands.

The research was being carried out by the Telecommunications Research Establishment (TRE) at Great Malvern, but on 7 June 1942, a month before Bennett's appointment, a disaster overtook the embryonic H2S when a Lancaster specially equipped – together with eleven men, a senior Bomber Command Liaison Officer, three vital employees of the manufacturer EMI, including the project leader, and the flight crew of five – perished when the aeroplane caught fire, lost half a wing and plunged to the ground upside down killing all on board. By a prodigious effort the project

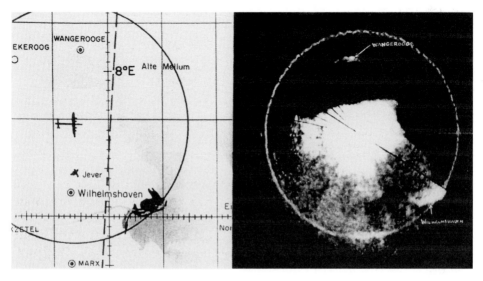

H2S picture showing the available returns over Wilhelmshaven and the island of Wangerooge.

continued with a delay of only two or three months. Bennett went down to Defford (the aerodrome belonging to TRE) and spent some time there doing a large amount of test flying with 'fairly good results'. Months later, when enough sets had been produced to equip a few squadrons, the War Cabinet suddenly decided that the magnetron could not be used over enemy territory, against which decision Bennett and his Commander-in-Chief fought hard.

In December 1942, the Pathfinders began to use 'Oboe' on operations, a device invented by the 'boffins' A.H. Reeves and F.E. Jones, as an enormous help for target-finding. It was a responder system worked by two stations in England (later moved to the Continent) sending out radar pulses. These were received by the aircraft and sent back to the ground station, which measured the time element and so calculated the distance, with an accuracy of about fifty feet. One station sent out a signal with dots on one side and dashes on the other to keep the aeroplane on track, while the other sent out signals that the target was coming near and finally sent out a long dash, the end of which signified the moment for release of bombs. One pair of stations was near Trimingham in Norfolk and one near Walmer in Kent so that they could operate two aircraft at a time, but there was one handicap. The beams could not be bent to follow the earth's curvature, and so they were limited to about 300 miles. This, however, was enough to reach the Ruhr. The first raid using Oboe was flown on 20 December 1942, and the captain was Hal Bufton, Sydney's brother. Thereafter for two months 109 Squadron operated 106 sorties with their Mosquitos for marking and test-bombing purposes, many of them in the Ruhr. Amazingly – for an aeroplane dismissed by many senior officers as useless – the loss rate was nil.

But this is to anticipate. Having found the target, the problem then was to mark it in such a way that the rest of the attacking force could – or would – not mistake it. The Germans made the task as difficult as possible by constructing dummy targets in the neighbouring countryside complete with guns and searchlights and letting off incendiary bombs to mimic an attack. The answer was the target indicator (TI) bomb, each consisting of a large number of pyrotechnic candles of great intensity and in a variety of colours or combinations of colours. They were set to burst by barometric fuses at relatively low levels, some 200–500 feet above ground, which meant that the main burning period was at ground level.

Stirling of No.7 Squadron being bombed-up at Oakington. It was the first squadron to receive 'heavies'. (*Aeroplane*)

A Lancaster of No.83 Squadron, the first such squadron in the Pathfinder Force. (Air Britain)

In addition, sky markers were produced consisting of parachute flares of various colours, with stars that would mark a patch of sky above the clouds over the target for three to five minutes. One of these would be put down by a marker aircraft fitted with Oboe or H2S so that, after it had burned half its time, it would have drifted over the target, at which point the main force could release their bombs. Other specialist aircraft would renew these markers as necessary.

The Pathfinder Force came into existence on 15 August 1942, with six squadrons in a group of aerodromes near Cambridge and its Headquarters at Wyton. These were:

7 Squadron	Stirlings	Wyton (from 3 Group)
35 Squadron	Halifaxes	Graveley (from 4 Group)
83 Squadron	Lancasters	Wyton (from 5 Group)
156 Squadron	Wellingtons	Warboys (from 1 Group)
109 Squadron	Wellingtons Mk V and VI	Marham

(109 Squadron was carrying out work on Oboe under Wing Commander MacMillan. His second-in-command was Squadron Leader Hal Bufton, Sydney's brother.)

There was also the invaluable Bomber Development Unit which Buf had sketched in his earlier paper:

On 18 August Harris sent Bennett this signal: '... All the crews of Bomber Command now look to the Pathfinders for a lead to their future objectives and will ensure the maximum infliction of damage on the enemy with the greatest economy of force. They will, I know, not be disappointed. Good luck and good hunting. Harris.'

Typically, Harris ordered them out that night with no period allowed for preparation or training.

The Force did not achieve immediate and striking success, as might have been expected. A careful study of results was made by Bomber Command of all PFF operations between 18 August and 21 November 1942: twenty-one against German targets and nine against Italian. In these the weather was good for fifteen, moderate for ten and bad for five, with the conclusion that the PFF have never succeeded in bad weather and have never failed in good. Success by the PFF in executing their planned technique has almost always resulted in an improvement achieved by the Main Force, and when the PFF have failed, the Main Force has never been able, by its own efforts, to improve upon expectation. The Main Force has invariably been diverted when the PFF have marked the wrong target. Judging by night photographs, the greatest percentage of aircraft bombing within three miles of the target was fifty-eight per cent at Bremen on 4–5 September. The overall average improvement has been 1.2 times.

One purpose of the study was to estimate the likely improvement with the use of H2S, and it concluded that with the PFF using it the average percentage within two miles of the target should be twenty to twenty-five per cent, and if the whole force were to use it, the figure should go up to about seventy per cent. The last figure was based on trials by the Bomber Development Unit, and represents a possible improvement of some three times. It involves, of course, the training of the average navigator in the use of H2S.

One decision that Harris made rather reluctantly to this end in the spring of 1942 was to implement a 'New Deal', abolishing one of the two pilots carried by bombers, and greatly reducing the number of pilots in training. By way of compensation, all bombers were to be equipped with automatic pilots; a flight engineer was to be carried in heavy bombers; one member of the crew, other than the pilot, was to be given enough training to bring the aeroplane back in emergency; the observer now became the navigator; and an additional member of the crew was to be the bomb aimer and also the front gunner. In addition, one of the two wireless-operator/air-gunners would become simply a gunner, and so save many weeks of training.

Amid all these radical changes and developments, Buf submitted a progress report on the Pathfinder Force to the Chief of Air Staff dated 21 November 1942. Since its formation on 16 August 1942, he wrote, it has carried out twenty-nine main operations. Its progress has been closely followed by Bufton's staff with numerous visits to PFF stations and constant discussion with the Force Commander and his staff. There is no doubt that the Force's operations have shown great promise.

Concerning the conception of the Force there is no common doctrine throughout Bomber Command. Group Commanders have favoured a 'House' rather than a 'School' outlook, and there has been some difficulty in getting crews. Although the Force Commander has visited the different Groups and given series of talks he feels that the PFF is getting only the second-best. 5 Group have a high degree of operational efficiency but they have always followed the PFF and could bomb in a period of illumination. The low wastage rate of the Lancaster Squadron has enabled it to produce many skilled crews, but it is most reluctant to surrender the best of these to the PFF.

The Headquarters is inadequate, the Force Commander badly overworked, and there are some unsuitable subordinate commanders.

When the PFF was formed, squadrons were transferred to it complete and a large proportion of the crews were still not capable of locating and marking the target. Operational Training Unit crews should NOT be posted direct: they must complete about 15 operations with the main force first.

The PFF should start illumination of target at zero -10 and prolong it to zero +10. At least six squadrons are necessary, and two Lancaster Squadrons should be added. Co-ordination with the main bomber force is a matter for concern: there have been cases where the main force started the attack before the Pathfinders arrived. The existing system of command appears to be fundamentally wrong, leading to a process of disintegration. The administration of the PFF by 3 Group HQ is unsound. Perhaps the present Force Commander is lacking in qualities of leadership.

The principle, however, has proved itself worthy and it will become more important when scientific aids are available. Second-best crews are not good enough.

Buf concluded with specific recommendations:

The PFF should be given the status of a Group, and it should consist of six squadrons plus 109 Squadron plus the Bomber Development Unit.

It should be commanded by an officer with enthusiasm, personality, and leadership of the highest order and his rank should equal that of other Group commanders.

He should be given authority to select the persons he requires for his staff and the staff of his squadrons.

Crews should be selected on the basis of efficiency displayed in their own squadrons.

OTU crews should be excluded.

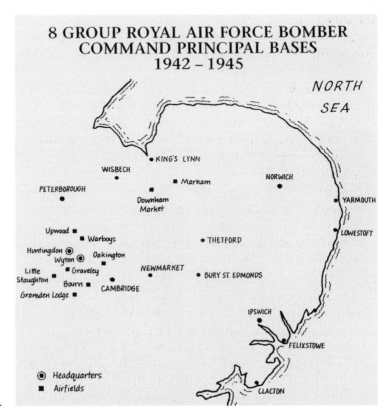

8 GROUP ROYAL AIR FORCE BOMBER COMMAND PRINCIPAL BASES 1942 – 1945

NORTH SEA

● KING'S LYNN

WISBECH ●

■ Markam

NORWICH ●

PETERBOROUGH ●

Downham Market ■

● YARMOUTH

Upwood ■

■ Warboys

● THETFORD

LOWESTOFT

Huntingdon ◉ Oakington ◉
Wyton ◉ ■

Little Staughton ■ ■ Graveley

Bourn ■ ● CAMBRIDGE

NEWMARKET ●

● BURY ST. EDMONDS

Gransden Lodge ■

IPSWICH ●

FELIXSTOWE

◉ Headquarters
■ Airfields

CLACTON

8 Group RAF Bomber Command bases.

Bufton added that he considered Air Commodore Embry admirably suited for Command, but this was not taken up and Bennett remained in command for the rest of the war. Buf's principal recommendation was swiftly carried out and the PFF became No.8 Group on 13 January 1943; Bennett became an Air Vice-Marshal. In May it received No.139 Squadron and the following month No.105 Squadron, both equipped with Mosquitos. Both had made history a few months earlier by carrying out the first daylight attacks on Berlin. No.105 was timed to disrupt a broadcast by Goering to the German people, keeping him off the air for over an hour. So much for Goering's boast that no enemy bomber would ever fly over German territory!

The arrival of the Mosquito on the scene marked a turning point in strategy. Greeted at first with suspicion, if not with contempt, the project was opposed by Ludlow-Hewitt, the then AOC-in-C of Bomber Command. De Havilland in 1939, with the experience of building the beautiful wooden four-engined Albatross air liner, proposed a wooden bomber powered by two Merlins, with a crew of two, a 1,500lb bomb load, a maximum speed of 405mph, a cruising speed of 320mph, and no defensive armaments. With considerable pressure and skilful manoeuvring, Wilfrid Freeman, the Air Member for Research and Development, managed to obtain an order from the Air Staff for fifty aircraft on the understanding that these would be used for photo-reconnaissance, and on 1 January 1940 the specification B 1/40 was drawn up. (It was not until July 1941

that the company was allowed to produce the bomber version.) On 25 November 1940, Geoffrey de Havilland, the company's chief test pilot, took off on a thirty-minute flight, starting a saga in aircraft history which saw 6,710 Mosquitos built during the war in England, Canada and Australia. On 17 September 1941 the first Mosquito, operated by No.1 Photographic Reconnaissance Unit, flew over Bordeaux and La Pallice.

The new No.8 Group received a signal honour with a visit by the King and Queen at Wyton on 26 May 1943. Bennett had indeed come a long way from his cattle-station at Toowoomba.

Above left: Mosquitos of 105 Squadron. (*Aeroplane*)

Left: Bennet, HM The Queen and Princess Elizabeth in 1944. (IWM)

CHAPTER 11

Ball-Bearings

Germany is a large country and a strategic bombing offensive was faced with a large choice of targets and a large number of changeable factors in the bomber force. The Combined Chiefs of Staff considered the broadest aspects of strategy (subject to Churchill's Defence Committee and ultimately to the War Cabinet) and made their recommendations to the appropriate body – in the case of bombing to the Air Staff, and so to the Directorate of Bombing Operations acting for the Chief of Staff. This department was responsible for the study and selection of targets in the light of intelligence and industrial reports, the study of photographic interpretation, information regarding enemy ground and air defences, and for the ensuing preparation of 'Directives' for Bomber Command which went out in the name of the Chief of Air Staff. These were, however, generally written by Norman Bottomley (Air Marshal), the Deputy Chief of Air Staff (who followed Harris in Command of No.5 Group from November 1940 until May 1941).

Harris at Bomber Command then had the task of translating these into action, considering the number of aircraft available, the weather, expected opposition, and then deciding on a target or targets. His staff would then work out details of squadrons, routes, likely opposition from aircraft and guns, diversions and timings, and communicate these to the squadrons concerned. As the Directives were issued with remarkable frequency – forty-five between April 1940 and April 1945 – Harris had to be flexible in his policy. He tended, however, to base this on a sweeping injunction of 9 July 1941:

> Subject to para. 7 below, I am to request that you will direct the main effort of the bomber force, until further instructions, towards dislocating the German transportation system and to destroying the morale of the civil population as a whole and of the industrial workers in particular. [Paragraph 7 allowed for 'diversionary attacks on objectives, the destruction of which is of immediate importance'.]

This gave Harris the basis for his policy of 'area bombing'. He had a list of forty, later expanded to sixty, principal towns and cities of Germany that he aimed to exterminate. They may have contained important factories, but he maintained that to destroy the workers' homes, along with their electricity, gas and water supplies, as well as some of themselves, was more important. This did not require precision bombing, which in any case was an impossibility when he took over.

He had no time for attacks on what he called 'panacea' targets, those deemed by the experts to be crucial for the German economy. The main such targets were ball-bearings, oil and transport, supplemented from time to time with submarine yards and aircraft factories.

In October 1941, the results of the bomber offensive were so poor that it was considered desirable to explain our intentions to the Americans, and a special review was prepared by the British Chiefs of Staff.

Our policy at present is to concentrate upon targets which affect both the German transportation system and civilian morale, thus exploiting weaknesses already created by the blockade. Since the targets selected lie within highly industrial and thickly populated areas the effect upon German morale is considerable. As our forces increase, we intend to pass to planned attack on civilian morale with the intensity and continuity which are essential if a final breakdown is to be produced. There is increasing evidence of the effect which even our present limited scale of attack is causing to German life. We have every reason to be confident that if we can expand our forces in accordance with our present programme, and if possible beyond it, the effect will be shattering. We believe that if these methods are applied on a vast scale, the whole structure upon which the German forces are based, the economic system, the machinery for production and destruction, the morale of the nation will be destroyed, and that whatever their present strength the armed forces of Germany would suffer radical decline in fighting value and mobility that a direct attack would once more become possible.

The Americans were not impressed. They did not take kindly to a bombing offensive aimed at civilian morale and urged that we should attack more specific objectives. When they came to join the offensive some two years later, their policy was precision bombing by day of such targets. When General Spaatz, Commander of the US VIII Army Air Force, and his staff arrived in England in April 1942, they visited Buf in his office and reported that in Washington the RAF was saying it could not operate by day. In a long discussion with Colonel Henry Berliner and Colonel Dick Hugh, Buf told them that they *could* operate in daylight, but only if they had fighter escort. (The standard US fighters, the Lightning and the Thunderbolt, did not have sufficient range to fly into Germany, fight battles with German fighters, and return to base.) The Americans ignored the warning and in 1943 suffered crippling losses. The climax came on 14 October with a daylight raid on Schweinfurt, deep in southern Germany, with the loss of sixty out of 288 heavy bombers.

Mr Churchill had some sympathy with their view:

It is quite possible that the Nazi war-making power in 1943 will be so widely spread throughout Europe as to be to a large extent independent of the actual buildings in the homeland. A different picture would be presented if the enemy's air force were so far reduced as to enable heavy accurate daylight bombing of factories to take place. This, however, cannot be done outside the radius of fighter protection, according to what I am at present told.

The problem of finding and hitting a target like a factory by night was a complex one. In a paper of January 1942 to be discussed with Bomber Command, Buf was concerned to try out the accuracy of Gee, which was just coming into service:

We do not know the accuracy *over Germany* and we must therefore check up, with two or three aircraft taking photos, say at Aachen, *before* the full-scale effort is launched; or by using flares at the beginning of the operation to make sure everything is OK. I favour the latter course, 'G' aircraft dropping flares for the fire-raisers ... The first raids should be in reasonably good weather so that all aircraft without 'G' can be effective ... As our initial raids must be in reasonably good weather, Essen may have to stand down in favour of Cologne, owing to the many heavy defences at the former. When the accuracy of 'G' is established Essen etc. can be attacked with blind bombing. If there are not thick clouds the 'G' aircraft could raise enough fire with 100% incendiaries to enable followers to bomb on reflections of clouds.

Buf concluded, 'we must make a case for switching from "Transportation and Morale" to "Morale", but as Duisberg and Cologne fall within the Transportation and Morale programme, we can tackle these first, in the hope of the results justifying the change.'

Much of this thinking is incorporated in Directive XXII of 14 February 1942, which refers to 'G' as 'a revolutionary advance in bombing technique'. It continues:

It has been decided that the primary object of your operations should now be focussed on the morale of the enemy civil population and in particular, of the industrial workers. With this aim in view, a list of selected area targets ... is attached.

This gives as primary industrial areas within 'G' range, in the Ruhr area, Essen, Duisberg, Dusseldorf, and Cologne, and in the northern coastal area, Bremen, Wilhelmshaven, and Emden, all with naval dockyards. A further list is appended of precise targets, synthetic rubber factories, power stations and synthetic oil plants.

Nine days later, Air Marshal Harris took over Bomber Command and would have found this directive on his desk. He would have welcomed it as giving him *carte blanche* for his policy of area bombing. This had been thrust upon him by the inefficiency of bomber aircraft up to that time, but he also argued that to kill or injure industrial workers, to bomb them out of their homes, to destroy or damage public utilities like water, gas and electricity, was as vital as hitting the factories themselves. On a larger scale, he argued, the effect on the population at large would be to break their morale and cause them to rise up against their Nazi masters. Events were to prove him wrong on both counts. The Air Ministry changed its mind, but Harris did not. By the end of the war, however, the distinction between 'area bombing' and 'precision bombing' had become largely academic.

In April 1942, Churchill wanted an unbiased assessment of the efficiency of the bombing campaign on Germany and the Defence Committee asked a judge, Mr Justice Singleton, to produce this, which he did within a month. On the bombing of factories, the photographic reports could not, he said, be regarded as satisfactory when it is remembered that the target area is a circle with a five-mile radius, i.e., an area of seventy-eight square miles. He spoke with two officers who had flown recently on night bombing attacks who were satisfied with the accuracy of TR 1335 (Gee), but only in capable hands. 'To assess the probable effect on Germany's war effort of different degrees of damage to different parts of her economy is difficult, but it is essential in the framing of an effective bombing policy.' The drop in the number of German fighters surprised Mr Singleton, but he realised that the Germans needed every aeroplane that could be spared for the Russian front, and intensified bombing would increase the demand for fighters on the Western Front. Similarly, a large number of men and guns are kept on anti-aircraft work in Germany and many more on fire-prevention. On the question of morale he wrote:

> I doubt whether our bombing ability is, or in the near future can be, sufficient to bring about a breach of morale in this way alone ... I prefer to ... envisage the bombing of an industrial area with important factories in the centre rather than the bombing of houses, and I think better results will be achieved thereby. Bombing ought not to be regarded as of itself sufficient to win the war or to produce decisive results; the area is too vast for the effort we can put forth. Much depends on Russia. But if Russia can hold Germany on land Germany may well not stand twelve or eighteen months of continuous, intensified bombing.

One of Harris's *bêtes noires* was the repeated demand that he should attack the German ball-bearing industry. The industry was, of course, vital for the production of aircraft, as well as tanks and other vehicles, and its production had been studied intensively by both British and American economists. It was first considered by the Target Committee in October 1941, and was recommended as a first choice by the Ministry of Economic Warfare throughout 1942. By the autumn of 1942 the location, the percentage of production and the special character of the factories was known with great accuracy, including the fact that fifty-two per cent of the German supplies were made in Schweinfurt in two large factories, one of which was partially controlled by a Swedish combine. On 21 November 1942 the Air Staff sent a very stiff directive to Harris to plan an attack for 'the complete devastation of the factories and town in one overwhelming operation.' It was to be on the heaviest scale and within four to six weeks. Accompanying the directive was a paper from the Ministry of Economic Warfare setting out the case for such destruction.

Harris replied with some sharp comments that the town of Schweinfurt, being fairly small (it had a population of some 60,000), could be dealt with by an incendiary attack by night, but the factories would need a low-level attack by night in good weather by trained and experienced crews, the target being more than 300 miles from the continental shore. The Commander reckoned he could produce 350 such bombers with a possible further 100 from other sources. He went on, however, to question the logic of the directive.

> If the remaining factories in German Occupied Europe could be made to increase their outputs, or if substantial stocks have in fact been built up, the effects of the operation might be very far from those envisaged in this paper. The conclusion that this operation should be carried out 'at whatever the cost' appears very dangerous.

In fact, Harris's doubts were justified. The stock of ball-bearings in the possession of the manufacturers amounted to between six and twelve months' supply, a fact that the Germans themselves only discovered twelve months later.

Harris held back, despite further explicit directives sent on 14 January 1944, 28 January 1944 and 17 April 1944. He was, however, forestalled. The American VIII Air Force arrived in England in late 1942 and its bombing policy was to attack precisely and by day. Their Fortresses (B-17) flew in close formation and the theory was that their heavy armament would deal with any German attackers. These, however, were armed with cannons and rockets, and by head-on attacks wrought havoc with the invaders. On 17 August 1943, 230 B-17s set out for Schweinfurt, and as soon as they had reached the limit of their own fighter escort (which could only fly to the German coast), they were set on by German fighters which shot down twenty-one bombers on the way out and a further fourteen on the way back. Another fell to flak over the target, giving a total loss rate of over fifteen per cent. Although the bombing was accurate and concentrated, repairs were carried out swiftly and output had recovered within two months.

Buf, who had become Director of Bomber Operations on 10 March 1943 with the rank of Air Commodore, persisted in pressing the case for selective attacks on ball-bearing centres and particularly on Schweinfurt. In the summer of 1943 he did his best to secure a follow-up night raid by Bomber Command immediately after the American day attack. He suggested that the bomber crews should be told immediately before take-off:

> History may prove that tonight's operation, in conjunction with the day attack which is taking place at this moment, will be one of the major battles of this war. If both operations are successful, German resistance may be broken and the war ended sooner than could be possible in any other way.

He wanted the crews to know that 'every vital piece of mechanism is dependent upon ball-bearings' and that, owing to extreme vulnerability to fire and water, 'literally millions' of bearings could be converted into 'so much scrap metal'. Finally, he suggested that the crews should be told that they had 'the opportunity to do more in one night to end this war than any other body of men.'

Harris took no notice and Buf continued the pressure. The Ministry of Economic Warfare regarded the German supply of ball-bearings as critical, and Buf pointed to further evidence: that in August 1942 Schweinfurt had been defended by only a few light gun batteries, but now, a year later, the town was covered by fifty-four heavy guns, fifty-seven light guns, forty-nine searchlights, three decoys and a very extensive system of smoke-screen generators.

The US VIII Air Force attacked it again on 14 October 1943 and made great claims for success, but suffered heavy losses. On 30 November Buf again pressed the matter on the Assistant Chief of Air Staff, stating that 'A completely successful attack would have an immediate and far-reaching effect upon Germany's war effort and incidentally upon her morale, as work in all kinds of factories would be held up through lack of ball-bearings.' On 17 December 1943, the Deputy Chief of Air Staff wrote to Harris asking for an early Bomber Command attack on Schweinfurt and repeated his request six days later. The result was a firm reply from Harris asserting that Schweinfurt was not a reasonable operation of war. The town was heavily defended, small in size, and difficult to find. He estimated that six or seven attacks would be necessary to destroy it, and even then the results would be dubious. Harris poured equal scorn on attacks on railways, on the Dams, on the molybdenum mine at Knaben and on the synthetic petrol sources. These 'panacea' claims, he said, are 'eagerly, if innocently, swallowed by those many people who like to have a finger in the bomber pie, while having no responsibility for it whatsoever as a military operation'. Schweinfurt, in short, would be a waste of effort.

Nevertheless, another directive was sent to Harris on 13 January 1944 stating: 'It is particularly important that you should do your utmost to destroy at as early a rate as possible, the town of Schweinfurt and the ball-bearing factories which it contains.' Again Harris prevaricated, pleading tactical difficulties, and again, on 27 January, he was ordered to attack. Finally, after further delay, on 24 February he sent off 734 bombers for the task by night, and the Americans sent 266 bombers to attack by day on the same date.

Riechminister Speer had appointed Dr Philip Kessler to be in charge of the whole ball-bearing field, and he reported to Speer on 6 April 1944:

Towards the end of February 1944 the main production places of the German roller-bearing industry, Schweinfurt, Erkner, Cannstatt and Steyr, had come to an almost complete standstill. Those works, which have remained intact, have embarked on the March production programme at full pressure and the severely damaged plants have in accordance with my directions made gigantic efforts to repair the damage and carry out further dispersal. In spite of all production losses, a March output of about 70% of the average output in the second quarter of 1943 was thus achieved despite all interruptions. In this connection I must point out that on that occasion the behaviour of the staff of the ball-bearing plants after these fearful attacks was splendid. The slogan which I emphasized at numerous meetings on reconstruction and on output is: 'Not a single fighter or panzer less through lack of ball-bearings!' Thus, requirements of roller-bearings for panzer and fighter production were met, also for the month of March, which, however, necessitated many superhuman efforts.

Speer's own post-war judgement on the Allied policy was precise:

At the beginning of April 1944 however, the attacks on the ball-bearing industry ceased abruptly. Thus, the allies threw away success when it was already in their hands. Had they continued the attacks of March and April with the same energy, we would quickly have been at our last gasp. As it was, not a tank, plane, or other piece of weaponry failed to be produced because of lack of ball bearings, even though such production had been increased by 19 per cent from July 1943 to April 1944. As far as armaments were concerned, Hitler's credo that the impossible could be made possible and that all forecasts and fears were too pessimistic, seemed to have proved itself true.

By April 1944 the position of Bomber Command (and the VIII Air Force) had changed radically, as plans were now being made for 'Overlord', the invasion of the Continent.

The other principal *bête noire* of Harris was the emphasis on the disruption of German oil production, another of his despised 'panaceas'. This, however, was to become a major issue in 1944 with the invasion of France.

CHAPTER 12

Hamburg

In January 1943, Buf submitted a detailed report to the Assistant Chief of Air Staff (Operations), with a copy to the Chief, on the first raid using H2S. It was against Hamburg on 30 January, one of a series, but that city was chosen in view of the priority of U-boat targets.

The Pathfinder Force consisted of seven Stirlings and six Halifaxes equipped with H2S and five Lancasters; the Main Force had 130 Lancasters (of which five failed to return and two crashed). The weather forecast was of variable cloud from two-tenths to ten-tenths and a wind of 100mph at operational height. The method of marking would be decided on arrival. The Stirlings carried a load of three red flares as landmark flares, three green flares as warning flares, twelve red flares with green stars as release flares and four red marker bombs as ground markers. The Halifaxes carried a similar, but slightly larger, load. The Lancasters (without H2S) each carried a 4000lb HC (High Capacity, thin case) bomb, two with four ground marker bombs and 360 4lb incendiary bombs and three with 900 incendiaries. The plan was to drop the red landmark flares on H2S response over Bremen, the green warning flares on H2S response over Wilhelmsburg to the south of Hamburg, and then either the sky marker flares or the ground marker bombs at the appropriate release point or aiming mark over Hamburg, depending on whether the target was obscured by cloud or clear.

The H2S aircraft operated at an average height of 18,000 feet and the equipment worked better than the crews had expected, although four of the six Halifaxes had to return with other technical trouble and three of the seven Stirlings had trouble with the H2S sets.

The first aircraft dropped its ground markers blindly on H2S. These lit up the ground brilliantly and the crew stated that they fell exactly at the aiming mark (the southern end of the Binnen Alster). Immediately afterwards a further red marker bomb was observed to drop very close to the original one. A good concentration of bombs then built up around these markers.

The target then became obscured by cloud and subsequent H2S aircraft reverted to the sky marking method and dropped their release point flares at the appropriate position. Group Captain Bennett was particularly pleased at the manner in which both the PFF and the Main Force were able to change smoothly from one marking method to the other in the course of the attack. Reports indicate that generally a good concentration was achieved. To summarise, in the words of Bennett, the operation was, in the light of the prevailing weather conditions, 'a brilliant success'.

This, however, for Harris was small fry, and six months later, in July 1943, he achieved one of his main ambitions, to lay waste to Hamburg, Germany's second city. During the previous six months his bomber strength had been greatly increased both in quality and quantity. By 24 July, 792 aircraft and crews were ready – 'all the available heavies' – as Harris put it in a preliminary letter dated 27 May to his six Group Commanders, whose intention was succinctly stated: 'to destroy Hamburg'. By this time, No.8 (Pathfinder Group) had grown to nine squadrons (and a Meteorological Flight) of which three and a half had Lancasters and three Mosquitos. On this day the RAF was authorised by Churchill himself to use 'Window' for the first time. This consisted of parcels of black paper strips with aluminium foil stuck to one side, measuring 27 x 2cm, which if dropped in quantity would render useless most of the enemy's radar sets, particularly the *Würzburgs*.

Hamburg was famous for its shipyards, which together produced over 400 U-boats during the war. These and most of the other industrial plants were sited on the south side of the River Elbe; the city proper lay on the north side. The armaments industry employed 66,000 foreigners of four groups: 'guest workers', mainly Dutch, French and Belgian; Eastern workers from Poland, Ukraine and Russia who were little more than slaves; prisoners of war; and the inmates of concentration camps, one of which had been built in 1938 twelve miles from the city centre. A total of 5,343 Hamburg Jews had left from a derelict station in goods wagons for death camps.

The attack over Hamburg was to be shared with the Americans – though not equally – in what was to be the Combined Bomber Offensive. Two days' planning was cancelled when the Mosquitos of the 'Met Flight' reported impossible weather. The first bomber, an ancient Stirling, took off a 9.45p.m. on 24 July, and the first ones to be heard over the city arrived at 12.51a.m. These were Pathfinders, and a German naval doctor reported:

> There were only odd bursts of Flak in the distance and the ghostly arms of the searchlights in the clear, starlit sky. Then, suddenly, there were yellow torches in the sky and the murmuring of engines coming ever nearer. Red and green marker bombs followed. They floated slowly towards the ground – boundary markers of death! The engine noise above us became louder and every gun of the Flak from Hamburg and of the ships fired. But still no bombs! It was so bright that one could have read the *Hamburger Tageblatt* without difficulty. And then it all started!

The Flak and the searchlights had been rendered fairly harmless because they were radar controlled and so crippled by the 'Window' strips. Small incendiary bombs hit the roofs of apartment blocks followed by larger ones to penetrate. Wardens called men from shelters to fight the fires but these were often killed by high explosive bombs which followed. Fires raged out of control despite the efforts of eighty-six fire-brigade units brought in as reinforcements.

The target had been the centre of the residential part of the city, but of the 617 photographs taken of the bombing, only 275 were within three miles of the aiming point, with 342 outside that distance. Most of this 'drift back' was up to seven miles to the north-east from where the attack had come and was to some extent due to red decoy flares laid in the open country. The Chief of Police estimated deaths at 1,500, and twelve bombers failed to return. The successful crews were delighted with 'Windows': 'On the night of Hamburg One our morale took a leap upward. We were all tickled pink with the crazy confusion caused to the defences'. But they knew it would not last.

Pyrotechnic candles. On the ground they produced a distinctive pool of red, green or yellow fire. (Creek)

At 4.10a.m. the Hamburg Fire Department reported a 'Major Catastrophe'. When dawn came, daylight did not, but only 'a big, black, greyish cloud, very low', as one schoolgirl remembered, observing the smoke.

The next day, Sunday 25 July, was the turn of the American VIII Bomber Command, but it was by no means a 'maximum effort', with 123 crews standing by. They flew in close formation of 'Combat Wings', and over the German coast were fiercely engaged by over thirty heavily armed fighters. Hamburg, however, was still covered by a dense cloud of smoke. The shipyards to the south were soon covered by an artificial smokescreen, but forty-nine aircraft of the leading wing probably bombed the Blohm and Voss yard and other harbour installations. Fifteen of the B-17s were shot down – over twelve per cent of the force – a rate of loss that could not be maintained.

On 27 July, Harris ordered another 'maximum effort' against Hamburg, and a Mosquito reported clear weather. The aiming point was to be the same as before but the approach, and therefore the creep-back, was to be from the north-east. This meant flying over Lübeck, and to lighten the load more incendiaries were carried in place of high explosives. As many as 787 bombers took off, with no less than five Station Commanders (Group Captains) and a very distinguished passenger, Brigadier-General Fred Anderson, Commander of the US VIII Bomber Command. By 1.00a.m. the attack was in full swing, the Pathfinder markers well concentrated with salvoes of yellow target indicators and the green markers of the Backers-Up. The Germans had chosen red flares for their decoys!

The burning of Hamburg that night was remarkable in that I saw not many fires but one. Set in the darkness was a turbulent dome of bright red fire, lighted and ignited like the glowing heart of a vast brazier. I saw no streets, no outlines of buildings, only brighter fires which flared like yellow torches against a background of bright red ash. Above the city was a misty red haze. I looked down, fascinated but aghast, satisfied yet horrified. I had never seen a fire like that before and was never to see its like again. [Flight Lieutenant A. Forsdike, 78 Squadron]

The leader of a fire-fighting team on the ground had tried to hold back the fire with hand extinguishers:

Then a storm started, a shrill howling in the street. It grew into a hurricane so that we had to abandon all hope of fighting the fire. It was as though we were

Some of the 40,000 Hamburg dead. (Creek)

doing no more than throwing a drop of water on to a hot stone. The whole yard, the canal, in fact as far as we could see, was just a whole, great, massive sea of fire.

The strongest of fires had to draw fresh air from the streets and from smaller fires. The area became a roaring inferno, the centre of which reached 800°C and the air sucked in reached hurricane force. That was the 'firestorm'. As the RAF bombing drew back eastwards, so the firestorm developed until it finally embraced an area some three miles from west to east and one and a half miles from north to south. Thousands of citizens, mainly old men, women and children, were trapped in basements when buildings above collapsed on top of them, and most met a merciful death by asphyxiation. Most of those who took to the streets perished horribly in the flames. In total, some 40,000 died.

Those who could attempted to flee on foot, either pushing little carts containing all their belongings, or hopping onto bicycles or any other vehicle that could be found, civil or military. Trains were almost impossible, as fifteen of Hamburg's eighteen stations were out of action. By nightfall, nearly two-thirds of the population had got away, one and a quarter million people, in a constant stream of misery.

This was not enough for Harris. After a night's rest he ordered another major raid on Hamburg and a Mosquito reported clear weather, though smoke was rising from fires still burning. The objective was the main remaining part of the residential area to the north of the city. This time 786 bombers took off, and as they flew across the North Sea they could see a faint glow on the horizon, the result of their raid two nights earlier. The Germans had by now put up a heavier night-fighter defence, and three Pathfinders went down before crossing the coast. An extensive area of the city was still burning, but the new attack drifted northwards mainly over the area of Barmbek, a suburban residential district. Probably fewer than a thousand citizens died. Twenty-eight bombers failed to return.

Harris ordered a fourth raid on 2–3 August, and again 737 bombers headed out for an approach to Hamburg from the south, but the weather worsened and over the German coast the raiders ran into a violent electrical storm, accompanied with heavy icing that brought down four, if not five, aircraft. Eight more fell around the city, and the bombing was scattered over an area a hundred miles long. Ten bombers were lost on the return flight. Altogether thirty-three aircraft were missing, with no serious damage caused anywhere – a sad anti-climax for Bomber Command.

In all, Hamburg was a great success for the doctrine of area bombing, but it was not considered politic to broadcast it in the British press or on the radio. All that was reported (on Government orders) was the destruction of industrial areas and the consequent enormous civilian casualties. There were a few voices raised in opposition, notably that of George Bell, Bishop of Chichester, in many speeches in the House of Lords. 'To bomb cities as cities', he wrote in his *Diocesan Gazette,* 'deliberately to attack civilians, quite irrespective of whether or not they are actively contributing to the war effort, is a wrong deed, whether done by the Nazi or by ourselves.' A few voices of protest against the Nazi régime were raised by those bombed, but they were soon silenced. As soon as the streets of Hamburg were cleared of rubble, lorry-loads of SS soldiers in uniform with rifles were patrolling to remove any signs of protest or those responsible, and morale was sustained. Indeed it was even raised, despite the awful suffering. One comment made by a Hamburg inhabitant some years after the bombing ran:

> When I was at the home of friends, after being bombed out, someone said over breakfast, 'This is the punishment for our attack on Coventry', and a teacher colleague of mine, a woman of very noble principles, said to me, later, 'I shouldn't really say this but I felt a wild joy during those heavy British raids. That was the punishment for our crimes against the Jews.' I could only agree with her.

Harris was so disappointed by the cool publicity given to his 'successful' raids that he wrote a strong letter to the Under Secretary of State on 25 October containing the following paragraphs:

> The manner in which the aim and achievement of the Combined US–British Bomber Offensive have been presented both in the Press and in public pronouncements by authoritative speakers both in Britain and the United States has encouraged the view that it is the nature of an experiment or side-show which is important but is not the major part of the United Nations' war effort in the European Theatre. Admittedly many people, even outside Germany, believe that the bombing of German cities is a much more serious matter for the enemy than minor military operations in Italy. But no one could possibly gather from casual reading of the British Press that the enemy openly admits the results of our bombing to be his most serious problem, i.e. of greater importance than the advance of the Red Army.
>
> ... To give the morale of our own crews proper support and encouragement, the following policy decisions are urgently required:–
>
> (a) The aim of the Combined Bomber Offensive, and the part which Bomber Command is required by agreed British–US strategy to play in it, should be unambiguously and publicly stated. That aim is the destruction of German cities, the killing of German workers and the disruption of civilised community life throughout Germany.
>
> (b) It should be emphasised that the destruction of houses, public utilities, transport and lives; the creation of a refugee problem on an unprecedented

scale; and the breakdown of morale both at home and at the battle fronts by fear of extended and intensified bombing, are accepted and intended aims of our bombing policy. They are not by-products of attempts to hit factories.

If Sir Archibald Sinclair wrote an answer there is no copy in the Bufton file. In all his public pronouncements Sir Archibald maintained a diplomatically neutral stance on this issue.

On 18 December 1943, Buf received a letter from the Chief Intelligence Officer of Bomber Command, Group Captain N.S. Paynter, accompanying a paper entitled 'RAF Bomber Offensive against Germany' that had been produced 'in an effort to maintain the pride of Bomber crews in their achievements. This has been written with the primary object of giving our aircrews, in simple non-technical language, a clear picture of what has been achieved and what remains to be done'. Buf wrote a courteous reply, congratulating him on the production with the comment, 'It cannot fail to do very useful work.' He then went on to refer to 'some divergence between the Air Staff as a whole and the Command as to how the bombing effort should be applied'. He continued:

While we have no doubt in our minds that writing off industrial centres one by one, and at the rate at which you are writing them off, would eventually bring about Germany's collapse, we feel that the time required to achieve her collapse this way and the effort which will be required to do so may be greater than seems possible at present. We are firmly convinced that the result could be achieved more certainly and more rapidly if Bomber Command's attacks could be more discriminating and could in some measure be concentrated on certain vital industries.

Buf added that this was a private and personal comment and a formal staff reply would follow after careful consideration of the letter and enclosure.

In December 1943, Buf wrote to the Deputy Chief of Air Staff to inform him that Harris had stated that if forty to fifty per cent of built-up areas were destroyed by 1 April 1944, Germany would capitulate. That implied no precise attacks on targets like Schweinfurt. The Intelligence department, however, reported that Hitler had boasted that he could control by means of his party organisations the morale of the population for some considerable time. A further letter to the Chief of Air Staff claimed that Harris's policy was undermining the Combined Bomber Offensive. The Americans were committed to precise attacks. Would this in turn open the way for the Americans to press for a Supreme Strategic Air Force Commander? Buf was not far off the mark.

CHAPTER 13

Alliance

In January 1943 Churchill, Roosevelt and their Chiefs of Staff – naval, military and air force – met in conference at Casablanca to make plans for the rest of the war, for a turning point had been reached. America, under General Eisenhower, had joined in the war in North Africa, though four more months of bitter fighting had to take place before von Armin surrendered in Tunisia. General Marshall stated at the outset that seventy per cent of Allied resources should be assigned to the Atlantic theatre and thirty per cent to the Pacific, a remarkably generous American allocation considering the vastness of demands for the Pacific war, but behind all this was a major problem – how best could their air forces be used in areas which up until then had been the arena for the RAF?

The conference produced a directive for the bomber offensive from the UK, dated 21 January 1943, applicable to the appropriate British and American Air Force Commanders:

1. Your primary objective will be the progressive destruction and dislocation of the German military, industrial and economic system, and the undermining of the morale of the German people to a point where their capacity for armed resistance is fatally weakened.
2. Within that general concept, your primary objectives, subject to the exigencies of weather and of tactical feasibility, will for the present be in the following order of priority:
   (a) German submarine construction yards.
   (b) The German aircraft industry.
   (c) Transportation.
   (d) Oil plants.
   (e) Other targets in enemy war industry.
   The above order of priority may be varied from time to time according to developments in the strategical situation. Moreover, other objectives of great importance either from the political or military point of view must be attacked. Examples of these are:
   (i) Submarine operating bases on the Biscay coast. If these can be put out of action, a great step forward will have been taken in the U-boat war which the CCS have agreed to be the first charge on our resources.
   (ii) Berlin, which should be attacked when conditions are suitable for the attainment of specially valuable results unfavourable to the morale of the enemy or favourable to that of Russia.

(iii) You may also be required, at the appropriate time to attack objectives
     in Northern Italy in connection with amphibious operations in the
     Mediterranean theatre.

(iv) There may be certain objectives of great fleeting importance for the attack
     of which all necessary plans and preparations should be made. Of these, an
     example would be the important units of the German Fleet in harbour or
     at sea.

(v) You should take every opportunity to attack Germany by day, to destroy
    objectives that are unsuitable for night attack, to sustain continuous pressure
    on German morale, to impose heavy losses on the German day fighter
    force and to contain German fighter strength away from the Russian and
    Mediterranean theatres of war.

(vi) Whenever Allied Armies re-enter the Continent, you will afford all possible
     support in the manner most effective.

(vii)   In attacking objectives in occupied territories, you will conform to such
     instructions as may be issued from time to time for political reasons by His
     Majesty's Government through the British Chiefs of Staff.

This directive was sent to Harris on 4 February 1943 and he replied in a letter two
days later saying that paragraph 1 provided full support for his policy of area bombing,
claiming: 'It states categorically that the "primary objective of Bomber Command will
be the progressive destruction and dislocation of the German military, industrial and
economic system aimed at undermining the morale of the German people to a point
where their capacity for armed resistance is fatally weakened."' In fact, it did not state
that, but Harris had subtly altered it to fit in with his own ideas.

The Americans did not understand it so. Their basic assumption was that 'it is better
to cause a high degree of destruction in a few really essential industries than to cause
a small degree of destruction in many industries'. The four principal target systems
were: submarine construction yards and bases, the aircraft industry, the ball-bearing
industry and oil production. General Eaker, the commander of the US VIII Air Force,
published a 'General Plan of Operations and Forces required' on 12 April 1943. Its
purpose was largely to state a case for the enlargement of his force from 944 heavy
bombers in the UK on 1 July 1943, to 1,192 on 1 October 1943, 1,746 by 1 January
1944, and 2,702 on 1 April 1944. This, he suggested, was an appropriate preliminary
for a continental invasion. The plan was, of course, based on the doctrine of precision
bombing, but he saw no difficulty in integrating it with RAF policy. 'All-out attacks
imply precision bombing of related targets by day and night where tactical conditions
permit and area bombing by night against the cities associated with these targets'.

The 'Eaker Plan' was in fact a plan for a combined bomber offensive, and it was
accepted as such by Harris, though with the rider that 'the Plan as it stands may prove
somewhat inelastic in the event. In practice, it could and would be modified as necessary
to meet developments in the general situation and to accord with new information as
to the effect of past attacks on different types of objective.'

March 1943 saw the beginning of a new phase in Bomber Command's offensive,
sometimes called the Battle of the Ruhr. On the night of 5 March, 442 aircraft of

Bomber Command were dispatched against Essen, the home of the Krupp works, with the aid of Oboe. The Ruhr Valley was a notoriously difficult target because it was generally covered in a thick industrial haze, but this attack was to be a precise one on a target that remained unseen throughout. The keys to success were the eight Mosquitos of 109 Squadron of the Pathfinder Force, though unfortunately three of these experienced failure of their Oboe systems, one being the Commanding Officer of 109 Squadron, Wing Commander H.E. Bufton, Sydney's brother.

The first salvo of red target indicators was dropped by a Mosquito two minutes before zero hour, was well placed, and immediately drew a shower of bombs from the leaders of the Main Force. Within minutes large fires were burning, and at 9.03p.m. the first of the backers-up went into action and dropped green target indicators accurately, followed at regular intervals for the next thirty-five minutes. Photographic reconnaissance on the second and third days after the raid confirmed its success, showing heaviest damage in the centre of the town and 450 acres in which at least three-quarters of the buildings had been demolished or damaged with the Krupp works suffering heavily. Fourteen aircraft were lost. The operation was a great success for the leadership of the Pathfinder Force, for its Mosquitos, for Oboe and for the training of all the crews who took part. A raid on Nuremburg three nights later nearly twice as far away had to rely on H2S and its bombs were scattered much more widely.

So the raids continued and mounted in size, against Essen and Duisburg with five each, Cologne with four, Bochum with three, and Dusseldorf and Dortmund with two each. One raid, however, was exceptional and unique, a low-level attack by Lancasters against the Möhne and Eder Dams.

For this, a special squadron was formed in 5 Group, No.617 with Wing Commander G. Gibson as its commander with authority to hand-pick crews for his nineteen specially adapted Lancasters. It was, and remained, a *corps d'élite* if ever there was one, Harris notwithstanding. The weapon it was to carry was the result of the private initiative of Mr Barnes Wallis of Vickers who had designed the R-100 airship and the Wellesley and Wellington, with their geodetic airframes. It was cylindrical in shape, designed to be dropped at a very low level – sixty feet – on to the water along which it would bounce over the protective anti-torpedo nets, hit the dam, sink to a pre-determined level and then explode. Harris, needless to say, needed some convincing. In a letter to Portal of 18 February 1943 he was 'prepared to bet' that this bomb was 'just about the maddest proposition as a weapon that we have yet come across'. Nevertheless training went ahead with constant low-level rehearsals by the light of the moon which, together with spotlights underneath the nose and tail of each to intersect exactly sixty feet below, enabled the crews to drop their bomb with unprecedented precision.

On 16 May, nineteen Lancasters took off from Scampton on Operation Chastise, led by Gibson himself. The first wave lost one aircraft on the way but the remainder succeeded in breaching the dam. Gibson then took the three still with bombs to the Eder Dam and that too was broken. The rest fared badly and had no success against the Sorpe Dam. Of the nineteen bombers, nine were lost, as were fifty-six out of 133 crew. So serious was the loss that the Squadron was out of commission for some time. Gibson was awarded the Victoria Cross for directing the whole operation by radiotelephone and drawing enemy fire to himself. Despite his dislike of a *corps d'élite*, Harris made it clear that 617 Squadron was not to become a part of the Main Force but was to be kept for specialist purposes.

The Dams raid was dramatic but not, for the Germans, disastrous. The towns of the Ruhr Valley were flooded, a thousand people drowned, over half of whom were workers from the East, half a dozen small electricity works were put out of action and transport was disrupted. After the war, Speer stated that 50,000 workers were drawn from the Atlantic Wall to repair the dams and this was achieved just before the autumn rains began. The total industrial loss was remedied within a month or two.

It seems that Buf did not play a major part in the planning of this operation, with Bottomley doing most of the committee work, but a few days afterwards he received a letter from the Ministry of Economic Warfare congratulating him on the successful outcome of 'Upkeep' and suggesting that it opened up all sorts of possibilities for attacks on German inland water transport, which carried 180 million tons of goods. To divert this to the railways, if it were possible, would seriously interfere with military traffic.

A meeting was therefore called, chaired by Bottomley and minuted by Buf, with representatives from his Directorate, from the Armaments Directorate, the Air Officer Commanding 5 Group of Bomber Command and Mr Wallis who had been working on designing ever heavier bombs. It was reported that the performance of the 'bouncing bomb' (as used on the Dams raid) over land was entirely satisfactory. When released from a height of 100 feet it made one initial bounce of 160 yards and after ten decreasing bounces ran smoothly on a straight course. An overall range of 1,000 yards was obtained with a release speed of 220–230mph. After a drop of 100 feet the damage to the bomb was slight and it was fit for use again. Trials would be carried out from heights of 150 and 200 feet.

Further details were discussed about the manner of dropping the bomb in order to breach the embankment, or the ship-lift in the case of Rothensee, and whether Lancasters or Mosquitos would be most suitable. It was agreed that most damage would be inflicted on the following targets in order of priority:

1. Rothensee ship-lift
2. Dortmund-Ems Canal (between Dortmund and the junction with the Mittelland Junction)
3. Mittelland Canal (probably near Minden)

Further information would be needed about defences and embankment

The Möhne Dam the morning after. The anti-torpedo nets were meant to protect the structure. (Creek)

heights, and it was agreed that the acquiring of special aircraft should wait on a complete economic and tactical survey of the main waterways of Axis Europe. In the meantime DB Ops would arrange for appropriate low-altitude dropping trials.

A week later Buf received a paper from Mr Brant of the Railway Research Section. He stated that traffic between the Ruhr industrial area and north-east Germany passed either via the Dortmund-Ems and Mittelland Canals or via one of four railway routes. If the Canals were blocked the railways would – theoretically – be capable of carrying the diverted traffic, but only at the expense of other traffic. In order to cause a major, and possibly catastrophic, dislocation of such traffic it would be necessary to cut some, but not necessarily all, of the railway routes. These were:

a) Ruhr–Münster–Osnabrück.
b) Ruhr–Hamm–Bielefeld–Löhne– Hanover
c) Ruhr–Soest–Paderborn–Altenbeken
d) Ruhr–Schwerte–Kassel

Of these routes, (d) had been cut by the flood caused by the destruction of the Möhne Dam and was likely to be interrupted for several months. Routes (b) and (c) had viaducts, the destruction of which would be likely to interrupt traffic for some months. These viaducts were on route (b) near Bielefeld and on route (c) immediately west of Altenbeken. Route (a) could only carry a fraction of additional traffic.

If rail routes (b) and (c) could be cut in addition to the canals, there would not only be a disastrous fall in the quantity of traffic that could be sent eastwards from the Ruhr, but also a serious interference with troops and other military movements between central and eastern Germany on the one hand, and between western Germany, Belgium and northern France on the other. The prediction was correct, but the attacks had to wait until Mr Wallis's new 12,000lb earthquake bomb, known as Tallboy, was in service. On the night of 23 September 1944, eleven Lancasters of 617 Squadron took off for the Dortmund-Ems Aqueduct near Münster, armed with Tallboys accompanied by another 125 Lancasters with smaller bombs and five Mosquitos to do the marking. The object was to breach the banks of the canal, and this was done successfully. Six and a half miles of it were drained and daylight photographs showed twenty-one barges stranded. Three further attacks on the Dortmund-Ems Canal and then on the Mittelland were successfully made in November 1944 and January 1945, not by the Dambusters but by 5 Group crews, demonstrating a level of accuracy never before achieved.

The US Air Force in its quest for precision bombing had not fared so well. Early in 1942 the US Army Air Force had started planning to operate 4,000 heavy bombers from England by August 1943, to be used in daylight operations, and once beyond the range of escorting fighters, to have to rely on close-formation flying and defensive armament (mainly 0.5-inch machine guns). Early in 1942, Bufton had warned the Americans that Fortresses would need escorting fighters, but the best of the present ones could just reach into France and certainly not into central Germany. Fortunately, in May 1940, Freeman in the USA had discovered the Mustang, P-47 fighter (which was not built to a USAAF specification and therefore suspect to the Americans) and had managed to order Merlin engines from Packards. He soon became convinced of the virtues of a Merlin-engined

Mustang IV of 19 Squadron in
1945. (*Aeroplane*)

Mustang. The Americans
needed some persuasion but
fortunately Arnold, having
seen the figures for the new
hybrid's performance, was
able to tell the President:
'Tests indicate that it will be a
highly satisfactory pursuit plane for 1943.' The Mustang Mk III (equivalent to P-5IC) had
a maximum speed of 442mph at 24,500 feet, a service ceiling of 42,500 feet, and a range,
with drop-tanks, of 1,710 miles, enough to take it to Berlin and back.

With the backing of Freeman, Roosevelt himself was persuaded to convince the US
Chiefs of Staff that there had to be a massive increase in the production of the P-5IC,
and by mid-1944 the monthly output of Mustangs rose from 200 to 700 and of
Packard Merlins from 1,400 to 2,400. Eaker was prejudiced against the new plane and
at the end of 1943 he was replaced by Major-General James Doolittle to command the
VIII Air Force. Before the end of March he had asked for all his P-47s (Thunderbolts)
and P-38s (Lightnings) to be replaced by Mustangs.

Tactics were changed accordingly, with the Mustangs able to fly ahead of the bombers
and sweep the enemy from the sky. This at once lessened the appalling casualties that
the VIII Air Force had suffered at the end of 1943, nearly bringing its operations to an
end. It is not surprising, therefore, that American strategy in that period was directed
against German fighters and their production. For them, ball-bearings were a central
feature of their manufacture, and the Americans paid heavily and unsuccessfully for
their destruction.

Now that the US VIII Air Force was engaged with Bomber Command it became
essential to plan operations jointly, especially the choice of targets. Ever since his
arrival in England in May 1942, General Eaker, the American Commander of the
VIII Bomber Force, had been on excellent terms with Harris, who gave him every help
in providing a headquarters (at Wycombe Abbey School for Girls) not far from his at
High Wycombe, and aerodromes in East Anglia for his bombers. He also invited him
to sit in on his 9.00a.m. staff briefings for Bomber Command's raids that night. The
Air Ministry and the US Strategic Air Forces in Europe had their own intelligence
and operational departments, and there was the Economic Objectives Department
of the Ministry of Economic Warfare that was required to give advice on, and assess
the results of, the strategic bombing offensive, and in so doing incurred the wrath
of Harris. The United States Embassy also had an Enemy Objectives Unit of the
Economic Warfare Division, and in addition there was the information gathered from
photographic reconnaissance that increased greatly in quality and quantity and
required skilled interpretation. By the middle of 1944, it became clear that closer
cooperation was needed, and new organisations were set up. The scene was radically
changed with the Allied invasion of Europe in June 1944, and in that change Buf was
to play a key role.

CHAPTER 14

Peenemünde

The raid on Peenemünde on the night of 17/18 August 1943 was an outstanding feat from several points of view.

In the first place, it was planned and carried out in the utmost secrecy, matching that in which the Germans had shrouded their research centre for jet- and rocket-propelled weapons far away on a small peninsula on the right bank of the River Peene, where it flows into the Baltic. Building began on the Military Experimental Station in 1937 and soon the scientists moved in, with the Luftwaffe building a small aerodrome next door. The commanding officer was General Dornberger, an excellent commander as well as engineer, and the leading scientist was Werner von Braun who, after the war, was commandeered by the Americans to lead their NASA programme.

The first test firing of the A-4, known familiarly as the V-2, had taken place in June 1942 and rich resources of money and personnel were poured into the project in which Hitler staked his bid for victory. In April 1943, plans were made for the production of 950 V-2 rockets per month by the end of that year, and also 2,000 V-1s, but Peenemünde was only used for test-flying the latter. The surroundings were beautiful and the company congenial, though not for the 10,000 or so foreigners who were imported to do the hard work, all sworn to absolute secrecy.

Information began to trickle through to London in December 1942, though it was confirmed by a bugged conversation between Generals von Thoma and Cruewell, captured in North Africa. Twenty-three days later, on 15 April 1943, the information reached Mr Churchill, who appointed Mr Duncan Sandys MP to take charge of the enquiry. Other information, more and less reliable, trickled in, but the name Peenemünde occurred frequently. The Mosquitos of 540 Squadron provided the key, with five flights on 20 May, 12, 21, 23 and 26 June. Detailed photographs of the site showed two V-2 rockets lying horizontally on a trailer with a massive tower above them, and gave details of every building. Churchill called a meeting of his Defence Committee (Operations) on 29 June and the first decision reached was that Peenemünde was to be handed over to the might of Bomber Command. (The photographs of 23 June also showed, to the skilled eye of the WAAF interpreter, Constance Babington Smith, the little tailless liquid-rocket fighter, the Me 163, and the fan-shaped jet-marks that it left on the airfield.)

Under a cloak of concealment Harris, who had been briefed by Portal, held a conference on 7 July 1943 for his group commanders outlining his plan, though the raid would have to wait for five weeks to allow for a sufficient period of darkness. Although Peenemünde was 500 miles away (or 1,250 miles in flight distance) it had the advantage of being reachable from the north through Denmark, thus avoiding most of the German fighter defences. It was beyond the reach of Oboe, but well sited for H2S, now fitted in all Pathfinder bombers.

Harris decided to put the whole operation under a Master Bomber, Group Captain Searby, Commanding Officer of 83 Squadron, who had flown under Guy Gibson. This was the first time that a Master Bomber had been detailed to superintend a 'maximum effort' operation involving every serviceable machine of the Command. On the evening of 17 August 1943, 596 bombers took off for a destination most of the crews had never heard of until their briefing. That was finished by a last-minute message from Harris that if they did not succeed in wiping out Peenemünde, they would go back the next night and do it again. The night was clear and the moon was bright.

The raid was to lead to a new form of German fighter defence. For two years they had used a system of boxes, each about thirty-five miles across, stretching from Denmark to France, each with its own radar and a 'fighter control officer', controlling twin-engined, long-distance machines (Ju 88s, Me 110s and Do 217s). But some smaller groups had been formed of single-engined fighters to protect a city under attack, the *Wild Boar* system. In all, 213 German fighters took off against the RAF, 158 twin-engined and fifty-five single-engined. Harris's plan, however, had allowed for this, dispatching eight Mosquitos from 139 Squadron to reach Berlin just before 11.00p.m., approaching from different directions. The German night fighters circled around, expecting the Main Force to arrive at any moment.

The bomber-stream, however, was approaching the coast of Rügen, forty miles to the north-west of Peenemünde on a clear moonlit night where every detail below showed up clearly, though the Germans had started to release their smoke screen. A complicated marking plan had been worked out for the Pathfinders: first, Red Spot Fires were to be dropped seven miles out as a signpost; second, the sixteen blind markers (i.e. marking on H2S) were to fly on and drop three red target indicators and sixteen illuminative flares each at the first aiming point; third, six visual markers were each to mark the exact aiming point with four yellow target indicators.

The first part, however, went badly wrong. The Pathfinders mistook the small island of Ruden and flew on for a further two miles, dropping six of their eight markers two miles to the south of the target right on to the Trassenheide labour camp with its foreign workers. The Master Bomber realised the mistake, and his deputy placed his reserve markers correctly. The Main Force began its bombing at 12.15a.m. and again this was divided into three phases, the first on the housing estate where the scientists lived, the second on the Production Works where the V2s were assembled and the third on the Experimental Works. The flak increased as the raid went on, mainly small-calibre fire because the bombers were low, at 6,000 to 8,000 feet.

By the end of the second phase, however, German fighters were beginning to appear, and the level of destruction to the Experimental Works was disappointing. At least twenty-five buildings were destroyed, but these were mainly administrative. The wind tunnel and the telemetry block (which measured the performance of the rockets in space) were spared, and the workshop where trial parts were made was 'only scratched'. Dornberger and von Braun went unscathed.

The German fighters apparently used their own initiative in flying to Peenemünde and perhaps not more than three dozen arrived, but circumstances could not have been better for them. One shot down three bombers and another (on his first operation) five or six. Twenty-eight bombers were shot down around Peenemünde, and altogether forty-four were lost.

This was the first occasion on which the Germans used their *Schräge Muzik* upward-firing cannons with tracerless ammunition. They attacked from below and aimed at an engine and the petrol tank behind it, avoiding the fuselage because it might have blown up. None of the crews after returning to base reported anything that might have led the authorities to support this kind of attack, though several reported 'scarecrows', supposedly pyrotechnic shells designed to frighten the bombers. These were probably exploding aircraft.

The V2 was Hitler's favourite secret weapon, designed to shatter England into submission. It needed no crew, there was no defence against it and its arrival was silent. At a top level meeting between Hitler, Speer and Himmler four days later it was decided that Peenemünde would not be rebuilt but left in ruins, with most of its activities moved far away: the test-firing of rockets to Poland; experimental work to caves in Austria; and mass production of rockets to huge underground caverns and tunnels in the Harz Mountains. It seems probable that the V2 programme was put back by some two months. The first rocket was fired operationally on 8 September 1944, three months and two days after D-Day.

It is, perhaps, not surprising that Peenemünde does not appear in Buf's file. No doubt this is due to the cloak of secrecy that surrounded the whole operation. There is equally no doubt that its success was largely due to his struggle over the previous twelve months to have the Pathfinder Force created and to see it equipped with appropriate flares, missiles, and navigation aids.

Bomber Command targets. (B. Harris)

CHAPTER 15

Berlin

Between 23 August 1943 and 24 March 1944, sixteen major night raids were carried out by Bomber Command on Berlin. This has come to be called 'The Battle of Berlin', but the name is misleading as during this period nineteen major attacks were also carried out on other German targets, including Frankfurt in the west, Augsburg in the south and Leipzig in the east.

'We can wreck Berlin from end to end if the USAAF will come in on it. It will cost us between 400 and 500 aircraft. It will cost Germany the war,' so said Harris to the Prime Minister in November 1943, and in a similar vein to Portal the next month, a calculation 'to produce in Germany by 1 April 1944 a state of devastation in which surrender is inevitable'. Harris's forecast was wrong, and he knew that the Americans could not come in on it because their day bombers were much too vulnerable. One result of his raids was the resurgence of the German night-fighter force that began to inflict intolerable losses on Bomber Command. His estimate of the fragility of German 'morale', was also wrong: it was much tougher than he suspected or wished, under the close supervision of the Nazi secret or security police. One English agent reported that 'the Germans were afraid of bombs but they were a damn sight more afraid of the *Sicherheistdienst* (Secret or Security police)'. Churchill had been keen on the bombing of Berlin, and Harris had close personal links with him, paying frequent visits to Chequers and supplying him with the latest photographs of bomb damage.

It was difficult to reconcile this policy with the Casablanca directive, drawing a comment from Buf, on behalf of the Air Staff: 'We didn't mind if Harris was able to mount a successful repetition on any industrial area, Berlin or anywhere else, as long as he intended to start towards the specific targets eventually.' It had been a good time for the RAF, with the Battle of the Ruhr, the devastation of Hamburg, and the raid on the rocket research establishment at Peenemünde, after which the Luftwaffe's Chief of Staff, Hans Jeschonnek, fearing the wrath of Hitler and Goering, shot himself.

A Lancaster of 101 Squadron bombing-up with a 4,000lb-er, four 1,000lb-ers and 4lb stick incendiaries. (Middlebrook)

Berlin was a difficult target. It was a 1,250-mile flight there and back, not counting diversions; it was also heavily defended by anti-aircraft guns in a belt forty-miles wide within a searchlight belt sixty-miles wide. There were two rings of guns, at the centre of which were three flak towers built in parks, enormous concrete structures, each with eight 128mm guns on top that could fire to 45,000 feet and had a lethal explosion area of 260-yards across. It was the largest city in Germany, the third largest in the world, covering nearly 900 square miles and a pre-war population of 4 million. It was the administrative centre of the new German 'empire', and also contained many war factories producing guns, locomotives, small arms, ammunition, electrical items, aircraft, aero-engines, cars, ball-bearings and cameras.

It was not, however, a good target to bomb. It was a sprawling area with few distinctive features and the new H2S Mark III sets were unreliable. The most successful raid was that on 22–23 November 1943 when 764 aircraft were dispatched – 469 Lancasters, 234 Halifaxes, fifty Stirlings and eleven Mosquitos – after an unpromising weather forecast affirming low cloud over most of Germany and broken medium-level cloud over Berlin. Three of the five new H2S sets in Pathfinder Mosquitos failed and their crews had to return to base. The remaining two were designated 'Special Blind Markers', and formed good fixes on Brandenburg, twelve miles away, and then in Berlin itself, marking the two wooded areas of Spandau to the north and Grunewald to the south. They marked four minutes behind schedule with a special type of yellow target indicators that went down right over the aiming point. These were followed up by nine ordinary blind marker aircraft, which dropped seventy-nine target indicators and sixty-eight parachute skymarkers, the latter illuminating above the thick cloud that reached up to 16,000 feet. The Main Force dropped 2,500 tons of bombs on the markers, with a massive explosion at the end. The red glow of fires reflected on the cloud could be seen from eighty miles away.

Four bombers were shot down by flak, two Pathfinder Lancasters from 83 and 156 Squadron and a Halifax from 57 Squadron with its Squadron Commander. Twenty-six other aircraft were lost on the way home. One unexpected result of the operation was Harris's decision to withdraw Stirlings altogether, since they had suffered a loss of over sixteen per cent. Thus, ten squadrons ceased to be an active part of Bomber Command, reducing the strength of 3 Group to two squadrons.

That raid of 22–23 November was the most successful with night fighters. The situation deteriorated in subsequent actions, as these losses indicate:

18–19 November 1943 – 2.0 per cent
22–23 November – 3.4 per cent
23–24 November – 5.2 percent
26–27 November – 6.2 per cent
2–3 December – 8.7 per cent
24–25 March 1944 – 9.1 per cent

In the second of these raids, delivered on the west-central part of the city, many government buildings were hit, as well as ten churches, a barracks, the Technical University, two hospitals, the zoo, railway stations, theatres, museums, and much else, with a death-toll of over 2,000. The raid that did most industrial damage, including the Alkett tank factory, was that of 27 November, and was the result of a miscalculation by a Pathfinder of 83 Squadron who dropped his yellow markers seven miles to the north of the city centre, north of the Tegel Forest – the site of weapons and munitions factories, metal works, oxygen and radar works, and aeroplane, motor and railway repair workshops, amongst other landmarks.

The final raid on 24–25 March 1944 was a disaster, mainly due to an unforecast wind of over 100mph over the North Sea. The bombers were met by a host of night fighters, and a gaggle, instead of a stream, of 700 aircraft spread over a frontage of some seventy miles arrived well to the west of Berlin, though the target was the north-east of the city. The Pathfinders were also scattered by the wind and hindered by low cloud so that target indicators and skymarkers were blown rapidly across the target. Some of the crews who had been blown past Berlin decided to return and bomb the markers, a decision which cost some their lives. A total of 126 communities outside Berlin reported bombs. Eleven bombers fell to German fighters over the city and at least nineteen more on the first part of the journey home, but the Me 110 units based in Holland had been kept for the occasion. With the benefit of their SN-2 radars they soon picked out scattered Lancasters and the upward-firing *Schrage Musik* 20mm cannons did devastating damage to engines and wings (though this was not known at the time). Altogether seventy-two bombers failed to return, forty-four Lancasters and twenty-eight Halifaxes, with the latter suffering a higher loss rate of thirteen per cent as against the Lancasters' 7.6 per cent. Of the aircrew, 392 were killed and 133 became prisoners of war. The German night fighters claimed sixty and flak twelve victims.

Even worse was to come. On 30 March, Harris ordered a maximum effort attack on Nuremberg, deep in the heart of southern Germany, with a full moon. It was the spiritual home of Nazism with SS barracks, other buildings designed by Albert Speer and a vast open area where Hitler held his grand parades before the war. The reasons for Harris's choice are unclear, except that he wanted to finish his 'Main Offensive' on a successful note. A weather reconnaissance Mosquito sent out that day reported that Nuremberg was likely to be covered in cloud, but that the route to the target was clear, offering no protection to the bombers. Even Robert Saundby, Harris's deputy, was foxed: 'I thought perhaps there was some top-secret political reason for the raid – something too top-secret for even me to know, but now I do not think that this was so.'

It was a perfect night for the German fighters on a 'Tame Boar' operation, deployed at radio beacons ahead of the bomber stream and given freedom to hunt by themselves. Few bombs hit the city and ninety-five bombers were lost, over twelve per cent of the force, with 545 men. It was Bomber Command's heaviest loss of the war, and a sad end to the Pointblank offensive designed to bring Germany to its knees. In January, the Japanese ambassador in Berlin reported to Tokyo (his messages were regularly decrypted at Bletchley Park): 'Internal collapse will certainly not be brought about by means of air raids'. On 24 February, a German businessman was quoted as saying that morale in Berlin had been badly shaken by the January raids but referred to a Finnish businessman believing that the situation there was best described as one of apathy. The word 'apathy' had appeared in a Foreign Office report on German morale of 8 February, so much so that Harris protested to the Air Staff against the growing use of the term as a description of the average German's reaction to heavy bombing, to which the Deputy Chief replied on 29 March: 'The word "apathy" is used by so many independent witnesses that we must tend to accept it as a fair description of the general state of mind'. This was not what Harris had wanted.

As German fighter defence by day was declining, so its night-fighter force was growing in size and efficiency. They had devised an air-interception (AI) set, SN2, immune from 'Window'. Its large aerial array limited it to twin-engined machines, Me 110s and Ju 88s, and it came into action in the autumn of 1943. These aircraft could emit a direction-finding note when in contact with the bomber stream so that other fighters could home in to it. Thus *Wilde Sau,* 'Wild Boar', developed into *Zahne Sau,* 'Tame Boar', whereby fighters hitherto limited to one box for fighting and landing were now free to roam the skies directed by a central controller. By chance a Ju 88 with SN2 landed at Woodbridge on 13 July 1943 from which its frequency was discovered as 85 m/cs, and within ten days a sophisticated form of 'Window' was devised to jam it.

This radar war of new measures and counter-measures demanded the best resources, and so a new 100 Group was formed in Bomber Command on 23 November 1943. Its first unit was 192 Squadron, which had been busy monitoring German radio and radar since January of that year. It was soon followed by 141 Squadron, which was in the process of converting from Beaufighter VIs to rather tired Mosquito IIs. On 9 December, 239 Squadron began to move in to West Raynham, and on 8 December, 169 Squadron arrived at Little Snoring, the third to be equipped with *Serrate.* 515 Squadron was added in December 1943, the last three all equipped with Mosquitos. By March 1945, the total number of squadrons had risen to thirteen and the Group had changed its name from 100 (Special Duties) to 100 (Bomber Support) Group. Its purpose was to strengthen and consolidate the various radar detection and jamming techniques that were being devised in this swiftly moving battle.

'Window', in order to be effective, had to be concentrated and so encouraged a tight bomber stream. This was watched by enemy radar and by *Korfu,* which picked up bombers' radar transmissions. This information now went to a single fighter controller to direct the night fighters on to the bomber stream. He had, of course, to guess their destination, and Bomber Command with diversions and spoof raids, made his job as difficult as possible. His 'running commentary' was transmitted by high-powered stations on unknown frequencies that were monitored in England. When one was discovered it was sent to selected aircrews who then jammed it, joined in October 1943 by high-powered ground stations under the code-name 'Corona'. An English voice speaking idiomatic German succeeded in throwing the fighter controller into an exceedingly bad temper. The Germans thought they could counter this by using a woman's voice, but the RAF were ready with a specially trained linguistic WAAF. It is said that her vocabulary expanded considerably.

Ju 88 at Woodbridge. (Cushing)

CHAPTER 16

'Overlord'

Allied planning for the invasion of Europe depended on a number of factors: sufficient land forces to overcome German army resistance; sufficient landing craft to carry these across the Channel; the elimination of the German Air Force from the skies above the landing areas; and favourable enough weather to permit the landing of the invasion troops and subsequent supplies. Harris had always maintained that invasion was not necessary, that the elimination of sixty or so principal German towns by bombing would be sufficient to bring Germany to its knees.

Alan Brooke, Chief of the Imperial General Staff, recorded in his diary for 11 March 1942, 'Long Chiefs of Staff meeting at which we discussed the naval and army calls on the air force. It resulted in rather a heated debate which did not lead us on to much! I expect some pretty stormy passages within the next few weeks.' He then added some later reflections:

> My expectations were certainly fulfilled! The Air Force was at this time engaged in an all-out air offensive on Germany and were putting every ounce of their strength into this effort. Many of them held the opinion that, given sufficient heavy bombers, Germany could be brought to her knees by air action alone. In these circumstances it is not surprising that the Air Ministry was anxious to develop its strength in those types of aircraft that were best suited for the attack on Germany. As a result the army was being starved of any types suitable for the direct support of land forces. We had gone to war with the obsolete Lysander machine, and since then nothing had materialized. Everything seemed to be devoted to the production of four-engine bombers which were unsuited for close cooperation with the army. All Air Force eyes were trained on Germany and consequently all personnel trained for long distance raids, and little interest was displayed in close cooperation with land forces.
>
> Many doubted that land forces would ever be again employed in large land operations on the Continent – why therefore provide for a contingency that would probably never arise? They could always produce the argument that the Air Force was at that time busy hitting the Germans hard – were they to reduce this effort for the problematical benefits to be derived by producing men and machines capable of cooperating with the Army in operations that were unlikely ever to take place! It was uphill work striving to obtain what I knew would be essential in the later stages of the war if we were ever to win!
>
> The Navy were also fighting for greater air support in the anti-submarine war which they were engaged in, and on which our very existence depended. Then again the Naval operations seemed purely defensive, promised no decisive

results of victory – were they therefore to be allowed to detract from the bomber offensive on Germany which might hold decisive promises of success?

A month later things were no better. 'A bad COS with much loss of time and interruptions trying to frame a reply for Marshall [his scheme for the invasion of Europe]. Then lunch with Portal and Freeman to settle "off the record" the differences between Army and Air Force. Evidently little hope of arriving at any sort of settlement.' Again, on 23 October 1942, he wrote:

Another long and difficult COS trying to arrive at agreement concerning future policy for the conduct of the war. We are getting a little nearer, but the divergence between Portal's outlook and mine is still very great. He is convinced that Germany can be defeated by bombing alone, while I consider that bombing can only be one of the contributory causes towards achieving that end.

Clearly at this stage Portal was on Harris's side.

By the beginning of 1944, however, the Allied leaders had agreed on 'Overlord', the operation to invade Europe by way of the French coast, and Harris wrote an eight-page paper headed 'The Employment of the Night Bomber Force in Connection with the Invasion of the Continent from the UK'. He starts with the reluctant admission that 'Overlord' must now presumably be regarded as an inescapable commitment, arguing that 'it is therefore necessary to consider the method by which our most powerful offensive weapon, the heavy bomber force, can be brought to bear most effectively in support of it.'

He stresses that the force had been developed as an independent strategic weapon for the destruction of the enemy's industrial centres with highly specialised aircraft and operational techniques. It was trained to operate only at night and would require at least six weeks of fair weather training to convert crews to day work. Even then, the aircraft were completely unsuited for anything but night operations, meaning that in no circumstances could day operations be undertaken. 'It is necessary', he wrote, 'always to use some form of Pathfinder technique. Oboe is limited by its short range and is unreliable; Oboe Mark II is in very short supply, but such marking is accurate to within 300 to 400 yards. H2S is unlimited in range but is not yet technically reliable and its accuracy depends largely on the nature of the target. A further instrument, G.H., is now becoming available, but only in small numbers.' He continues:

The choice of target is chiefly governed by the weather. The smaller the target the more important the weather conditions. It is not possible to use the Pathfinder Force in strength for more than two nights running without greatly impairing its effectiveness. For a period of about twelve days it would be possible to work two nights out of every three without undue fatigue. The maximum effort which the force can sustain is approximately 5,000 sorties or eight full scale attacks per month.

The heavy bomber force is quite incapable of being brought into action quickly against 'fleeting targets' because some seven daylight hours are necessary between the decision to bomb a given target and the take off of aircraft to attack it. 'Programme bombing', except over a long period and in most general terms, is thus ruled out.

Consequently, he claims:

... anything like a planned schedule of bomber operations designed to give immediate assistance to ground forces engaged in effecting a landing or operating in the field would be extremely unreliable and almost wholly futile. In the event of favourable weather conditions, a 'drenching' attack on selected beaches immediately before the assault would be practicable. 'Area' bombing of objectives further back would similarly be entirely dependent on weather conditions and would be very unlikely to achieve sufficient accuracy to be material assistance to the Army. Nor is the heavy bomber force suitable for cutting railway communications at definite points. It is essential for any bombing designed to assist the army to be planned on the broadest possible lines.

'With strategic bombing', Harris claimed, 'the effects are cumulative: the bomber offensive is sound policy only if the rate of destruction is greater than the rate of repair. Remove the bombing and the shortages would comparatively soon be remedied at least in sufficient measure to put an entirely new complexion on the war on land.' He concludes:

It is thus clear the best and indeed the only efficient support which Bomber Command can give to 'Overlord' is the intensification of attacks on suitable industrial centres in Germany as and when the opportunity offers. If we attempt to substitute for this process attacks on gun emplacements, beach defences, communications or dumps in occupied territory we shall commit the irremediable error of diverting our best weapons from the military function, for which it has been equipped and trained, to tasks which it cannot effectively carry out. Though this might give a specious appearance of 'supporting' the Army, in reality it would be the gravest disservice we could do them. It would lead directly to disaster.

Buf circulated this paper to his colleagues, asking for comments. These included reference to successful day operations already carried by Bomber Command, to an over-narrow view of the possibilities of H2S and Oboe, and chiefly to the fact that in the preparatory phase of 'Overlord', all or part of the forces of Bomber Command would be at the disposal of the Supreme Commander, in conjunction with advisers from Bomber Command. It would therefore be the duty of the Commander-in-Chief to do his best to fulfil these tasks.

A week later, on 22 January 1944, Buf felt himself compelled to write a stern, if not despairing, note to the Assistant Chief of Air Staff (Operations) about Harris's intransigeance in ignoring Air Staff Directives. He had been sent, a week before, instructions that 'whilst first priority must now be accorded to the destruction of

Schweinfurt, high priority must also be given to the destruction of those towns associated with the assembly of fighter aircraft, particularly, Leipzig, Brunswick, Gotha and Augsburg.' Yet, on 21 January, Bomber Command had been sent against Magdeburg, and this was not because of the weather (Buf had checked with the Senior Forecaster at Dunstable).

> I am forced to the conclusion that the selection of Magdeburg demonstrates clearly that Bomber Command does not intend to comply with the instructions of the Air Staff. This state of affairs cannot be permitted to continue during the critical months ahead, when it is essential that the closest cooperation should be maintained. I consider that the problem should be resolved immediately in order that the Air Staff may know where it stands.

On 30 January, Buf commented on Harris's doctrine of attacks on German towns that, as far as morale was concerned, results so far showed apathetic resignation from fear of the Gestapo, and the general destruction of housing was not necessarily affecting production of aircraft for the German Air Force. A greater effect would be produced by cumulative damage to many factories in one industry. Buf quoted the estimated reduction of aircraft production from March to October 1943 by the US Army Air Force as fifteen per cent compared with Bomber Command's 0.5 per cent.

Harris's worst fears were confirmed. The Admiralty were pressing for more attacks on German submarine bases in France. Then he received a polite paper from Morley of the Air Staff 'suggesting' the allocation of six squadrons from Bomber Command for daylight operations in preparation for 'Overlord':

> It is concluded that serious consideration should now be given to the initiation of a training programme for daylight operations for certain Squadrons from your Command. A force of six Squadrons might, it is suggested, be set aside for this purpose. They would, no doubt, have to be withdrawn from night operations. This would be a serious loss of effort, but if required training programme was initiated immediately, these Squadrons would be fit to operate by D-day of operation 'OVERLORD'. The advantages to that operation which the employment of these Squadrons by day under strong fighter escort in France and Belgium might give in the period immediately after D-day are considered greatly to outweigh the disadvantages of their withdrawal from your night operations in the immediate future.

In December 1943, the appointment of General Eisenhower as Supreme Commander of 'Overlord' was decided, and Leigh Mallory (formerly of Fighter Command) was appointed as Commander-in-Chief of the Allied Expeditionary Air Force, though this gave him no control over the strategic air forces. On 6 January 1944, Churchill suggested that Air Chief Marshal Sir Arthur Tedder, who had just been appointed Deputy Supreme Commander, should be the real Commander-in-Chief of the Air. This was Eisenhower's plan for achieving unified Command, but it did not go down well with the Chiefs of Staff who were concerned with maintaining control over their own Commands. By the end of February, however, Eisenhower and Portal reached agreement about the strategic air plan in preparation for 'Overlord': it was to be framed by Tedder in consultation with Harris and Spaatz. Tedder was to be the real supreme commander of the air, with the approval and authority of Eisenhower behind him.

Tedder was not a typical RAF Commander. He had neither a DFC nor a DSO; he had not been to Haileybury but he did have a degree in history from Cambridge; he did not go hunting, fishing and shooting; his appearance was often untidy – he seldom wore a peaked cap; whenever possible he had a pipe in his mouth; and in the desert he liked to sit with the men of a squadron to hear what they had to say. He was convinced, particularly from his experience in the Western Desert, that battles could only be won by cooperation based on reliable intelligence. Discussion, for example, with Admiral Cunningham, had been difficult because his headquarters in Alexandria were 125 miles away; and he soon discovered that army commanders in the desert sometimes did not actually know where their units were. Freeman wrote to Rosalinde, his wife, 'I now feel that things will look up for us in the Middle East for at last there is at least one man of real intelligence at the top'. Tedder had served as Deputy to Freeman in the late 1930s when Freeman was Director-General of Research and Development until Beaverbrook was appointed in his place. Tedder managed to escape by being posted as Deputy to Longmore in the Middle East Air Command. In May 1941, he took over the command and began a difficult and distinguished task, often with inadequate resources.

On 8 November 1942, the Americans landed in Morocco and Algeria to attack Tunisia from the west, while the Eighth Army battled on from the south, a situation that caused large problems about overall control of operation, particularly in the air. Eisenhower, the supreme commander, had not yet recognised the importance of a combined headquarters, and called a conference of senior airmen on 26 November to discuss air operations. In January 1943, Tedder had to take part in the Casablanca Conference of Allied leaders (twelve days after his wife had been killed in an air crash) at which it was decided that he was to command everything with wings between Gibraltar and Palestine under the overall direction of Eisenhower. February was spent in working out a complicated organisation for a combined British–American headquarters. The Tunisian campaign that provided a painful training ground for the Americans confirmed Tedder's reputation and

Tedder. (IWM)

ensured that he would hold high command for the rest of the war. General Carl Spaatz wrote to George Stratemeyer (Chief of Air Staff in Washington) that in their American set-up it was hard to treat aviation as co-equal with the army and navy, whereas the RAF will not submit to it being considered in any other way. It will not accept that air support 'belongs' to an army commander, or that he may dictate its employment. That was a hard lesson for the Americans to learn, and it is a tribute to Tedder's insistence that within a couple of years after the end of the war, the Americans had abandoned 'the US Army Air Force' in favour of 'the US Air Force'.

It is not surprising that, on 6 January 1944, Air Chief Marshal Sir Arthur Tedder was appointed Deputy Supreme Allied Commander to Eisenhower for Operation 'Overlord'. He and Portal agreed that the strategic air plan was to be framed by Tedder in consultation with Harris and Spaatz, the latter having been given command of United States Strategic Air Forces in Europe (USSTAF). Leigh-Mallory's concern was with two principal objectives: air superiority and the disruption of rail communications in France and Western Germany. The early stages would be more 'strategic' and the latter ones 'tactical'. Spaatz, however, favoured oil as the prime objective, but Tedder saw this as a long-term objective rather than an immediate one for the invasion. Tedder had learned the long-term importance of attacking enemy communications both in North Africa and in Sicily and Italy, and he argued that a sustained attack on the railway system of German occupied Europe could, in the long term, wreck its industry.

A conference was called on 15 February 1944 to settle these issues with Tedder, Harris, Leigh-Mallory, Spaatz, Anderson, Oxland and other staff officers, along with Professor Zuckerman, a specialist adviser on transport to Tedder. Leigh-Mallory laid great emphasis on the necessity for interrupting the railroad communications from the beachhead all the way to Western Germany (the minutes were produced by an American officer), but Spaatz found this incompatible with the 'Pointblank' directive which laid down as first objective the destruction of the German fighter force, second, the reduction of the will and means to continue the war, and third, the direct support of 'Overlord'. Harris stated that he would give a written guarantee that the proposed plan for interrupting the railroad communications would not succeed, and that the Army would then blame the Air Forces for their failure. Tedder then suggested that a Joint Planning committee be formed with adequate representation from RAF Bomber Command, US Strategic Air Forces, and Allied Expeditionary Air Force to draw up a plan to suit the capabilities of all concerned. Spaatz and the others agreed.

Harris's objections were by now beginning to wear a little thin, and so Portal decided to have a trial of strength. He suggested a directive be sent to Bomber Command with specific orders to attack six railway objectives in France under the heading 'Attacks in preparation for "Overlord"':

> To provide data for the final detailed planning for 'Overlord' and in order to contribute materially to the requirements of 'Overlord' during periods when 'Pointblank' operations are not practicable, attacks should be carried out against the following railway objectives using a ground marking technique: Trappes, Aulnoye, Le Mans, Amiens, Courtrai, Laon ... Other railway targets will subsequently be detailed when the 'Overlord' plan is finally formulated.

These marshalling yards were all attacked between the 6th and the end of March with outstandingly successful results, proving that Harris's estimate of his own force's capabilities were far short of the mark, and he confessed himself to be surprised at the accuracy of the operations.

The argument continued between Spaatz's favouring of oil and Tedder's of transport, and in particular railways, as the prime objective of the heavy bombers, but the decision had to be shaped by the particular demands of 'Overlord'. So Eisenhower called a meeting for 25 March 1944 in which he took part (it was chaired by Portal), along with Tedder, Spaatz, Harris, Leigh Mallory, and representatives of the War Office, the Joint Intelligence Staff, and the Ministry of Economic Warfare. Tedder opened with his case for railway bombing, but this was severely attacked with doubts about its efficiency for interrupting troop trains. The alternative was oil, but Mr Lawrence of the Ministry of Economic Warfare pointed out that the Germans had considerable reserves of oil on the Western Front, and strategic attacks on oil production would not produce visible results for four or five months. Eisenhower took up Tedder's claim that 'it was only necessary to show that there would be *some* reduction, however small, which won the day'. The communications plan was reluctantly accepted.

In fact, there was no fundamental dispute between these two objectives. Both were equally necessary, and the immediate criterion was help for the invasion of France. Tedder should now have been in a position to issue his orders to Harris, but the way was not yet clear. The bombing of seventy-four French and Belgian railway targets would incur civilian casualties, officially estimated at 40,000, and Churchill could not accept this. He referred the decision to the War Cabinet, which passed it to the Joint Intelligence Committee, which then referred it to the Defence Committee. Eisenhower, however, could not brook this prevarication. He reminded Churchill that he had registered no opposition to the heavy bombing of the French U-boat bases in 1943, and he did not think that the number of civilians killed would exceed 10,000–15,000.

Churchill was still not satisfied, and sent a message to Roosevelt saying that the British Government was seriously disturbed, and asked the President whether such raids would embitter the French against their liberators. Roosevelt replied brusquely that the decision was a military one, which must necessarily be left to the commanders.

On D-Day, while Allied assault forces were tossing on the dark waters of the Channel en route for France, the night bombers which were to herald their approach passed overhead. Shortly after midnight the bombing commenced, and by dawn 1,136 aircraft of Bomber Command had dropped 5,853 tons of bombs on ten selected coastal batteries lining the Bay of the Seine between Cherbourg and le Havre. As the day broke the US 8th Air Force took up the attack, with another 1,763 tons of bombs on the shore defences.

During the remainder of the day, the heavy bombers concentrated their attacks on the key centres of communication behind the enemy's lines, through which he would have to bring his reinforcements. Allied fighters and fighter bombers roamed over the entire battle area attacking German defensive positions and known headquarters, strafing troop concentrations and destroying transport. During the twenty-four hours of 6 June the 'heavies' flew 5,309 sorties to drop 10,395 tons of bombs, with very light losses, while the aircraft of the tactical air forces flew a further 5,276 sorties.

Thus, Bomber Command was redirected. In March 1944 its aircraft dropped over 27,000 tons of bombs, of which about seventy per cent fell on Germany. In June, 57,000 tons were dropped, of which about 5,000 tons were aimed at Germany. In the final offensive of the last year, the Americans gained superiority in the air, and although the German night fighters were never completely overcome, the casualty rate fell dramatically after September 1944. In addition, the Command developed the ability to hit small targets both at short and long range. As the Allies occupied France, the German night-fighter force lost its early warning areas, and the radar transmitters for the direction of Bomber Command moved forward almost to the Rhine. Such were the consequences of the decisions taken for 'Overlord', and the decisions were the result of highly complex negotiations between two powerful nations and two powerful air forces, in which Buf played an active part.

After one such meeting, Buf was tapped on the shoulder by Bottomley and told that Churchill wanted to speak to 'the little Air Commodore'. He asked Buf if he had been involved in any recent accidents. Buf said he had not, and asked the reason for the enquiry. Churchill said he had noticed that Buf often differed from some of his senior officers and that there was always the possibility that he might be run over by a bus. He went on 'to make an order that you report to me in person once a fortnight so that I know no accident has befallen you'. Buf thanked the Prime Minister for his concern, but said he did not think it was necessary!

On 27 April 1944 Buf wrote in a letter to Sue, 'By the way there was another C [Cabinet] Meeting last night and (Norman B. [Bottomley] told me) Winnie asked about the Air Commodore again – supposed he'd been "banished" as he wasn't there. Keep this to yourself.' Buf had obviously made an impression on the Prime Minister.

The first tactical use of heavy bombers in France was planned by Buf. He recalled that he went down to Portsmouth to talk with General de Guingand, Montomery's Chief of Staff, and introduced him to Oboe and to the overlays from the War Office with their best estimate of the layout of the enemy defences. He said, 'Look, if you want to bust through the ground defences this is what you do,' and threw them down on the map several times.

On the day, 8 July, Buf and de Guingand with two other officers landed on the beachhead and were taken in a jeep to a slit trench from which the Huns had recently been evicted, 2,000 yards from the most northerly of five aiming points. At 6.00a.m. a marker bomb came down on it from a Mosquito, and then three Lancasters appeared against the dawn sky, then five, then ten, until the sky was filled, each one dropping fourteen 1000lb bombs. 'In five minutes you couldn't see 20 yards for dust, but the markers could be seen from above.' Buf reckoned that 2,000 tons of bombs were dropped. Then the Tactical Air Force took over and carpet-bombed all the area in between the aiming points with fragmentation bombs so that there would be no cratering to impede the tanks of the 11th Armoured Brigade. These moved up to the farthest point, but were then held up by two 88mm guns that had not been knocked out.

By 10 July all of Caen north of the river was gained, and Churchill sent a telegram with 'many congratulations' to Montgomery. He replied, 'Thank you for your message. We wanted Caen badly. We used a great weight of air power to ensure quick success and the whole battle area leading up to Caen is a scene of great destruction. The town itself also suffered heavily'.

CHAPTER 17

Rockets and Jets

Hitler put great hopes on forms of bombardment that required no pilot. Research on rockets had been going on since 1934, but it was intensified in 1942 when a swift victory in Russia was seen to be impossible. The first weapon was known as the V1 from the German *Vergeltungswaffe*, retaliation weapon, though the German designation of the V2 was the A-4, and Hitler's plan was to produce 950 of the latter per month by the end of 1943. Fortunately this proved impossible, and the first was fired on 8 September 1944. The RAF raid on Peenemünde had put back production by a couple of months.

Five days before this, on 12 August 1943, a report was received about the production of pilotless aircraft, and further investigation was handed over to Bottomley, the Deputy Chief of Air Staff. More reports were coming in concerning a new experimental unit soon to move to northern France under the command of a Colonel Wachtel, to be known as Flak Regiment 155W, designed to operate 108 'catapults' on an arc from Dunkirk to Abbeville. Larger concrete emplacements were being constructed in the Pas de Calais and near Cherbourg. On 28 October, another report arrived about a 'concrete platform with a centre axis pointing directly to London'. Photographs showed, in addition to this 'platform' three other buildings and a pair of long constructions looking like skis turned on their side. These became known as 'ski sites'. By the end of 1943, seventy-two of these had been identified in northern France and seven in the Cherbourg Peninsula. On 28 November, a photograph was taken at Zempin (adjoining Peenemünde) of a pilotless aircraft on such a launching ramp. In May 1944 a prototype crashed in Sweden, revealing a wingspan of seventeen and a half feet, a fuselage length of some twenty-two feet and a propulsion unit of just over eleven feet. The warhead contained about 1,870lb of high explosive and the tank 130 gallons of a new fuel to drive a simple jet-propulsion engine. Gyroscopes provided directional control.

In the autumn of 1943, the Air Ministry set up a new Directorate to co-ordinate all information on 'Crossbow' (the code-name for measures to deal with the bomb) and propose appropriate action. Between 5–31 December, fifty-two ski-sites received 3,216 tons of bombs, dropped partly by the Second Tactical Air Force and partly by Bomber Command and the VIII Air Force. Precision was absolutely necessary and the most successful results were obtained by very low-level attacks by Spitfires, Mustangs and Mosquitos of 2 TAF. By the end of May 1944, 103 out of 140 sites had been destroyed and probably less than ten remained capable of launching a bomb. This was an undoubted success, greatly reducing the severity of what could have been a major attack.

Wachtel, however, was not to be deflated, and devised a simpler form of launching ramp, abandoning the ski shape and camouflaging the place to look like farm buildings: these were called 'modified sites', but soon became known to Allied agents and spies. By 12 June 1944, six days after D-day, the day on which the first flying bomb was launched, thirty-six 'modified sites' has been identified. Three days later, 244 bombs were launched from fifty-five ramps, and by 21 June the thousandth one was dispatched to London. The English reaction may be summed up in the name 'doodle-bug', with which they were christened.

The Chiefs of Staff Committee had to decide whether the forty-two sites now identified in the Pas de Calais should be attacked, and on 13 June decided that nothing must impede the invasion of France, now seven days off. The Americans decided to set aside 200 bombers to attack the sites, forty-seven of which had now been identified, but Tedder argued for a mass attack on Berlin with 1,200 American bombers by day and 800 British by night. The defences in England were greatly strengthened, in guns, fighters and balloons.

Bomber Command did drop 3,000 tons of bombs on a major flying-bomb depot at St Len d'Esserent on the nights of 4 and 7 July. These landed on store caves in the valley of the Oise, after which the commandant reported that many of the underground passages had collapsed and the roads and ramps leading to them had been ruined. Despite some vacillation by the Directorate of Bomber Operations and appalling weather from 3 to 6 August, twelve attacks were made by Bomber Command, and in one week nearly 15,000 tons of bombs fell upon depots or launching sites. One last attack with 500 tons on a storage depot was the last because the Allied Armies had, by then, cut communications with Germany. Between 15 June and 15 July, 1,280 flying bombs fell inside the London area, the worst hit urban district being Penge where, in eighty days, every one of its 6,000 houses was either destroyed or damaged, and one in twenty of its population (after the evacuation of women and children) was killed or injured. In August the heavy defence guns were moved to the coast, all 412 of them, though the fighters had to patrol on both sides, and on the night of 27/28 August,

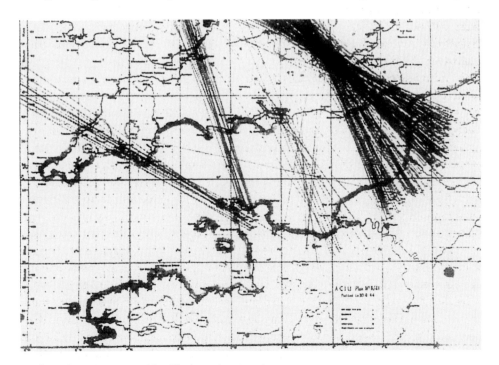

V1 firing lines in France, identified on photographs.

eighty-seven out of ninety-seven bombs reported approaching England were destroyed. By 5 September, the Allied armies had overrun most of the sites.

On 7 September, Mr Duncan Sandys declared that the Battle of London was over, 'except possibly for a few last shots'. The next day, a loud explosion occurred in Chiswick, followed by the sound of a large object rushing through the air. The first V2 had arrived, the first of 1,000 in the next six months. On 31 August and 1 September, Bomber Command dropped 2,897 tons on nine suspected storage depots, but between 8 and 16 August, twenty rockets arrived in England, ten of which were in London. The bases were now seen to be in Holland and between 25 September and 3 October Norwich suffered sixteen missiles. In the next eleven days, thirty-nine 'incidents' were reported there and in London. By the end of November, 160 people had been killed in England.

A main launching site was identified and bombed in the Haagsche Bosch, a wooded area on the outskirts of The Hague, along with a hotel in The Hague that was thought to be accommodating rocket crews. These attacks were mainly by bomb-carrying Spitfires, and a decline in the number of rockets in February raised hopes. But the frequency then increased and a severe attack by medium bombers on 3 March caused much damage in the city of The Hague, and many casualties. The last rocket fell in Orpington on 27 March, the last of 1,115 to hit the United Kingdom, causing 2,855 deaths as compared with the 6,139 caused by flying bombs. The official history comments:

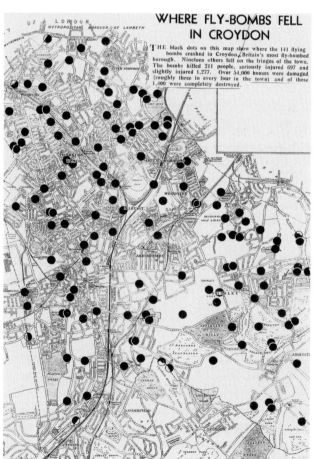

WHERE FLY-BOMBS FELL IN CROYDON

THE black dots on this map show where the 141 flying bombs crashed in Croydon, Britain's most fly-bombed borough. Nineteen others fell on the fringes of the town. The bombs killed 211 people, seriously injured 697 and slightly injured 1,277. Over 54,000 houses were damaged (roughly three in every four in the town) and of these 1,400 were completely destroyed.

Savage though they were, they were not aimed, and that sporting instinct, indigenous in the male Londoner, came to his rescue. In the case of the rocket, whether a citizen was hit or not was soon seen to be a matter of chance, and to a male population which delighted to take its pleasures at the race-course, or the dog track, the element of gambling was to a certain extent reassuring.

Locations of bomb sites in Croydon.

ME 163. (Crick)

Jets and rockets, however, were not confined in Germany to bombing. In the summer of 1944, new jet and rocket aircraft were coming into service, of which the Messerschmitt Me 163 posed the most immediate threat to Allied airforces. The Me 262 entered service as a bomber in August 1944. An Enigma decrypt of 26 July stated that the Me 163 would operate with immediate effect round Leipzig in defence of the Leuna hydrogenation plant. A decrypt from the Japanese Naval Mission in Berlin in July stated that the Luftwaffe would be receiving them at the rate of 1,000 a month from January 1945, whereas the USAAF was not expecting jets of its own until October 1945. (The RAF received its first jet Gloster Meteors in July 1944 and the first V1 to be brought down by one fell on 4 August, but the early Mk 1 Meteors only had a top speed of 385mph at sea level.)

Plans for the Me 163, however, were not fulfilled: at the end of September, Air Intelligence learned that production had been set back by damage to the Jumo factory at Dessau. In November, the Japanese Naval Mission reported that production of the components of the fuel was only one-tenth of the planned amount, and in December, Enigma revealed that the number of Me 163 pilots completing their training, which had been thirty-eight in October, had dropped to nil. Such were the results of the Allied air offensive against German communications and of their attacks on oil targets.

So much for Hitler's assurance given to assembled military leaders in June 1943 that the Germans had only to hold out to the end of the year. By this time, he thought, London would be levelled to the ground and Britain forced to capitulate.

CHAPTER 18

Oil

Petroleum products, oil and petrol and allied chemicals are the lifeblood of a country at war: without them, armies cannot move, submarines cannot go to sea and aeroplanes cannot fly. Germany had little natural source of oil, and had to rely on extracting it from coal, of which there was a plentiful supply. This synthetic oil then had to be transported by rail, road or canal, and so transport was as necessary as production. Germany's conquests eastwards provided extra sources, in particular the rich oilfields of Ploesti in Rumania until it was overrun by the Russian advance in August 1944. It was just within range of heavy bombers flying from southern Italy, as were the oil refineries in Austria and Hungary.

The task of calculating German resources had been pursued zealously by Allied oil committees throughout 1943 and into 1944, and their figures were fairly accurate. Stocks of aviation spirit, motor petrol and diesel oil had grown by May 1944 to one and a third million tons, of which over half a million was aviation spirit. The supply, however, was vulnerable, because a large proportion of the most valuable production was centred in a small number of targets: ninety per cent of aviation spirit came from the Bergius hydrogenation plants, and one third of this from two large plants in Leuna and Pölitz, both in East Germany. Much synthetic production was concentrated in the Ruhr, and these plants had already been subjected to heavy attacks by the Eight Air Force in May and by Bomber Command in June.

Germany alleviated its energy problem by a feat of chemical alchemy in turning coal into oil with an enormous expansion of the synthetic oil industry. The gigantic chemical companies like I.G. Farben, sympathetic to Hitler's conquests and racial cleansing, relied increasingly on slave workers from conquered countries and inmates from concentration camps. I.G. Farben built one of its synthetic fuel and rubber plants in Poland, next to Auschwitz. The chemical process produced not only liquid fuels but also ninety-nine per cent of Germany's synthetic rubber and nearly all its synthetic methanol, ammonia and nitric acid – the raw material for military explosives.

A high percentage of petroleum production was concentrated in a few Bergius hydrogenation plants that were the sole source of high-grade aviation petrol. Nearly one third of Bergius production was concentrated in two plants at Leuna and Pölitz in Polish Silesia, the former ninety miles south-west of Berlin and the latter seventy miles north-east of the capital. Leuna covered three square miles of land, employing 35,000 workers, 10,000 of them prisoners or slave labourers, with millions of tons of brown coal from local pits fed into it. What might have been a straightforward target for daytime bombers was obscured by black camouflage smoke sent up from hundreds of small ovens. The Bergius process, named after its inventor, Friedrich Bergius, a Nobel Prize-winning chemist, used hydrogen under high pressure and extreme heat in the presence of a catalyst to convert brown coal into the high-grade petrol used in tanks and aeroplanes.

The Ruhr Basin produced nearly two-thirds of Germany's bituminous coal – different from lignite or brown coal – which produced the coking coal, the key ingredient for smelting iron, and was thus vitally important for the great Krupps armament works and other lesser works. It also supplied the industries of central and southern Germany, requiring a vast transport system mainly of rail and canal. Tedder's insistence on the bombing of this system caused a coal famine which nearly brought the entire economy to a standstill in early 1945, despite the 200,000 workers Speer had engaged in repair work in the Ruhr alone.

On 24 May 1944, Buf wrote a paper on 'Selection of aiming points for Bomber Command in the Ruhr/Rhineland Area'. It was concerned with the following eight to ten weeks when short periods of darkness would confine attacks to that area. 'The problem', he wrote, 'will be to select aiming points which will result in the maximum degree of "destruction and dislocation of the German military, industrial and economic system" and at the same time have the maximum effect upon the enemy's military operations this summer.' He quotes the conclusion of a paper of the Ministry of Economic Warfare:

> There is no question that at the present time the destruction of the major synthetic oil plants of the Ruhr would do more to embarrass the enemy's military operations than the destruction of any other targets in this area. The enemy has already shown, as a result of recent operations, that his oil situation is so difficult that any damage must be met by an immediate cut in military consumption so as to maintain the distributional minimum essential for the mobility of his active forces ... The attack of at least four major synthetic plants in the Ruhr, and if possible, the remainder as well, therefore demands the most serious consideration as a primary objective for the summer offensive.

The Ministry of Economic Warfare paper then lists ten such plants, of which the first four are:

Gelsenkirchen-Nordstern (Bergius)	400,000 tons per year
Gelsenkirchen-Scholven (Bergius)	375,000 tons per year
Wesseling (Bergius)	200,000 tons per year
Homberg (Fischer-Tropsch)	190,000 tons per year

The total capacity of all ten amounted to 1,785,000 tons, nearly half of Germany's total synthetic production.

Buf pointed out that the VIII US Bomber Command had already begun its attacks on those targets and in May had severely damaged some of the larger plants, such as Leuna, Zeitz, Bohlen and Pölitz. These, together with XV US Bomber Command's attacks on Rumanian and Central Germany's refineries were exerting considerable pressure on the enemy's oil supplies.

Buf's conclusions were that these targets were the most profitable, under the Combined Bomber Offensive Plan, for the attack in the immediate future. He pointed out that such attacks were complementary to the attack on his rail transportation system. Since these were the only plants within effective range of RAF Bomber Command during the coming weeks, they should be undertaken as soon as possible.

Buf followed this up with a paper to the Deputy Chief on 7 June recommending, in the light of information just received about the 'acute position in the supply of oil to the enemy's armed forces', that Bomber Command should deliver attacks on a heavy scale and at the earliest opportunity against the four major synthetic oil plants in the Ruhr, and if these were successful, against the remaining six as rapidly as possible: that is, subject to the Supreme Commander's (Eisenhower's) agreement about the immediate demands of 'Overlord'. Buf considered that an effective weight of bombs on such a target would be produced by some 250 Lancasters, and he considered it advisable to achieve sufficient damage to stop production at all the plants, rather than achieve long-term damage at just one or two.

Such a policy was anathema to Harris, as were the demands of 'Overlord', because they distracted his force from their 'proper' function of devastating large German towns. The demands of 'Overlord' had been considerable. First there had been the softening up of the German coastal defences and their air bases. Then, when the British forces came to a halt at Caen with fierce German resistance, it was decided to bring in the 'heavies' and on the evening of 7 July, 457 aircraft of Bomber Command dropped 2,363 tons of bombs on selected targets north of Caen. The infantry attack by British and Canadian troops brought them into the city, but not through it. Montgomery's armour could not move through the streets because of the craters and rubble caused by the bombing. A still greater attack was considered necessary and was provided by Leigh-Mallory. Ten days later, on 18 July, 1,570 heavy and 349 medium bombers of Bomber Command, the US VIII Air Force and the Allied Expeditionary Air Force dropped 7,700 tons of bombs on Colombelles, another suburb of Caen. It was the heaviest and most concentrated air attack in support of ground forces ever attempted. Though half the city was destroyed, the Germans fought on, but their General von Kluge, who had succeeded the wounded Rommel, was near despair. On 21 July he wrote to Hitler:

> There is no way by which, in the face of the enemy air forces' complete command of the air, we can discover a form of strategy which will counter-balance its annihilating effect unless we withdraw from the battlefield. Whole armoured formations allotted to the counter-attack were caught beneath bomb-carpets of the greatest intensity so that they could be got out of the torn-up ground only by prolonged effort and in some cases only by dragging them out.

Four more such daylight attacks were made by Allied heavy bombers, which did much to aid the conquest of Normandy, though there were some casualties caused by the inevitable errors, including one Canadian general who was killed in a fox-hole in the front line.

After the first attack, General Montgomery sent this signal to Harris, with a copy to Buf:

> Again the allied Armies in France would like to thank you personally and Bomber Command for your magnificent co-operation last night. We know well

that your main work lies further afield and we applaud your continuous and sustained bombing of German war industries and the effect this has on German war effort. But we also know well that you are always ready to bring your mighty effort closer in when such action is really needed and to co-operate in our tactical battle. When you do this your action is always decisive.

Please tell your brave and gallant pilots how greatly the Allied soldiers admire and applaud their work. Thank you very much.

Another top-level issue was now occupying Buf's attention: the best method of controlling the Strategic Bombing Force in the new stage into which the war was now moving. He wrote a paper to the Deputy Chief on 20 July pointing out the 'considerable difficulties' that arise for the Air Staff in ensuring close day-to-day control of the bomber forces. Corresponding difficulties were experienced by the Commands themselves. The present system may have been essential for the early stages of 'Overlord' but was wholly unsatisfactory as a long-term arrangement. Buf proposed, therefore, that the Commanding General of the US Strategic Air Forces should be appointed as 'Deputy Chief of Air Staff (US)' as advisor to the Chief of Air Staff on matters affecting the Americans, particularly in view of the fact the US Strategic Bomber Force amounted to 3,500 heavy bombers compared with Bomber Command's 1,200. There is, he said, a risk that the Americans may wish to break away from RAF control, which would threaten the close collaboration essential to the success of our strategic plans.

This paper was accompanied by a lengthy 'Note' for the Chief to present to the Combined Chiefs of Staff that they should resume control of the strategic-bomber force, particularly because the Supreme Allied Commander was mainly concerned with the land battle and not with 'Crossbow' (operations against V1 missiles), or with the overall planning of operations against oil, the countering of flying-bomb attacks on Britain, or with the planning of a possible overwhelming 'morale bombing' of major German cities. The matter went to the Chiefs of Staff Committee in August and was agreed. On 6 September Portal, with Arnold, resumed control of the heavy bombers, ending Tedder's authority to *require* heavy bomber support; henceforward he would have to *ask* for it.

Combined air operations against German oil supply continued remorselessly during the autumn of 1944. The Joint Intelligence Sub-Committee produced a fortnightly report on the state of enemy oil in Europe and their figures were proved remarkably accurate by post-war comparison with German figures. In their report of 30 October 1944 they stated that, in the six months from April to September, the total output of all products was estimated to have fallen from 1,344,000 tons to 316,000, and of petrol from 532,000 tons to 106,000, though there may have been a slight rise in October due to bad weather.

They acknowledged that since Speer's appointment of his principal lieutenant, Geilenberg, as Special Commissioner for organising the repair of the oil industry, repair efforts had been redoubled. Aerial photographs had revealed the presence of new labour camps alongside the principal plants, no doubt for permanent repair gangs, and the flak defences at Stettin and Pölitz now numbered 310 heavy guns as compared with Berlin's 325. The daily allowance of petrol for the two Army Corps on the Western Front appeared to be roughly five tons of petrol per division as against a normal allowance of about thirty tons in active operations. The acute shortage of aviation spirit continued to restrict German air operations, and even for testing aircraft engines petrol was sometimes not available.

Researching and evaluating possible targets for three air forces was a crucial task and now called for a new body, the Combined Strategic Target Committee, set up on 13 October 1944. Its members were to be kept to a minimum, with representatives from Bomber Operations and Intelligence Directorates of the Air Ministry and of the US Strategic Air Forces, the Foreign Office and Ministry of Economic Warfare, the Enemy Objectives Unit of US Embassy, and Supreme Headquarters, Allied Expeditionary Force. The Chair would alternate between the two Directors of Bomber Operations. Thus, Buf occupied a key position in Allied policy.

It is perhaps not surprising that the Navy felt left out and their Director of Plans wrote to Buf on 7 November suggesting that, as a matter of principle, all three services should be permanently represented. Buf replied in a diplomatic tone that 'The work of the Committee is almost entirely restricted to considering ways and means of attacking those target systems laid down for attack by the Chiefs of Staff. Should it be decided by the Chiefs of Staff ... that some part of our effort is to be diverted against Naval targets ... we would of course rely upon expert guidance from the Admiralty ...' This seemed to pacify their Lordships.

Tedder, at least, had no doubts about his priorities, and he set them forth in a paper of 25 October:

1. As I see it there are two methods of ending this war; one is by land invasion, and the other is by breaking the enemy's power and control behind the lines. I myself do not believe that these two courses are alternative or conflicting. I believe they are complementary. I do not believe that by concentrating our whole air effort on the ground battle area we shall shorten the war. Nor do I believe that we would shorten the war by putting our whole bomber effort against industrial and political targets inside Germany.

2. As regards the land campaign, the primary objective is the Ruhr. The Army groups have now made it clear that what they would like the air to do is to interrupt enemy reinforcements and supplies across the Rhine. As a secondary object they wish the enemy ability to withdraw heavy equipment across the Rhine reduced to a minimum. Up to the present the direct strategic contribution towards this has been the oil plan, the successful attack on the Dortmund-Ems canal and some attacks on ordnance and MT depots. The other action, by the tactical forces, has been line-cutting and attacks on trains by fighters, and some (largely abortive) attacks on bridges.

    I am not satisfied that on these lines we are using our air power really effectively. The various types of operations should fit into one *comprehensive pattern,* whereas I feel that at present they are more like a patchwork quilt.

3. With regard to the direct attack on Germany, here again I feel our efforts are rather patchwork. The various targets (oil, cities, depots, marshalling yards, canals, factories, etc.) do not together build up into a really comprehensive pattern.

4. My views as to what should, or can, be done are as follows:

   The one common factor in the whole German war effort from the political control down to the supply of troops in the front line is communication. Leaving on one side signals communications as being relatively invulnerable to air attack, road, rail and water communications are the common denominator. The city populations may have gone underground, but without surface communications they will starve. Industries may have gone underground, but their lifelines remain on the surface. Industries have been dispersed, but the more they have been dispersed, the more they depend on good communications. Governmental control depends to a very large extent on efficient road and rail communications as is only too evident to-day in Belgium and France. The Army's dependence on communications needs no comment.

5. In my opinion, our primary air objective should be the enemy's communications. Road, water and rail are interdependent and complementary and our air operations should play on that fact. The present oil plan is the key to movement by road and air and, moreover, directly affects operations in the battle area. It is supplemented by fighter attacks on mechanised transport. The river and canal system in west Europe has been examined and targets indicated. The successful attacks on the Dortmund-Ems canal is being followed up by attacks on further vulnerable points. The practicability of mining the Rhine and stopping the extensive barge traffic is being examined.

6. Except for a few incidental attacks on German railway centres, the only systematic operations against the enemy rail systems have been extensive fighter-bomber line-cutting attacks, covering a period of more than six weeks. There has also been a certain amount of 'shooting up' of trains. Only within the past few days have these operations begun to show dividends. There have been a number of attacks on Rhine and Moselle rail bridges, but these have been largely abortive.

7. It is abundantly clear from French and German railway records (the latter kept with typical tidy thoroughness) that:

   It was the heavy attacks on rail centres and marshalling yards which were the main factor in paralysing the railway system in Northern France', and:

   The effect of these attacks was far more rapid and final than had ever been anticipated.

8. It is essential not to apply too literally to Germany the lessons of France and Belgium. In occupied territories it was possible for the enemy to maintain a flow of military traffic while the non-military and economic traffic died out. In Germany *all* loss of traffic is a dead loss to the war effort. In France and Belgium the enemy had prepared for precisely the form of attack he experienced by introducing large bodies of special labour and railway workers. In Germany now all the indications are that all manpower that has not been thrown into the army is fully employed in defence digging, and that even the normal running personnel of the railways have been drastically combed ... In France and Belgium all available repair and salvage material and personnel could be concentrated on repair of railways.

In Germany all such facilities are already more than fully occupied in repair and salvage of factories, public services, etc. In France and Belgium, the programme of attacks on railheads was severely limited, both as regards selection of targets and as regards weather conditions, by the need to avoid civilian casualties. No such limitations affect attacks on German rail centres.

9. I do not consider it necessary to spread attacks all over the German rail system. I am convinced that, with Germany in her present condition, we can obtain immediate results which have every prospect of being decisive. In my opinion, our main strategic concentration should be against the Ruhr; rail centres, oil targets, the canal system, and centres of population. I believe that in such a system it should be possible to maintain the attack under all conditions in which the heavies can operate. Alternatives and supplementary targets should be selected, with the same primary object in view, in the appropriate alternative weather areas of the middle and upper Rhine, including Bavaria.

10. The tactical air forces' operations against trains, embankments, selected bridges, etc., will be complementary to the strategic operations and will continue with a far greater prospect of producing immediate effect than they have in the past while the heart of the rail system has been relatively untouched. The combined strategic and tactical air forces will, in fact, be operating towards one objective.

11. I believe that the execution of a *co-ordinated campaign* against the communications system of West Germany such as I have outlined would rapidly produce a state of chaos which would vitally affect not only the immediate battle on the West Wall, but also the whole German war effort.

At a meeting on 27 October, in Tedder's own words:

I subjected the Director of Bombing Operations, Air Commodore Bufton, to a heavy cross-examination when he defended the prevailing directive. The net effect of our meeting, which was also attended by Spaatz, Bottomley, and Robb, was an agreement to amend the existing Directive so that oil should remain the first priority with transportation and rail centres in particular as the second priority. The next day, Portal, who was visiting our Headquarters as Eisenhower's guest, said that he thought my paper was the right answer to Marshall's request for air support to the armies.

So, on 1 November new directives were issued to the Strategic Air Forces. Oil was to have first priority, and transportation alone the second priority. Thus, the necessary concentration was to some degree achieved (in Tedder's words), though area bombing continued for some time.

Both priorities were put to the test by a surprise counter-offensive carried out by von Runstedt over Christmas 1944 through the wooded Ardennes, with twenty-four divisions in a plan remarkably similar to the great breakthrough against the French four years before. He launched his attack, in complete secrecy, on 16 December, and advanced some 20km a day in atrocious weather. On the 23rd the weather cleared, and the tactical air forces flew nearly 600 sorties mainly against enemy vehicles. The next day Allied fighters shot down nine German aircraft, including one Messerschmitt 262, the new jet fighter that could fly at 500mph, faster than any Allied plane. The 'heavies' were called in and Bomber Command caused havoc among troop concentrations at St Vith on Boxing Day, by which time the offensive had been contained. By 16 January it was over, although on New Year's Day the Luftwaffe made one last desperate onslaught on Allied airfields. As many as 144 aircraft in the British area were destroyed and eighty-four damaged, with 137 German aircraft claimed and another 115 American. After the war, General Galland, a leading German fighter pilot, described the day's work as 'the final dagger thrust into the back of the Luftwaffe.'

The main strategic blows, however, had been delivered both on the railheads that had been pushed back behind the Rhine so that all military supplies had to come up by road, and on petrol supplies, which were very short. The Germans were relying on captured fuel dumps, but these were few. So the argument between oil and transport was unreal; attacks on both were equally important, for both were equally vital to the enemy's war effort.

Road and rail, however, were not the only means of transport: a great deal of industrial freight, particularly coal from the Ruhr, was carried by water, notably the Dortmund-Ems Canal and its junction with the Mittelland Canal. In June 1943, a high-level meeting was called with Mr B. Wallis and chaired by Buf to consider the use of the special Dams bombs against it. It was successfully breached on 23 September 1944 and revisited, after repairs, on 4 November and again on 21 November. Two further attacks followed on 1 January 1945 and it was again drained by the Lancasters of 5 Group.

Many similar attacks were made on railway centres. Mr Wallis, however, was not satisfied by a Tallboy of 12,000lb. He went on to design the 'Grand Slam' of 22,000lb, which needed a specially adapted Lancaster (less two crew) to carry it. Its production, however, was cancelled in September 1944 in view of the War Cabinet's expectations that the war would be over by Christmas, but fortunately it was rescued by Wilfred Freeman who was then Chief Executive at the Ministry of Aircraft Production. On 14 March 1945 it was dropped by 617 Squadron on the railway viaduct at Bielefeld, which carried the main line from Hamm to Hanover, accompanied by fifteen other Lancasters bearing Tallboys. It is not certain which bomb did the crucial damage, but the viaduct was wrecked over a length of more than a hundred yards.

In the autumn of 1944 a major policy conflict developed, principally between Harris and Portal, though behind Portal was Bufton, who was, after all, Director of Bomber Operations for the RAF, a post which Harris himself had set up in the Air Ministry. The conflict centred on the bombing of oil installations in Germany. Tedder wanted the emphasis on communications, Harris on the blitzing of major towns and Bufton on oil.

The first shots were fired by Harris in a letter to Portal on 1 November 1944. It opposed a recent paper by Tedder which advocated a concentration of bombing against the Ruhr and certain rail centres, oil and canals as principal targets, these objectives being interlocked. Harris rejected any suggestion that the war had not been shortened by area attacks, and maintained that it would have been shortened more if he had not had so many diversions. He complained again about the number of cooks engaged in stirring the broth. 'The Tirpitz has got within range and the Admiralty has resuscitated

A famous photograph showing Bielefield Railway Viaduct after bombing in March 1945. (H.M.S.O.)

a U-boat threat. The ball-bearing experts have again become vocal ... and even the nearly defunct SOE has raised its bloody head ...' (The Special Operations Executive in assisting the French underground planned to drop a large quantity of munitions in preparation for 'Overlord'.)

Bufton was asked by Portal to comment on this letter and he wrote three pages answering Harris's contentions. Portal was clearly impressed and asked Buf to draft a reply that ran to over four pages. Portal accepted the difficulties that Harris faced in choosing targets and agreed that the final decision was his. But Portal sought assurance from Harris that the apparent magnetic attraction of German cities was not deflecting him from the designated priority targets. He sought confirmation that whenever a reasonable opportunity appeared, Bomber Command would attack an oil target. The aim, he said, should be to put them out of production for three months. He rejected Harris's contention that operations in the Ruhr would mean enormous losses for his Command by quoting Buf's figures (without acknowledgement) as, apart from the raid on Bochum when the loss rate was 3.7 per cent, the average loss rate in the Ruhr since 1 September 1944 was 1.3 per cent.

Harris wrote again to Portal on 12 November, but on a different tack: that of acceptable losses to bomber crews. In 1942 and 1943 the average loss was three to four per cent, and it was unreasonable to expect this to continue. Amazingly, Harris argued that crews became bored by having to attack the same targets night after night. This Portal would not accept, and a swift end to the war might demand a loss rate of up to four per cent. By way of increasing fighter support for the bombers he promised Harris an additional five Mark XXX Mosquitos per month. Again Buf wrote a draft reply, four pages long, to which Portal added in writing: 'Agree as slightly amended'.

Harris replied on 12 December, claiming that his own Operational Research Section had calculated that to knock out the forty-two oil installations in the west of Germany would require some 9,000 sorties per month, all at the mercy of the weather. The targets in central Germany were a harder proposition. All depended on the weather, and records showed that during December, January and February on average only eight days and eight nights would have clear conditions. For central Germany, the figure would be three or four. He concluded that the figures produced by the Ministry of Economic Warfare were quite unreliable. Buf analysed Harris's argument in eight pages and submitted a draft reply for Portal, which he accepted. Portal concluded: 'It would be a tragedy if, through any lack of faith or understanding on your part, the RAF Bomber Command failed to take the greatest possible share in the supreme task of driving home our attacks on enemy oil.'

Harris fired another salvo on 28 December and, as usual, Portal requested Buf's comments, which he produced in a comprehensive memorandum. Buf stressed it was clear that Harris had no faith in the oil plan – 'another panacea'. Later he wrote, 'I am sorry that you also imagine my staff cannot be devoting its maximum thought and energy to the oil plan because of my views. I do not give my staff views, I give them orders. I have told them to miss no opportunity of prosecuting the oil plan, and they have missed no worthwhile opportunity'. Buf's handwritten comment was: 'This is rot. Of course they must know his views.' He amplified this somewhat in his draft letter: '... it is difficult to see how, with his views, he can be enthusiastic about it. If he is not, his Staff will not be enthusiastic ...'

He also had to deal with familiar points concerning possible bomber losses, and Harris's lack of faith in the Ministry of Economic Warfare's figures about oil. He was able to quote figures about the great increase of defences at places like Leuna, now with 475 heavy guns and 360 light guns. Portal (Buf) trounced Harris's description of the Ministry of Economic Warfare's record of 'amateurish ignorance, irresponsibility and mendacity', describing it as 'an unworthy and inexcusable travesty of our conduct of the war to suggest that our policy is determined on that kind of basis ...' Portal left Harris in no doubt about the importance of the oil offensive: 'Your determination to destroy it [enemy oil production] matters more than that of all of us put together.' Again, Portal's response is almost exactly borrowed from Buf's memorandum.

Portal's letter is dated 8 January 1945, and on the 18th he received Harris's reply, the bitterness of which can best be ascribed to the stomach ulcer that plagued him. He resented Portal's suggestion that he failed to discuss policy matters with his staff and he noted 'no inclination on your part, or anywhere else in the air Ministry, for that matter, to discuss with me ... such matters as the strategic policy applicable to my force ... I am merely sent lists of targets by the Air Ministry, made out in priority by a committee presided over, where the RAF is concerned, by an ex-Station Commander of my command ...' This must have been a snide reference to Bufton.

The rest of this bitter letter is a replay of his old arguments about panaceas. About oil he wrote, 'we pursue a chimera and we will not overtake it. The oil policy will not succeed. If it fails, the enormous force diverted will achieve nothing. It is for such reasons that I am glad to have no share of responsibility for a decision which I am convinced is utterly wrong ...' His final thrust was to offer his resignation. 'I therefore ask you to consider whether it is best for the prosecution of the war and the success of our arms, which alone matters, that I should remain in this situation.'

Portal did not give this letter to Buf, for obvious reasons, but he wrote a long-suffering reply saying that there had been no suggestion of disloyalty, and he expressed the hope that there would still be enough punch remaining in Bomber Command to flatten some of the German cities named by Harris in his letter, including Dresden. Portal declined to accept Harris's offer of resignation (it was not the first he had received) and concluded, 'we must wait until after the end of the War before we can know for certain who was right, and I sincerely hope that until then you will continue in command of the force which has done so much towards defeating the enemy and has brought such credit and renown to yourself and to the Air Force.'

CHAPTER 19

Joint Control

For the support of 'Overlord' it had been decided in March 1944 that the Supreme Commander of the Allied Expeditionary Air Force (Eisenhower) should take responsibility for the strategic air forces operating out of the UK, which happened on 14 April. By July, it seemed desirable that this control should revert to the Chief of Air Staff (Portal). The main reasons given were that the Supreme Commander was concerned with the land battle and not with particular demands such as 'Crossbow' (attacks on V-weapons) or attacks on the enemy's oil supplies, then in a critical situation. In order, however, to maintain the closest possible relations between the British and American Air Staffs it was proposed in July 1944 that the Commanding General of the US Strategic Air Forces (Spaatz) should be appointed to the British Air Staff as Deputy Chief of Air Staff (US). He could then act in Portal's absence as agent for the Combined Chiefs of Staff.

Portal's note proposing this revolutionary step emphasised the German critical situation in regard to oil supplies. 'To ensure that the bomber effort ... is directed to full effect, it is essential that control should be exercised through the American and British Air Staffs who have jointly acquired the experience of planning and developing the combined bomber offensive over the past two years'. The proposal was put formally to the Chiefs of Staff in August and was duly carried.

In that month, Portal laid a plan before the Combined Chiefs of Staff for a catastrophic blow on Germany, not as a means of bringing about its defeat but of inducing an organised surrender, though with the passage of time the motives for such a strike (probably on Berlin), code-named *Thunderclap*, changed. Buf prepared a paper on 20 August giving the view of the Air Staff that to achieve a positive effect on morale would necessitate a maximum heavy bombing effort on a limited critical area with a 100 per cent chance of destruction. The target must have the maximum associations, both traditional and personal, for the population as a whole to convince them that the government was powerless to prevent a repetition. This meant the administrative centre of Berlin, some two and a half square miles, as a spectacular and final object lesson to the German people of the consequences of their aggression. Its effectiveness would be increased by day bombing by the US XV Air Force and an all-incendiary night attack by Bomber Command on the heaviest scale on the remainder of the city.

In a second report, of 25 January 1945, the Joint Intelligence Committee doubted whether such an attack would lead to a breakdown in the German will to continue the war. It might, however, 'materially assist the Russians in the all-important battle now raging on the Eastern Front', which was producing a flood of civilian refugees. The same day, Bottomley phoned Harris to discuss its implications since it would need coordination with the American Strategic Air Forces. Harris replied that Berlin was already on his programme, and he suggested that similar operations should be mounted against Chemnitz, Leipzig and Dresden, also focal points of communications behind the Eastern Front and all of which were receiving a flood of refugees from the east.

The matter was pressed by Churchill who, on the night of the 25th, asked the Secretary of State what plans the RAF had for 'basting the Germans in their retreat from Breslau', and the next day Portal, accepting the advice of his staff, replied that 'Oil should continue to have absolute priority', but subject to that, 'we should use available effort in one big attack on Berlin and attacks on Dresden, Leipzig, Chemnitz, or any other cities where a severe blitz will not only cause confusion in the evacuation from the East but will also hamper the movement of troops from the West.'

Churchill again pressed the matter as he was about to leave for Yalta in the Crimea to confer with Stalin and his staff about the coming end of the war and thereafter. On 6 February, Portal sent a message from Yalta to Bottomley saying that the British Chiefs of Staff had approved the recommendations of the Vice-Chiefs and, subject to General Spaatz's approval, should be embodied in a directive to Bomber Command. The Americans had already acted, with a massive daylight attack on Berlin on 3 February, which indicated that General Doolittle had received from Spaatz the same instructions as those conveyed by Bottomley to Harris.

The Combined Strategic Target Committee (CSTC) had its first meeting on 18 October 1944 at the Air Ministry, chaired by Buf, with representatives from the Directorate of Bomber Operations, the HQ of the US Tactical Air Force, Air Intelligence, HQ of Supreme Allied Commander, the Foreign Office and Ministry of Economic Warfare, Economic Objectives Unit (US). In addition there were four 'Working Committees' for specialised areas: oil; army support; the German Air Force; and any other requiring examination. Tedder remarked that it was an odd way of conducting a major war by a committee with sub-committees, but it seems to have worked.

Its task was to make recommendation about priority of targets within different systems and between different target systems, about any change in the current directive, and about proposals submitted by SHAEF, the Admiralty or the War Office about the employment of the strategic-bomber forces. It had also to issue weekly priority lists of strategic targets for attack under the current directive and to submit to the Deputy Chief of Air Staff and the Commanding General of USTAFE joint proposals on specific situations.

As for oil, they maintained that it was important that October should maintain September's level: without attacks, it would rise from twenty-three to thirty-seven per cent, and so major plants should continue to be attacked even if their status was unknown. The Ruhr/Rhine area was still producing forty-three per cent of Germany's synthetic oil and two-thirds of its benzol supplies. As far as the German Air Force was concerned, jet aircraft were so far only a potential menace. Germany was conserving its fighters, which had been largely withdrawn from their armies for defence of the Reich. The shortage of fuel had compelled the closure of many elementary flying training schools, leading, in turn, to a shortage of pilots also. The Americans saw the end of the war by late 1944.

At its second meeting, on 25 October, it was reported that Hungarian crude oil was being sent to German naval bases, perhaps indicating a shortage of fuel for U-boats. The question was raised about re-attacks on targets without positive proof of their recovery. Autumn weather was not good for photographic reconnaissance – perhaps low oblique photography would succeed. A paper entitled 'Plan for Attack on Communication Targets' was considered (which had apparently been vetted by Tedder). Of the four sections, the first was the Ruhr: on this the maximum weight of effort should be directed, both on communications and also on industrial areas – as in the 'Hurricane' plan. The rest of Germany was divided by a line running from Hanover through Wurzberg to Ulm, and the second section dealt with communication targets west of this, with important communication centres in this area and on the west bank of the Rhine being recommended for attack, with those north of Koblenz given priority. As for targets to the east, the third section, a more limited number of transportation centres were recommended south of Koblenz in the area between the dividing line and the Rhine. The fourth section dealt with vulnerable points on waterways and trunk railway lines, with the familiar names of the Dortmund-Ems and Mittelland Canals and the Ruhr-Paderborn and Bielefeld Viaducts given. Fifthly, fighters returning from escort duties should contribute by shooting-up communication targets, with moving trains as first priority.

At its next meeting, on 8 November, Buf as Chairman was able to report that the Communications Plan had been approved by Tedder, by the Deputy Chief of Air Staff and by the Commander General of USSTAF. A warning note was sounded that Germany's oil production was probably back to forty per cent for November, and an encouraging report told of good results from the mining of the Danube. An appendix gave details about recommended attacks on the canals and viaducts already given, as well as other viaducts and vital railway marshalling yards.

At its fifth meeting, on 15 November, it was reported that Germany had announced that U-boat construction had now stopped: this was as significant as the transfer of experienced air personnel from bombers to fighters. General Bradley with his Twelfth Army Group heading towards Koblenz had asked for oil targets within a radius of 30,000 yards of the Rhine for his artillery to deal with.

At the sixth meeting, on 22 November, the Committee learned that recent photographs showed that the synthetic oil plants of the Ruhr were finished. The question of close support for the army as it prepared to cross the Rhine was discussed. As for the bombing of industrial areas when attacks on particular targets were not possible, in the western area priority was given to areas associated with the oil industry and leading communication centres, whereas in the east priorities were given to important centres of war production which remained substantially intact, as well as communication centres. Berlin was excluded from the priority list as 'best reserved for that stage in the war when disaster within the capital might reasonably be expected to tip the scales in favour of organised capitulation.' In the west, the first three important industrial areas selected were Harburg, Hanover and Ludwigshafen, and in the east Magdeburg, Chemnitz and Halle, followed by Dessau and Dresden. In an appendix on the bombing of Romanian oil from April to August 1944, normal production would have been 584,000 tons, but the actual production was 213,500 tons, representing a loss of sixty-four per cent of normal production.

On 29 November, Buf said it was not proposed to issue the weekly priority list. The relative priority of area targets was not as important as oil and communications. As and when Command considered one centre had been successfully dealt with, they should strike it off their list.

On 6 December, it was noted that the Russians were approaching Lake Balaton in Hungary, south-west of Budapest.

At its tenth meeting, on 22 December 1944, Buf expressed his concern at the decline in the intensity of Allied attacks on oil targets as against the rising number of attacks on communications by both Bomber Command and the US VIII Air Force. They learned that Germany had been able to increase their fighter-aircraft production by 100 to 200 per cent in recent months; that food production in Germany was not as bad as in 1917 (the Ruhr used to rely on Holland for food); and that 30 to 40 million tons of coal per month were being moved for domestic use.

On 16 December, an altogether unexpected attack was launched by Rundstedt with ten Panzer and fourteen infantry divisions against a weak point in the Allied extended front in the Ardennes, with the aim of breaking through and swinging north to capture the port of Antwerp and so cut the lifeline of our troops in Germany. Fortunately, Montgomery in the north and Bradley in the south successfully resisted this thrust (though with mainly American troops), assisted by total control in the air when the winter weather allowed, and by 16 January the Germans were forced back behind their frontier with nothing to show for their effort except 120,000 casualties and ruinous losses of material. Shortage of fuel had played a key part in this operation.

At the thirteenth meeting of CSTC, on 10 January 1945, chaired by Colonel Maxwell, the main item was the future of the oil offensive. The Chairman asked Mr Lawrence about the accuracy of the Oil Working Committee's estimates and the answer was that the margin of error was not more than fifteen to twenty per cent. The Chairman reported that USSTAF considered the situation to have altered so much that the whole strategic-bomber offensive needed to be reviewed. The enemy had gained sixty days in which to re-equip his forces and build up reserves. Jet aircraft, the new type U-boats, tank production and secret weapons were mentioned. Would another process of 'softening-up' be necessary? The Chairman believed that if the bomber offensive were directed exclusively to the attack on oil over the next thirty to sixty days, reducing production to ten per cent, the enemy's recovery would not take place. This would, of course, have to be approved by the Supreme Commander who would be able to modify it for emergencies. Mr Lawrence's conviction was that if the remaining synthetic oil plants and the two or three leading refineries – i.e. the ten first targets on the current priority list – were put out and kept out for three months, further resistance by the enemy would be impossible.

On 17 January, Buf was able to report a great series of attacks on oil in the previous week. As for attacks on communications, since it was impossible to dislocate the whole, the attack should be on the economic system that might be better achieved by blitzing cities. Attacks on communications in the short term should be close to the battle area.

At its fifteenth meeting, when they had considered a report from the Joint Intelligence Committee which concluded that the immobilisation of major oil producers would, in about six weeks, immobilise the German Army and Air Force, the Combined Committee concluded that the present oil situation demanded an all-out effort to complete the bombing programme.

Buf received powerful support for his argument in a German Air Force signal dated 24 January 1945 (referring to a Top Secret message from the Supreme Commander of the Luftwaffe dated 19 January) concerning Economy of Aircraft Fuel. It stated:

(A) Of approx. 19,000 cubit metres issued for consumption in January some three-fifths was consumed in the first half of the month. Since only small allocations can be counted on for February in view of the general fuel situation, a further fifth will be set aside from the January allotment.

   The 4,000 cubic metres which will thus remain available for use in January will, in addition to a general reduction of consumption, be distributed to as small a number of airfields as possible, flying formations shifting their locations accordingly, so as to make this quantity readily accessible when required. To this end it is ordered:

   (a) Every transport flight, including the evacuation of the wounded, must be authorised by the Commander of Luftflotte Reich ...
   (b) Personal journeys and recce flights are strictly forbidden unless Commander of *Luftwaffe* Reich expressly orders them to be carried out.
   (c) Fighter formations will be employed by *Luftwaffe* Kommando West only when there is a sure prospect of success. It is forbidden to make attacks on opportunity targets in areas where enemy dispositions are not definitely known.
   (d) Aircraft will not take off except when there is lively fighter-bomber activity in the area of operations or when a state of crisis exists at the front.
   (e) Employment for purposes of Reich defence:
      (1) By day, only when contact with the enemy is absolutely assured.
      (2) By night, under the same conditions, but in principle with front gunners only.
   (f) Fighters and night fighters will be employed in support of the Army only when operations are of decisive importance or at times of crisis.
   [...]
(B) The low level of stocks and continual attacks by the enemy on the petroleum industry and on fuel storage depots necessitate a severe restriction of all consumption which is not vitally necessary.

   The need of the hour is more than ever to achieve the highest possible performance with a small consumption of fuel.

   Commanders of air districts and of airfields, as well as formation commanders, are once again urged to use all the means at their disposal to prevent every sort of waste.

On 2 February, the Committee had to consider a new situation arising from the swift Russian advance westwards. It had already been agreed by the British and American Air Staffs and the Deputy Supreme Commander that Berlin, Leipzig, Dresden and other cities associated with the movement of evacuees from, and of military forces

The result of fuel shortage – a Fw 190 trainer being dragged by oxen into position. (Crick)

to, the Eastern Front should be given a priority for bombing second to that of oil. On the proposed attack on Berlin, Spaatz wanted particular focus on industrial plants and administrative headquarters, but this was not considered to be in line with the main objective.

At its seventeenth meeting, on 7 February, Buf reported a request from the Chiefs of Staff for increased bombing of U-boat assembly yards at Bergen and Trondheim. Buf considered that too much importance was being given to the threat of German jet fighters: the attack on oil and communications was slowing production. Why was the enemy confining jets to ground attack and reconnaissance? As for the Eastern Front, some alteration of priority was made on towns for bombing: 1) Berlin, 2) Dresden, 3) Chemnitz, 4) Leipzig … (ten in all), and for their industrial importance: 1) Kassel, 2) Nuremburg, 3) Hanover, 4) Zwickau … (17 in all). As Berlin had suffered a series of raids, sixteen major operations, between 18 November 1943 and 24 March 1944, with a notable lack of success and a heavy casualty rate amounting to 9.1 per cent in the last raid, the emphasis moved away from the capital to the other cities on the list. The next was Dresden.

CHAPTER 20

Dresden

I t is appropriate at this point to break the narrative of the Combined Strategic Targets Committee with Buf as its co-chairman to consider the joint Anglo-American attack on Dresden launched on 13–14 February 1945. For this, Buf must bear his share of responsibility as the RAF's Director of Bomber Operations, although, as has been shown, that responsibility was shared between the Prime Minister, the Combined Chiefs of Staff, the intricate network of command of the air forces on the Continent and, of course, Bomber Command.

Dresden was a beautiful Baroque city, 'Florence on the Elbe', much favoured by the British who even had an Anglican church there. At no point in the planning is there any trace of a plea for it to be declared an 'open city' on that account, unlike Florence and several other historic cities in Italy. Before the Second War the name 'Dresden' brought to mind dainty porcelain shepherdesses (though these were not made in Dresden but in Meissen, twelve miles down the river), but ever since that raid, the name sums up the horror of aerial warfare.

The raid was a model of its kind, the result of over three years of trial and error, with a grievous loss of life among the aircrews of Bomber Command. On 14 February, Harris, its Commander-in-Chief, having considered with his staff all the circumstances, particularly the weather, the phase of the moon and likely German opposition, and in consultation with the Commander of the US Strategic Air Forces, issued his order for a double attack on Dresden that night. Under 'Intention' it read, 'to destroy built-up areas and associated rail and industrial facilities'. (Originally the plan was for the Americans to strike first by day, but the weather did not permit.)

By night the weather had improved, the defences were few because most of the anti-aircraft guns had been moved to the east where they could be used for anti-tank purposes, and night fighters were few. The initial attack, timed to begin at 10.15p.m. was scheduled to last for twenty-five minutes. No.5 Group (Harris's *corps d'élite*) provided 246 Lancasters and nine Mosquitos, the Lancasters providing blind illuminations using navigational radars to show up the city on the Elbe for the visual markers. These were the Mosquitos that dived down to 1,000 feet or less to drop bright-red target indicator bombs on specified aiming points. Circling above was the Main Force of over 200 Lancasters due to follow over the next twenty-five minutes, each carrying a load of 2,000lb or 4,000lb high explosive and the balance of smaller incendiary bombs. The second attack was due to start at 1.30a.m. with 551 Lancasters led by the Pathfinder Force, No.8 Group, and when the red and green marker bombs had been dropped, the Main Force were to follow in five successive waves, each of three minutes.

The first force, concentrating on the Altstadt, the centre of the old part of the city, caused most destruction, with fires taking hold of buildings when roofs were destroyed and windows blown out. The inferno caused violent up-draughts that sucked in oxygen from the surrounding area, causing in turn gale-force winds at ground level, a veritable firestorm. Tar melted on the streets and large quantities of carbon monoxide penetrated to the basement shelters where thousands were seeking refuge, and hundreds died. The second force added a quarter of a million incendiary bombs, making fire fighting almost impossible. Six bombers failed to return.

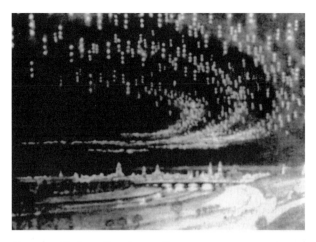

Above and below: Dresden on fire.

The heat was so intense that crews at a height of 12,000 feet felt it through the floor, and the light so bright that navigators could read their charts without desk lamps. It was a horrifying spectacle,

Funeral pyre in the Altmarkt. (Sächsische Landesbibliothek)

and at least one crew were so appalled by the sight that they deliberately overflew the target to drop their bombs.

At daybreak (though it became little lighter) the fires were still raging, but more was to come. Shortly after midday, 316 Fortresses of the US VIII Air Force flew over the unhappy city still covered with a pall of smoke. Some of their bombs were directed on to the railway marshalling yards to the south and west of the city, but then the cloud obscured their targets and aiming became less accurate.

The death toll was impossible to calculate, despite official efforts to identify bodies burned beyond recognition. The Chief of Police's report gave 18,375 dead, and the city authorities recorded 21,271 corpses buried or cremated. Many more were never found and the number of refugees was unknown. Probably the final figure was around 25,000. The slaughter was so great largely because the *Gauleiter*, Martin Mutschmann (an old friend of Hitler's), ignored instructions to build concrete shelters for the citizens, though he had a solid one constructed for himself in his garden.

As for industries in Dresden, the 1944 edition of the German High Command's handbook of weapons, munitions and equipment listed 127 factories. The largest employer was Zeiss-Ikon AG, famous in peacetime for its cameras, but almost every lens in the German armed forces came from there, not to mention time-delayed fuses for U-boat torpedoes. Three of its factories were destroyed along with three others making similar equipment. Universelle Werke employed 4,000 workers, many from occupied countries, including, from 1944, 700 women from Ravensbruck concentration camp, making machine guns, searchlights, directional guidance equipment, torpedo tails, and much more. A fifteen-year-old Polish Jewess was sent from Auschwitz to a factory in Dresden to make cartridges, twelve hours a day, seven days a week, sleeping in a bunk in the factory under guard.

The other major incentive was transport. The Dresden area of the National Railway Administration (*Reichsbahnsdirektion*) controlled more than 100,000 railway workers by the end of 1943, including some 12,500 foreign workers living in camps around Dresden, mainly employed in repairing the damage caused by air raids. One of the first officials to arrive from outside was General Erich Hempe, plenipotentiary for the Restoration of Railway Connections, and even he was appalled by the slaughter at the station and its underground shelters. On the 15th, repair gangs, mainly Allied prisoners of war, began work round the clock to mend the track. Around 800 coaches and wagons had been burned out by the RAF, and the American raid that followed on the 14th knocked out the Friedrichstadt passenger station completely and demolished forty-five tracks in the marshalling yards. Nevertheless, two weeks later, the service was back to a reasonable level, though the complex railway network suffered from having no functioning telephone system, and the availability of qualified staff was much reduced. The final devastating blow was delivered by the Americans on 17 April with nearly 600 Fortresses dropping some 1,500 tons of bombs on the railways. From that day until the end of the war, Dresden remained out of action as a major rail junction. What was left of the city fell to the Russians on VE Day, 8 May. On that first day of peace, Dresden passed from one totalitarian government to another.

How is one to assess the raids? For the RAF it was one attack among many, and a very successful one. In overall terms of destruction it cannot compare with the fire-raid on Tokyo by 334 US bombers on 9–10 March 1945 when some 83,000 people died and over fifteen square miles of the city was destroyed, or with the atomic bomb on Hiroshima which killed some 70,000. The American principle of precision bombing suddenly became area bombing as soon as their B-29 bombers had secured bases within reach of Japan on the Mariana Islands. At Nagasaki, the victim of the second atomic bomb, the young ladies attended their college classes in the morning and assembled fighters at the Mitsubishi factory in the afternoon. Were they 'civilians' or 'munition workers'?

The bombing of Dresden gave Goebbels good propaganda material for foreign consumption: by 25 February the Swedish newspaper *Svenska Dagbladet* ran a headline 'Rather 200,000 than 100,000 Victims'. On 16 February, the referral of the RAF's press officer to destroying 'what was left of German morale', interpreted by the Associated Press correspondent in Paris as 'deliberate terror bombing', amazingly passed by the censor. It was promptly denied by Supreme Headquarters, but the damage was done, leading, eventually, to a debate on 6 March in the House of Commons. Even Churchill was having doubts about the policy he had been so strongly advocating, and he wrote an unfortunate minute to his Chiefs of Staff, dated 28 March:

> It seems to me that the moment has come when the question of bombing German cities simply for the sake of increasing terror, though under other pretexts, should be reviewed ... The destruction of Dresden remains a serious query against the conduct of Allied bombing ...

The Air Staff took strong objection and Portal drafted an alternative minute, which finished: 'We must see to it that our attacks do not do more harm to ourselves in the long run than they do to the enemy's immediate war effort.' This was accepted by his colleagues and also by the Prime Minister, and the original remained secret for some time. The Chiefs of Staff produced their reply on 4 April, which did not agree to abandon the principle of area bombing altogether; it might, they said, be necessary if resistance stiffened again or if Nazi leaders established new centres of power.

Let the last word be with Alan Brooke who, as Chief of the Imperial General Staff, probably did more than anyone to direct the course of the Second World War. He wrote in his diary on VE Day, 8 May 1945:

> The suffering and agony of war in my mind must exist to gradually educate us to the fundamental law of 'loving our neighbour as ourselves'. When that lesson has been learned, then wars will cease to exist. We are however many centuries from such a state of affairs. Many more wars, and much suffering is required before we finally learn our lesson. However humanity in this world is still young, there are still many millions of years to run during which high perfection will be attained. For the present we can do no more than to go on striving to improve more friendly relations towards those that surround us.

CHAPTER 21

Victory in Europe

At the eighteenth meeting of the Combined Committee on 16 February there was no mention of Dresden. It was just another attack, and a very 'successful' one at that. A request had been received from the Admiralty for a repeat of attacks on Bremen and Hamburg where U-boat construction was still under way, some of it under concrete protection. (By the end of April, after a series of devastating attacks, production had virtually ceased.)

On 21 February, a heavy raid on the oil plant at Pölitz in the far north-east of Germany was reported, which was to put it out of production for two to three months. By 2 March, it was calculated that petrol production from benzol plants had been reduced to 5,000 tons per month, though they were to remain on the list. (Colonel Maxwell commented that the Committee were known to be 'oil fanatics'.) The Luftwaffe had to ban all training on twin-engined aircraft, and petrol shortage was having a crippling effect throughout their air force. Bomber Command had again succeeded in cutting the Dortmund-Ems Canal, with the result that goods from the Ruhr to the rest of Germany were reduced by three-quarters.

The twenty-first meeting, on 7 March, 1945 heard reports from the Working Committees. Coal from the Ruhr, which was reckoned in the year ending July 1944 to be 2.5 million tons a month, since December was quoted by the Joint Intelligence Committee to be down to one million tons, or perhaps even half of that. The 11th Panzer Division started to move on 13 February from Trier, near Luxembourg, to the Cologne area, a distance of less than 100 miles, and it did not begin to arrive until 27 February – and then only piecemeal and short of ammunition. The Bielefeld bypass was now only single track. The production of tanks and self-propelled guns was given as 600–800 for January, and this was now raised to third priority for Allied attack.

On 14 March, production of Hungarian crude oil was given as 60,000 tons per month: perhaps this was a target for bombers based in Italy. On the 21st, documents found at Krefeld revealed a programme for hulls of all kinds of vehicles including 870 for tanks; this was a sharp drop since September 1944. U-boat construction was given as eighty at Kiel, forty at Bremen and forty at Hamburg. A shortage of the special J2 fuel for the Me 262 and the Arado 234 was reported at around 5,000–10,000 tons per month, but this was considered sufficient for the time being. (The Arado Ar 234 was a twin-jet bomber/reconnaissance aeroplane which only entered service early in 1945 because of delays in the delivery of the Jumo 004 turbojet engines. It had a formidable performance with a top speed of 461mph and a range of 1,100 miles.)

The meeting on 21 March considered a report on Communications which stated:

In attacks on interdiction targets Bomber Command, employing their new 22,000lb bomb for the first time, scored signal successes on the Bielefeld and Arnsberg viaducts, each a key target on the two most important lines from the Ruhr. Six of the central spans on both of the twin Bielefeld viaducts were destroyed in the daylight attack of the 14 March whilst in the last of four attacks on Arnsberg, in which a total of 255 tons were dropped, the viaduct, already damaged, was finally breached.

Altogether, twenty attacks were made upon targets in the current CSTC Priority List. In Western Germany, in the week 12/13 to19/20 March 1945, Bomber Command dropped 1,557 tons of bombs by day and 3,081 tons by night, and the 8th USAAF dropped 1,948 tons by day.

At its twenty-fourth meeting, on 29 March 1945, the Committee learned that Leuna was now producing five per cent of its capacity, which was equal to the largest producer of petrol (gasoline) in Germany. It also received a daily intelligence signal on enemy airfield activity, and accordingly recommended attacks on fighter bases. On the naval side it was reported that Kiel had seventy-eight U-boats, two heavy cruisers and one light cruiser, which invited a very heavy attack. Over sixty U-boats were still at sea. (On the next day, the 30th, American bombers sank the *Köln* at Wilhelmshaven, and on 9 April British bombers sank the *Scheer* in Kiel Harbour. When the British entered Kiel on 3 May, scarcely a building was untouched, and the cruisers *Hipper* and *Emden* lay stranded and heavily damaged by bombs.) As for communications targets, these should be specific and limited, preferably in the Ruhr, and not widespread.

On 4 April, ordnance and tank depots were raised to second priority, next only to oil. It was reported that thirty tanks of 11th Panzer Division had been captured having run out of fuel. The sinking of the *Köln* was also reported. On 11 April, the Committee learned that the Germans had transferred four prisoner-of-war camps to the neighbourhood of Falkensee tank plant at Berlin, and consequently the US VIII Air Force was reluctant to bomb it. It was agreed that attacks should be suspended.

At its twenty-seventh and final meeting, on 18 April, Buf suggested that the Working Committee on oil should produce a brief outline of the Allies' attack on enemy oil. An officer who had visited the ordnance depot at Kassel/Bettenhausen reported that the destruction was terrific: he had counted 300 guns from 75mm to 155mm destroyed or seriously damaged.

On 1 May, Hitler committed suicide; by 3 May the German front in Italy had surrendered; on 4 May Montgomery met Keitel and received the surrender of North Germany, Holland and Denmark; and on 7 May the final documents were signed with the Russians. On 8 May, Victory in Europe was celebrated. On 4 May Bottomley, Deputy Chief of Air Staff, and the Commanding General of the US Strategic Air Force, General Arnold, had sent two letters of appreciation, one to Bufton and one to the Combined Committee through its joint chairmen.

To: Air Commodore Bufton
1. As the work of your committee is coming to an end I should like to place on
   record my appreciation of the very valuable services the Committee and its

Working Sub-Committees have contributed to the direction of effort of the strategic air forces in Europe.

2. The work of the Committee has always been characterised by the thoroughness of its examinations and investigations. I know what a great amount of labour and thought has been involved in the various tasks of the Committee and I have always admired the enthusiasm and zeal with which its labours have been undertaken.
3. The work of the Committee has been of the greatest help to me in the execution of the duties which have been laid on me jointly with General Spaatz. I feel sure also that General Spaatz would speak similarly of the Committee's work.
4. I consider that its work has been of supreme value in the conduct of the strategic air offensive during the last eight critical months.
5. I would like you to convey to Brigadier-General Maxwell, the American Joint Chairman and the Chairmen of the various Working Sub-Committees my sincere thanks for its thorough series of investigations and its wise recommendations.

To: The CSTC through the Co-Chairmen, Air Commodore Bufton and Brigadier-General Maxwell

1. At the close of the strategic offensive of the Allied heavy bomber forces, I desire to express my sincerest appreciation and gratitude to the Combined Strategic Targets Committee and personnel, military and civilian, of the various Allied intelligence and reconnaissance organisations which contributed to the outstanding work of the Targets Committee. I am especially grateful to Air Commodore Bufton for his outstanding guidance of this committee throughout its difficult task.
2. The results of the air offensive speak for themselves; the outcome would have been less sure without the invaluable aid of the Committee. The brilliant work and infinite pains which these organisations have shown in piecing together the multiplicity of intelligence information, have raised the selection of strategic targets to the stature of a science. The consistently sound recommendations which this committee and its subsidiaries have submitted to the Deputy Chief of Air Staff, RAF, and have been largely responsible for the decisive execution and successful conclusion of the Strategic Air Offensive in Europe.
3. The congenial atmosphere and general unanimity of opinion coming from this mixed group of British and American officers and civilian personnel, working together for the defeat of Germany through the determination of sound operational principles and targets, has been an inspiration to all of us and a model for future combined organisations.

From 13–16 May, five days after VE Day, Buf flew with a group of Staff Officers on a survey of bomb damage in Germany. The group included Wing Commander John Strachey, who had given a series of War Commentaries on the BBC. On 20 May, he gave this broadcast:

Within a minute or so of flying over the German frontier you see Cologne. I can't hope to convey to you the impact of that first sight of a ruined city. We had flown out over

The centre of Cologne as seen by groundcrews visiting after the war.

London and looked carefully at the patches of bomb damage as we passed; but the moment we saw Cologne we realised that we had never yet seen devastation. One's first sight is of the six long bridges – all down – some destroyed by bombing, others blown by the retreating Germans, with the Rhine washing white in foam against the wreckage. As the aircraft drops lower you can see that the bombs have ploughed into the railway centres and cut the lines as well as crashed through the factory roofs. And then there is nothing but acre after acre of roofless, gutted, crumbled buildings passing slowly under you as the aircraft circles.

Next Krupps was beneath us. One by one the great, square workshops of Europe's largest munition plant went by. Not one had its roof on and in many the walls had crumbled down upon the rows of machine tools. Over the expanse of dull red rust of these ruined plants, there shone and glittered little points of light. I think it was the shattered glass thrown about like confetti by the bomb bursts.

We flew on up the Ruhr, that valley which rang and trembled with the flak barrage and the bomb bursts. Now it lay silent and dead in the sunshine. We passed the places where the two Gelsenkirchen oil plants had stood, and then the shell of Dortmund. We turned left along the broad thread of the Dortmund-Ems canal. After a few miles the canal ran dry and empty, and then the neat clear outline of the embankment, which carried the water some twenty feet above the surrounding country at this point, was abruptly swallowed up into what looked like a morass. The yellow subsoil had been spread over the countryside, covering as area of perhaps a square mile. Four violent attacks on this one point had obliterated one of the greatest of the inland waterways of Europe.

How well I remember the time when we first began to consider the problem of how to cut the water and rail communications of the Ruhr; of how to breach the Dortmund-Ems canal and break the massive spans of the Bielefeld railway viaduct. Neither the techniques of bombing nor all the appropriate weapons were then in existence. The four track, trunk railway crosses the valley at Bielefeld on two long viaducts, several yards apart. Two-thirds of the way across the valley seven piers are now missing from <u>each</u> of the viaducts. They are neither damaged nor broken. They've simply gone. The railway tracks droop and sag over the gaps – like iron hammocks slung between the remaining piers. What happened was that in one of the attacks, a special Squadron of Bomber Command put one of the ten-ton deep penetration bombs exactly between the two viaducts. The bomb drove deep into the earth, as it was designed to do, and uprooted the piers of both viaducts. The ten-ton bomb is a weapon the uses of which are only beginning to be explored.

From Bielefeld we flew on East past devastated Hanover and Brunswick, and then turned South for Cassel and its industries, I can only say simply that they have been destroyed. I saw some houses which were habitable in the suburbs, but in the city proper I did not see one in which people could live, at any rate above ground. But people <u>are</u> living there; no doubt in the cellars, for one sees them in the streets. Moreover, I must report a remarkable fact about these people. Amidst these heaps of rubble they appear neat, well dressed and healthy. They are mostly women, young children and old men, of course, but they don't look in the least like the shattered or ragged survivors of a catastrophe. The Bomber offensive wasn't of course designed to kill or wound civilians but to destroy the enemy's centres of production: at Cassel it certainly did that.

We'd landed, on what only a few weeks ago, had been a German Night Fighter station. But the night fighters had not been able to save Cassel, though on that night in October 1943, when the greater part of the town was destroyed, we lost forty bombers. As we were driving back, we passed several garages by the roadside. Over their petrol pumps was written the word 'Leuna'. It was from the mighty synthetic oil plant of Leuna, then, that this part of Germany got its petrol. Next morning we set course North-East for Leuna. After about an hour's flying, the biggest industrial plant I have ever seen in my life loomed up under our port wing.

As we circled Leuna, nearly three miles long by a mile wide, with the labour camp built beside it so that thousands of workers could be rushed in to repair after every bombing, we realised that what we were looking at was one of the main battlefields of this war. Leuna lies hundreds of miles from the Normandy beaches, the Siegfried Line or the Eastern Front. Nevertheless, this was the scene of one of the great victories of the allies in this war.

We looked down on this new kind of battlefield, and saw the debris of battle – wrecks of our own aircraft which had been shot down, as well as shattered chimneys and gas holders. For the advantage of this battle of Leuna had swayed first one way and then another – it had not swayed backwards and forwards as a land battle does, but rather up and down, for this was a ground-to-air battle on the vertical plane; the defence and the repair squads on the ground now gaining the advantage, then the attacking bombers coming down from above to inflict another wound.

Don't let us forget these air battlefields of the Second World War – Cassel, Leuna, Pölitz, Brux, Hamburg, the Ruhr and Berlin. Here the air crews fought savage battles to shatter the main supports on which the structure of German war economy rested. As, one by one, those supports were shattered, the German war effort sagged and drooped – much as I saw the railway sag and droop over the gap in the Bielefeld viaduct. It was thus that the Allied Armies were able to win their magnificent and indispensable victories without suffering the terrible casualties of the last war.

From Leuna, we began to fly back South-West towards the cities of the upper Rhineland. But on the way we found something for which we weren't looking – we found a hollow hill. It was a short, steep ridge or hill – hogsback as we should call it in this country. But there was something peculiar about this hill. Even at first glance we saw that the top of it had been sliced off to make a runway for the take-off of aircraft. We went down to investigate: we saw workings all round the hill. Shafts ran into it at half a dozen points. There was no doubt about it. The hill was hollow. Inside the Germans had been building one of their new under-ground aircraft plants. Rocket or jet fighters were no doubt to be assembled in that hill, raised on lifts to the runway and flown off the top.

Some of these underground plants were already working this spring. One of our party had the opportunity of examining perhaps the largest of them in a place called Niedersachswerfen. Here, twenty-thousand foreign slave workers, driven by five-hundred German foremen, were only last month turning out V. 2 rockets in the underground galleries. Now the slave workers are camping in the huge tail sections of the rockets while they wait till they can get back to their homes. Such is the crack-up of the final Nazi plan to win the war by fantastic new weapons. It brought home to us all that the devastation done by our bombers, far from being too much, might well have been too little and too late, had we slackened or paused in our air attack for a single week.

Frankfurt, Darmstadt, Pforzheim, Stuttgart, Karlsruhe, Saarbrucken were merely further examples of devastation in varying degrees of completeness. The destruction of the industrial area at Bremen is a complete job. One section of Hamburg, lying away from the docks and factories is relatively <u>un</u>damaged, but all the rest has gone.

Landing on a nearby airfield we motored into Hamburg and there we confirmed something which we'd noticed in all the other places which we'd passed through. Germany, until V.E. Day, was covered with Nazi posters, stickers, streamers and slogans scrawled and painted on the walls. Now, every one of them had gone; to the outward eye, it's as if Nazism had never existed in Germany – and this within six days of the surrender. It must have been done by the Germans deliberately and to order immediately before the end, for I am told nothing of this sort was done in the towns which we occupied before the surrender. On the contrary those towns were still covered with Nazi posters and inscriptions; now they have all been wiped away as if by magic; too quick a conversion by half, we thought.

From Hamburg we flew on to Kiel. A long, thin, red shape lay alongside one of the quays. For a moment we couldn't identify it; then we realised it was the bottom of the *Scheer*, one of the last of Germany's capital ships. There she lay capsized in what, until the coming of the bomber, would have been the ultimate safety of Kiel harbour.

From Kiel we set course for home; but we'd one more call to pay. We crossed Holland, and below us lay the countryside, on which the Dutch cities depend for food, sodden and flooded, by the dykes which the Germans had broken. Our pilot was a Dutchman, one of the highly skilled men of the K.L.M. Air Lines, who have flown with us throughout the war. We were passing Amsterdam, looking down with relief on an undamaged city, when once again, and this time unexpectedly, we felt the aircraft losing height and beginning to circle. We passed low over a house on the outskirts of the city, turned, passed over it again – a third time – and then a fourth time. On that fourth circuit a woman and boy ran out of the door of the house; it was the pilot's wife and son whom he'd not seen for five years. Worse, he'd not had any word from them since last November; and that meant that he didn't even know what had happened to them in these last months of famine which the Dutch people suffered under the German occupation.

If all the ruins we'd seen had made any one of us feel that our bombing of Germany had been too ruthless, that incident at Amsterdam would have served to remind us why we had to destroy West Germany. It would have been an unpardonable crime to withhold a single bomb, the bursting of which on Germany could shorten the Nazi tyranny over Europe by an hour. The punishment which fell upon the German people was severe indeed, but that punishment was inflicted, inevitably but incidentally, in the course of the combined bomber offensive. In the words of the Prime Minister's message to Sir Arthur Harris, the purpose of that offensive was, to make 'a decisive contribution to Germany's final defeat'. And that purpose was accomplished.

After the conclusion of hostilities, a number of high-ranking Luftwaffe officers were interrogated about Allied policy. In answer to the question, 'What is the general opinion of effectiveness of US strategic bombing of the aircraft and fuel industries of Germany?', these were the answers:

Galland
The heavy attacks by US strategic bombers on the main centres of German aircraft production early in 1944 practically destroyed the German fighter production for a short period, but at that time their dispersal programme was already under way and after a short period it was possible again to maintain production. The figure for fighters, night fighters and fighter bombers in 1944 reached a total of 3,050 aircraft per month whilst the average for 1943 was about 2,500. In Galland's opinion it was the Allied bombing of the oil industries that had the greatest effect on Germany's war potential; reduction in the quantity of available petrol forced the curtailment of supplies for training. From the autumn of 1944 onwards plenty of training and operational aircraft were available and there were enough pilots up to the end of 1944, but lack of petrol did not permit the expansion or proper training of the fighter force as a whole. Galland wondered why we waited so long to attack German oil production.

Massow
Strategic bombing of the aircraft industry was a blow which was soon overcome

by dispersal, but the attack on German oil production which, according to von Massow, was opened in July 1944, was in his opinion the largest factor of all in reducing Germany's war potential.

Kolb

This general considers that at the opening of the bombing of aircraft industry the Germans were caught short by having left their factories vulnerable to air attack, and dispersal to the underground sites should have started far earlier than it did. This prisoner of war could not understand why the Allied bombing of oil refineries and fuel depots started as late as it did.

Von Rohden

Strategic bombing was the decisive factor in the long run. This prisoner of war, however, made the proviso that had the Luftwaffe been reorganised on a ninety per cent defensive basis at an earlier date than actually was the fact, Allied strategic bombing might not have been as successful.

Spies

This prisoner of war's comment on strategic bombing of aircraft and fuel industries in Germany was in the form of a counter-question – 'Why did you not begin bombing the oil industry earlier?' The industry was always a weak point in Germany economy, and targets like Leuna were easily damaged. Once the bombing had begun it was extremely effective and Allied intelligence was such that they knew exactly when a target was ready to recommence refining and immediately opened further attacks. He considers that US bombing attacks on the aircraft industry, whilst very successful and effective, had not such a far-reaching effect as attacks on oil.

It is perhaps worth repeating that he particularly praised the accuracy of both day and night bombing from about 1943 onwards. It was quite obvious to him that a lot of thought had been put into the question of which target should be attacked – for instance the ball-bearing industry – and in his opinion the only mistake we made was that oil was not made the primary target from the beginning.

Untrieser

This general also echoed the opinion that attacks on the fuel industry were more effective than those on the aircraft industry, since the latter case dispersal of assembly plants followed almost immediately. As proof of this, prisoners of war pointed out that aircraft production was maintained at a high level up to the last months of the war.

Germany was defeated, but this was by no means the end of the war. Japan had to be dealt with and the Americans had already decided that the mainland would have to be invaded, starting in November 1945. Churchill was keen to have full British participation of land, sea and air forces, and the Chiefs of Staff were suggesting a land force of some five divisions.

By the end of 1943, Buf's Directorate was already drawing up tentative plans for a Very-Long-Range Bombing Force to augment America's campaign. This assumed bombers with a range of 1,500 miles operating from possible bases in Burma, China, Formosa (Taiwan), the Philippines and the Marianas. Consideration had to be given to flight refuelling, and on 16 February 1944 a conference was held with Sir Alan Cobham, the pioneer of flight refuelling, and representatives of Avro, and work was soon started on adapting Lancasters for this purpose with a view to twenty squadrons as bombers and twenty as tankers. The Lancaster IV, which became the Lincoln, was to be in full production by December 1944 and 1,000 flight refuelling sets were to be ready for them.

On 21 August, the Air Officer Commanding-in-Chief of Bomber Command was informed of the Chiefs of Staff's decision and he was not pleased, but by December the first test operation by hose between two Lancasters had been successfully carried out. These plans and trials were reported to President Roosevelt and his Chiefs of Staff at Quebec in September 1944, and on 27 October official approval was given subject to the availability of suitable air bases. By November, twenty-four bomber squadrons had been earmarked, with a substantial contribution of Canadian personnel, based on the assumption of refuelling in flight.

Tankers and bombers would fly as pairs until each had consumed 1,200 gallons of petrol, at which point, about 1,000 miles outbound, the tanker would refuel the bomber and return to base, allowing the bomber an extra 1,000 miles of flight or a correspondingly greater weight of bombs. If the Lincoln could be cleared to operate with a load of 83,000lb its performance would be comparable with the B-29.

The time required to deploy was first considered in detail in May 1944, and the end of the European war was considered, optimistically, as 1 October of that year. A nucleus planning staff of Tiger Force – its code name – was set up in February 1945 with Air Marshal Sir Hugh Lloyd as its Commander Designate. Flight refuelling, however, was abandoned in April along with the use of Lancasters – in favour of Lincolns – and experiments were made with increasing its fuel load, first with bomb-bay tanks below the fuselage and then with saddle tanks above, with the upper turret removed.

As the Americans drew nearer Japan, the need for extra fuel became less necessary, and in June 1945 the Americans offered a base on Okinawa initially for ten British squadrons. With the ending of the German war in May 1945, the main force was to consist of tropicalised Lancaster VIIs modified to operate at an all-up weight of 72,000lb, the first eighty to be ready by July and another eighty in August. The training of crews began in May, with one British and one Canadian Group. On 6 June, the bomber element was reduced to eight RAF squadrons, eight RCAF and two RAAF, with a special request from General Spaatz for the two special Tallboy Squadrons, Nos 9 and 17. The first five squadrons were expected to be operational by 1 December, though this was optimistic.

The first of seven convoys, comprising eight ships carrying mainly airfield construction personnel and equipment, sailed for the Ryukyu Islands at the end of June 1945 via the Panama Canal, followed on 6 August by the Advanced HQ Party. On that day the atomic bomb was dropped on Hiroshima, with a second on the 9th on Nagasaki, and the next day the Force Commander announced that they would not now be required to bomb Japan. The elements of Tiger Force that were on their way to the Far East were diverted to Hong Kong to form a new HQ there, and on 22 August the

Air Ministry decreed that all the Tiger Force squadrons, none of which had yet moved, were to return to the control of Bomber Command.

One remarkable feature of this episode is that, throughout these extensive preparations, no mention was made of the likely deployment of an atomic bomb. It was indeed kept a closely guarded secret. Despite the terrible slaughter, largely of civilians, it was as well because if the Allies had had to invade, the Japanese Army would have fought to the last man. Churchill envisaged the possibility of a million American casualties and half that number of British – if they could get there in time.

There were other threats to a peaceful settlement, so much so that Churchill named the last volume of his history 'Triumph and Tragedy'. He saw Russia as a looming threat, as did the Chiefs of Staff. In his diary for 27 July 1944, Brooke recorded that he spent an hour with the Secretary of State and suggested that Germany should be gradually converted to an ally to meet the Russian threat in twenty years' time. This the Foreign Office could not admit (2 October). On 24 May 1945, Brooke wrote:

> It may be remembered that a few weeks earlier, when examining the desirability of dismembering Germany after her defeat, the C.O.S had then looked upon Russia as our future potential enemy (see 2 October 1944). This paper had created a considerable stir in the Foreign Office, who considered it very remiss of us to look upon our present ally as our probable future enemy. We might even have been asked to withdraw this paper had we not asked for an interview with Anthony Eden, who approved our outlook. Now only a few weeks later, Winston had come to us expressing his anxiety at seeing 'that Russian bear sprawled over Europe', and instructing us to examine from the military point of view the possibility of driving him back to Russia before the Americans and ourselves demobilized our forces! I asked him if he took charge of all the political aspects of launching a war on our ally! He said we could leave that aspect and concentrate on the military problem.

In fact, Churchill told his Woodford constituents that he had telephoned Montgomery in May 1945 'to be careful in collecting the German arms, to stack them so that they could easily be issued again to the German soldiers whom we would have to work with if the Soviet advance continued.' Fortunately matters did not turn out as badly as that.

On 15 September 1945 Harris relinquished his appointment with Bomber Command, and in the following month he submitted his 'Despatch on War Operations, 23 February 1942 to 8 May 1945'. Not unexpectedly, it contained some Harrisian views which were so slanted that the Air Ministry allowed it only a very limited circulation, and it was not published in full until 1995. The Air Ministry prepared a Confidential Memorandum giving alternative views of the Air Staff and other senior officers concerned, and this was attached to the Despatch when it was first circulated, and also when it was finally given general publication. 'It [the Despatch] contains ... a number of statements, opinions, and criticisms, from the personal standpoint of the Commander-in-Chief, which call for comment. An Air Staff Memorandum has therefore been prepared which amplifies some and corrects certain others of the statements made in the text'. (The hand of Buf may be clearly discerned.)

The most obvious correction concerns the formation of the Pathfinder Force. The Appendix states, with reference to Harris's paragraph 20:

17. The Air Staff cannot accept this description of the circumstances attending the formation of the Pathfinder Force. Nor can they agree with the suggestion that a better solution would have emanated from Bomber Command if they had been given a free hand. The argument may appear plausible, but it is, in fact, misleading, as it neglects to give due weight to the time factor.

18. The Air Staff discussed with members of Bomber Command staff in November 1941, the idea of forming a special target finding force. The C-in-C held a conference with his Group Commanders on the subject, at which (as also at later ones) the proposal was turned down unanimously. It must be pointed out, however, that this major and purely tactical problem was discussed, and a decision made, in the absence of any person from the Command with the relevant operational experience. The only officer present with experience of night bombing was an Air Ministry Air Staff Officer who was attending as an observer, and he felt strongly that if the issue had been put fairly and squarely to a conference of experienced operational personnel, the opposite decision must have been reached. The matter was considered of such importance that, shortly afterwards, in order to confirm this opinion, the scheme was outlined, separately and individually, to some 12–16 of the most experienced operational officers in Bomber Command, who were found to be, without exception, enthusiastically in favour of it.

[...]

20. The statement that 'the Commander-in-Chief was overruled at the dictation of junior staff officers in the Air Ministry' must, of course, be refuted. The idea of a Pathfinder Force (and its accompaniment of a Bomber Development Unit) was fully discussed within the Air Staff and with Bomber Command. The arguments for and against were carefully weighed by the Air Staff, after which the Chief of the Air Staff, after full consideration and discussion with the C-in-C himself, in a letter to the Air Ministry dated January 6th, 1943, requested that the PFF should be formed into a separate Pathfinder Group, and formal Air Ministry approval to this step was given on January 28th, 1943.

21. But for this prolonged discussion, the PFF might have been formed at least six months before it was – in August 1942. Had it been, it would have had the advantage of unjammed 'Gee', and the good weather of the summer to give it a good start. Nevertheless, its formation was fully justified by results, as within four months it had brought to light many points of operational importance, and it was formed in time to enable OBOE, the marker bomb, and H2S to be immediately and effectively exploited.

At the end of the war, Harris was a deeply disappointed man. On 13 May, Churchill broadcast to the nation and Harris and Eaker listened to it together, but with mounting incredulity. Of the strategic bombing campaign, or indeed of any bombing operations, there was not one word, apart from a side reference to damage done to Berlin. Harris fought long and hard for a campaign medal to be awarded to all the personnel of Bomber Command, but it was refused. The aircrews would receive the European campaign medal, but all the ground personnel would only qualify for the Defence Medal. In a letter to Trenchard he added a postscript: 'I started this war as an Air Vice-Marshal. That is my substantive rank now. With that and the 'Defence' medal I shall now leave the Service as soon as I can and return to my country – South Africa. I'm off.' Furthermore, he was not awarded a peerage, as were most of the high commanders. It may be that he was offered one, but turned it down on account of the insult he considered had been done to his men. On 1 January 1946 – after he had retired – he was promoted to Marshal of the Royal Air Force, but this served only to add fuel to the flames: he regarded it as a 'contemptuous sop' thrown after him. On 14 February 1946 he and his family set sail in the *Queen Elizabeth* from Southampton.

Harris was, without doubt, a remarkable commander. He inherited a meagre and demoralised bomber force and built it up to devastating strength and efficiency with an organisation that had to deal with aircraft, their crews, and their weapons, their servicing, their bases with ground personnel, the further training of aircrews, and the planning of aerial attacks against a clever and resolute enemy. He had to send young men out on missions with certain knowledge of heavy casualties and seldom visited them at their bases, yet drew from them a devotion almost amounting to affection.

It must, however, be said that most of the assumptions underlying his policies were wrong. He maintained that air attack by itself could bring victory, a view certainly not shared by the Chiefs of Staff, nor by the Americans; he opposed the loan of six of his squadrons to Coastal Command in 1942 at the height of the U-boat war, oblivious of the fact that those convoys were bringing the fuel on which his bombers depended; he maintained that area bombing of towns and cities would break enemy morale and make them sue for peace, but he gravely underestimated their toughness, the efficiency of the Nazi Security Police, and the availability of an almost unlimited slave-labour force for repair work; he poured scorn on the recommendations of the Ministry of Economic Warfare and on the intelligence sources which they used, labelling them 'panaceas' from ball-bearings to oil; he was not too much concerned about accuracy in bombing because at the beginning of his command his aircraft were not able to pinpoint targets, and later with the invasion of Europe when his bombers had to switch to daylight bombing on precise targets he admitted how surprised he was that they could succeed; and he bitterly resented being overruled from London, even by the Chief of Air Staff, on the issue of a target-finding force. Poor Bufton in the Air Ministry was ground between the upper and the nether millstone.

On one issue, however, he was right, though it concerned the winning of the peace rather than of the war. He was concerned to teach the Germans such a lesson that they would never again start a war of aggression. After 1918, within five years Hitler had established himself as a dictator bent on avenging defeat in the First World War. This had been a defeat of the German armed forces, not much felt by the German people at large. The Second World War, with its area bombing of towns, was quite different, and the Germans clearly learned their lesson.

CHAPTER 22

Forgotten Wars

'Iam not worried about the war; it will be difficult but we will win it; it is after the war that worries me. Mark you, it will take years and years of patience, courage, and faith.' So said General Smuts in 1941, quoted by Tedder in his memoirs *With Prejudice*. Tedder followed Portal as Chief of Air Staff in 1946 with the gigantic task of reorganising the Air Force. By April 1947, just under a million men and women had been released from the RAF and the WAAF and another 60,000 were due out by the end of that year. Only 2,250 officers who had held permanent commissions before the war were still serving, and so the quality of pre-war short service officers and those who entered during the war and were now being selected for permanent commissions would determine the character of the RAF for many years to come.

The quality of officers chosen was high and by the end of the year, numbers were sufficient. Not so with non-commissioned ranks. There was an urgent need for more trained men to re-engage and for 100,000 new men by the end of 1946 in more than 100 different trades. It had always been policy to move around senior officers every two or three years to different branches of the service to give them a broad view of the field, and so Buf, who had opted, and was chosen, to stay on, found himself posted on 7 July 1945 (a month before the atomic bomb had been dropped) to Egypt as Air Officer Commanding, though with a reduction in rank to Group Captain, on 1 January 1946. The Far East was in a state of turmoil, and remained so for years, and our vital line of communication passed through the Suez Canal. The Middle East also was troubled, not least in Egypt.

Following the completion of the Suez Canal in 1869, Egypt had fallen heavily into debt to European powers and, on the pretext of protecting its investments, Britain, in 1882 seized control of Egypt's government and in 1914 declared a protectorate over the country. After 1919 there was a series of revolts that forced Britain to give Egypt its independence in 1936, but Britain kept much control. In 1953, the Egyptian Republic was declared with Nasser as President, who, in 1956, nationalised the Suez Canal, prompting the Suez Crisis.

So Buf entered a very troubled country. Civil disturbances were soon expected at Regina Mansions, the residence of Air Headquarters, Egypt, and Buf gave orders that British troops should protect British persons and property but should not, if possible, come into contact with demonstrators. The police force in Egypt had previously been dominated by British advisers, but these were now being sent packing and officials were complaining of 'oriental slackness' in security.

Soon after his arrival in Egypt at the end of June 1945, whom should he meet in the Heliopolis Palace Hotel but his 'very dear old friend B. H. [Bert Harris] and his wife.' He found himself a flat in Cairo, and in August was busy organising an RAF contingent for the celebration of VJ Day, and in the evening a dance in a hangar for the other ranks. At the end of that month came the good news of the birth of Carol, their first child, on the 26th, though he did not hear of it until he received a signal of congratulations from the Chief of Air Staff, Tedder, on the 29th. For some reason the telegram from Sue's entourage did not arrive. Buf enjoyed himself with squash and swimming and reported to Sue that the temperature had gone down to 92°F. In September he managed a holiday in Palestine and sent Sue an olive leaf from the Garden of Gethsemane. The next month he had some home leave and was able to meet Carol, his young daughter. He did not neglect flying, for he had his own little Percival Proctor for the inspection of RAF units, and in October he managed three flights, each of one and a half hours in a Wellington.

There was another period of unrest in November, and Cairo was declared out of bounds. In February 1946, when Buf was preparing to hand over to Air Vice-Marshal Toomer, serious rioting broke out, starting with civil demonstrations at No.1 Base Personnel Office. After the main door had been broken down by crowd pressure, shots were fired by a Provost policeman and the crowd drew back. Two possible casualties were observed. There was no attempt by the Egyptian police or army to prevent the mob's attack. Just down the road from the Air HQ was the Midan Ismailia Camp, and a large and hostile mob attacked the hoardings that formed part of its perimeter. Five days later fire was opened by RAF personnel, killing one Egyptian and wounding four or five others. This was a very different Egypt from the one where Buf had trained in the 1920s.

Buf left Egypt at the end of February 1946 to attend a course at the Imperial Defence College (it dropped the 'Imperial' in 1971 to become the 'Royal College of Defence Studies'). This was where selected senior officers studied strategy, international relations and major issues of defence policy. Its basic assumption was that the RAF's principal function was defence on a worldwide scale, and in a world that was rapidly changing. Since the dropping of the atomic bomb the whole question of armaments had to be re-thought, and the jet engine had revolutionised the design and performance of aircraft.

The meeting of officers from the three services and from Australia, Canada and New Zealand with lectures by prominent political, civil and service chiefs was particularly important, not least because of the situation in the Far (and not so Far) East. On 15 August 1947, Parliament created the new dominions within the Commonwealth – Pakistan and Hindustan-India – and with it ended the Raj and also the Indian Army with its British officers that had done gallant service in the war. This partition resulted in the slaughter of tens of thousands of citizens in communal riots, but the old Indian Army remained aloof from this mayhem. The British Imperial presence lasted in Malaya until 1957 and in Hong Kong for another forty years, but by 1949 British Asia – the great crescent of land that four years earlier had linked Suez to Sydney in one swathe – had collapsed, and its last great proconsul, Louis Mountbatten, had left the region.

After 1945 conflict was far from over, with a new series of intense wars that raged throughout Indonesia, Burma, Malaya and Vietnam as a wave of nationalism, supported by communist China, swept the old colonialism aside. The disturbances even reached the RAF. Discontent was growing in Karachi, Delhi and Singapore at overcrowded conditions, inadequate leave facilities, poor rations and disappointment at the slow rate of repatriation. In Karachi, Air Marshal Barratt, Inspector General of the RAF, was howled down when addressing a large assembly of men at RAF Drigh Road. On 26 January 1946, the men at Seletar on Singapore Island had downed tools (there were more than 3,000 men in uniform there with 1,600 civilians). Air Marshal Sir Keith Park, the Allied Air Commander-in-Chief, arrived to address them. The next day the strike was resumed, and unit commanders explained the measures being taken to remove their grievances. The men were also told that the Government took an extremely serious view of their action and that unless they returned to work by 2.00p.m. the 'strike' would be regarded as mutiny. The trouble was over.

Two squadrons, Nos 205 and 230, were based at Seletar and No.88 was based at Hong Kong, all still flying Sunderland flying boats that had been in service for nearly ten years – the last operational flight took place on 15 May 1959. They were busy flying mail and supplies to the occupational forces in Japan. One load was an aircraft full of curry for Indian troops, and another was a load of Japanese war criminals, guarded by Ghurkas, being brought for trial. Such were the circumstances, military and political, that senior officers had to deal with.

On the last day of 1946, Buf was posted to the Central Bomber Establishment at Marham to command its Tactics Wing with nine subsidiary sections. There was also a Development Wing to try out the recommendations from the tacticians. The primary aim of the Establishment was 'to increase the efficiency of the bomber crew, aircraft and equipment in all offensive roles, and in defence against enemy opposition.' The methods were set out as follows:

(a) The development of tactics and operating procedures, including target finding and target marking for day and night attacks by heavy, medium and light bombers, primarily for strategic operation but additionally for sea and land warfare, using information, experience and intelligence gained in all theatres.

(b) Study of the progress of bomber development, in collaboration with the appropriate research and development Establishments, and the making of recommendations for the improvement of aircraft and equipment to increase the striking power of the bomber and to lessen its vulnerability in face of all forms of enemy action.

(c) To undertake tactical trials of aircraft and all ancillary equipment, in order to assess their tactical value and define their best tactical employment.

(d) The formulation of proposals and recommendations on bombing procedure, bombing methods, and training methods both for specific operations and for general adoption in the Royal Air Force.

(e) The formation of a tactical school where potential commanders and specialist leaders can be given a sound appreciation of current and future tactics, with practical demonstration and exercises.

These staff instructions might have been written for Buf!

By way of an exercise on 23 June 1947 he laid on a replica, somewhat shortened, of a meeting of the Combined Strategic Targets Committee. He explained how it came into being in the autumn of 1944 when control of the RAF strategic bombing reverted to Portal from Eisenhower, with weekly meetings in Whitehall (in Buf's office) for about eighteen members equally divided between British and American, with Bufton and an American colonel taking turns as chairman. Since meetings had averaged between three and six hours and the demonstration was limited to forty-five minutes, the agenda was reduced to four items but the material was drawn from its sub-committees. The subject matter and the methods used were then open to discussion.

In February 1948 (four months before the Berlin Airlift), Buf produced a comprehensive paper on 'The Development of Bomber Aircraft and Tactics'. He started by emphasising that, despite all the experience gained in the Second World War, we could not rest on our oars for three good reasons: the potential enemy was no longer Germany and therefore operating conditions were likely to be greatly different; the advent of jet aircraft had largely made our knowledge obsolete; and the advent of atomic weapons had made the solution of these problems a matter of overriding importance.

We did not expect a war with Russia, but it would be a waste of effort to design our bombers to any lesser requirements. This meant an operational radius of action of 2,000 nautical miles with a bomb load of 10,000lb. Buf then sketched the main features of the new bomber requirements already under construction: (a) B3/45 – the transitional or interim jet bomber; (b) The 'insurance' Medium-Range Bomber; (c) The Medium-Range Bomber; and (d) The Long-Range bomber. His comment on (a) was that it might well have a limited life as a strategic bomber but it had potentialities as a tactical bomber, trainer and photographic reconnaissance aircraft. How right he was! The Canberra came into service in 1951 and lasted until 2007.

The Medium Range Bomber was a different matter. Its design had to embody new aerodynamic features such as swept back or delta wings in order to achieve the speed and ranges required, and this involved some risk of serious teething troubles with delay in production. To guard against this the 'insurance' bomber was being built on more traditional lines in order to hasten production. (This turned out to be the Vickers Valiant, the prototype of which flew in May 1951, but it did not come into service until 1955. The more advanced designs produced the delta-winged Avro Vulcan, which entered service in 1956, and the Handley Page Victor with swept wings, entering service in 1957. The latter had a maximum speed of 647mph at 40,000 feet with a combat radius of 1,725 miles, but its maximum range was 3,500 miles with a service ceiling of 60,000 feet. It was designed to carry the Blue Steel nuclear missile.)

Buf spelled out the flight plan of the B3/45 (Canberra) as follows:

The fuel consumption is 120 gallons per hour when taxiing; and again at low levels consumption is 3 to 4 times that at operating height. When maximum range is required it will be essential to reduce pre-flight taxiing to a minimum, or eliminate it altogether by ranging aircraft on the end of the runway before starting up. It will no longer be possible to employ low level approach to enemy territory as a tactical

Three prototypes, clockwise from top left: four Canberras, one Valiant and one Valiant and two Victors. (*Aeroplane*)

Opposite: A 75 Squadron Lincoln flying over Lincolnshire in September 1945, painted white for tropical service in the Far East. (*Aeroplane*)

method; jet bombers will have to climb from base at maximum power to operating height if maximum range is to be achieved; indeed altitude must be increased progressively as fuel is used and bombs released. Thus the B3/45 should be climbed to 40,000 feet in the first 120 miles; climbed progressively to 44,000 feet over the target; when bombs are released a rapid climb should be made to 47,000 feet, followed by a progressive climb to 52,000 at a point some 150 miles from base, when height is then reduced. The jet bomber will involve some loss in tactical flexibility.

At such speeds, heights and ranges, navigation presented its own problems. Gee would not be of much use, nor H2S with its range of thirty-five miles, but the Navigation and Bombing Computer (NBC) promised to keep the aircraft and track until it came within H2S range.

As for actual bombing itself, Buf wrote:

This N.B.C./H2S combination should make it possible to use H2S to maximum advantage despite the fact that at 40,000 feet and 500mph with a 35 mile H2S range there is only an interval of some 3 minutes from the time the target response first appears to the time of bomb release. The blind bombing accuracy of the combination in the B3/45 is unlikely to be much better than 1 nautical mile. In addition the serviceability at the target is estimated at only some sixty per cent, at least initially. For these reasons, and because a number of important strategic targets may give no appreciable H2S response anyway, it has now been decided to fit the B3/45 with a visual bombsight. The sight will be a simple periscope one, not very accurate. Subsequent jet bombers will however be provided with a highly accurate visual bombsight. This will entail the development of new Pathfinder equipment and technique.

Concerning tactics (still then limited by the sonic barrier), Buf reckoned that the margin of speed between fighter and bomber would be between 30 and 100mph, and added 'a personal guess' that the fighter would maintain a minimum of 50mph until a supersonic fighter appeared less than ten years later (1948). Manoeuvrability of both bomber and fighter would be low, with a slight advantage to the latter. Jet bombers would also be unarmed, for to attempt to arm them would make interception relatively easy. Tactics must be based on evasion.

One further item made the future even more difficult to predict: that of guided or homing missiles, supersonic, and launched from either ground or air. Scientists working on them were confident that they would have the answer to the bomber within ten years or so, while those working on electronic countermeasures were equally confident that they would be able to defeat them.

The last item Buf mentioned was the problem of homing and landing large numbers of jet bombers returning to base from operations. Jet aircraft would not be able to circle base for a long time as some bombers had to in the Second World War, but he was confident of a successful solution.

Another aim of the Central Bomber Establishment was to pay a regular visit to each major Dominion in turn. The programme consisted of Australia and New Zealand in October 1947, South Africa in February 1948 and Canada in May 1948, with the purpose of bringing their staffs up to date with the latest planning and equipment of the sort Buf had been dealing with at Marham. The journey was in an Avro Lincoln, a somewhat enlarged version of the Lancaster, which arrived just too late for the war in Europe. It entered service in August 1945 with No.57 Squadron and was preparing to join Tiger Force to bomb Japan when the atomic bomb was dropped, and subsequently served in Malaya and Kenya.

Buf's team consisted of eight other officers, all specialists in various aspects of bombing and three non-commissioned officers to supervise maintenance work on the 'Crusader' (see front cover). They took off on 26 October 1947 and flew via Castel Benito in Tripoli, Habbaniya in Iraq, and Karachi to Ceylon, where there was a delay of six days because of engine trouble, then on to Singapore, Darwin and Sydney. Finally, they arrived at Whennapai, in New Zealand. Ten days there covered Wellington, Ohakea and Woodbourne and the return journey allowed visits in Australia.

On 21 November they reached Melbourne, and after a day of golf met the Chief of Air Staff, Air Marshal Jones and lectured to an audience of sixty. Buf met up with one Group Captain Noble, whom he had known at Heliopolis in 1928. In Sydney his audience was over 100. On to Brisbane on 7 December and Darwin on the 9th, then to Singapore on the 10th and home on the 14th via Bombay, Castel Benito in Libya, Cape Bon, Istres near Marseilles, Manston and back to Marham in Norfolk. On several occasions Buf noted 'self at controls'.

The South African trip lasted thirty-three days, from 17 February to 21 March 1948. It took Buf from Marham to Castel Benito, Shallufa, Khartoum, Nairobi, Palmietfontein, and Brooklyn (Cape Town). An additional visit to South Rhodesia was arranged in a Dakota of the South African Air Force, and everywhere they were greeted with great kindness and hospitality. The main themes of their lectures were bomber tactics and the development of the RAF in the Middle East, and of the Rhodesian and South African Air Forces. The flight enabled them to practise the technique of long-range reinforcement by standard heavy bombers, for such was their Lincoln II, minus its mid-upper turret plus three bunk beds and a divan. It was equipped with the latest Gee H2S Mk III G, but they did not find it much good over central Africa. Buf and his two colleagues took turns at flying the bomber. From Zwartkop they flew home via

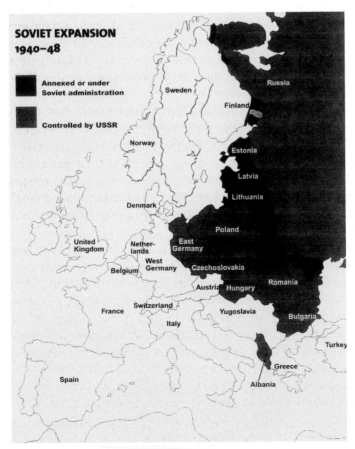

Map of Soviet expansion. (*Aeroplane*)

Kisumu, Khartoum, Castel Benito and Manston. They had enjoyed sixty-eight hours of flying time.

Buf's merits had been widely recognised towards the end of the war and after it had ended. In January 1945 he had been made a Companion of the Order of the Bath (Military), and in December he had been made a Commander of the Legion of Merit conferred by the President of the USA. In November 1947, he was appointed a Commander (with Sword) of the Order of Orange Nassau conferred by the Queen of the Netherlands. In December 1948, he was promoted to Air Commodore on his appointment as Assistant Chief of Staff to the RAF Element at the Headquarters of Air Forces Western Europe. The sky was already darkening over Eastern Europe. In March 1946, in a speech delivered at Fulton, Missouri at the invitation of President Truman, Mr Churchill (now not in office) had proclaimed:

> From Stettin to the Baltic to Trieste in the Adriatic, an iron curtain has descended across the continent. Behind that line lie all the capitals of the ancient states of Central and Eastern Europe, Warsaw, Berlin, Prague, Vienna, Budapest, Bucharest and Sofia, all these famous cities and the populations around them lie in what I must call the Soviet sphere of influence.

In January 1948, Bevin, the Foreign Minister, helped to bring about the Brussels Treaty, producing a defensive alliance between Britain and France with Belgium, Luxembourg and the Netherlands. A little later the western allies agreed to link their three zones in Germany economically, and despite vehement Russian protests introduced a new currency, the Deutschmark. On 24 June the Russians stopped all access to Berlin by rail, road or waterway along the agreed corridors of East Germany, and a week later declared that the western allies had no right to be there. Stalin began to move Soviet armour into East Germany, assembling forty divisions by mid-July as against the West's ten. On 16 July, the Third Air Division of the United States Air Force in Europe was established at Marham in Norfolk. On 21 June, General Lucius Clay, the Allied military governor in Berlin, ordered an all-out effort to relieve the siege of Berlin, and so began the famous airlift. (In January 1946, Spaatz and Tedder had made a gentlemen's agreement that certain airfields in England would be available and equipped to handle Boeing B-29s in the event of an emergency.)

The Berlin Airlift was the biggest air supply operation ever undertaken. On 26 June the first Dakota left Wunstorf for Berlin, Gatow, and the first of many US Air Force Douglas C-54 Skymasters flew along the southern corridor to Tempelhof. On 3 July, Yorks joined the contest (a transport version of the Lancaster), and two days later Sunderland flying boats from two squadrons joined in, alighting on Havel Lake. On 28 October, a Combined Airlift Task Force was established with an American General in command and an Air Commodore as his deputy. Flying continued throughout the winter and the one hundred thousandth sortie was flown on the last day of 1948.

Food was the main commodity carried, the RAF aiming to convey 40 tons daily for the garrison and 1,300 tons for civilians. For obvious reasons most of the potatoes, milk and eggs were dried. On 16 April a record tonnage of 12,941 was flown in, but that was exceptional. In April 1949 twelve nations, troubled by Russian belligerence,

A No.201 Squadron Sunderland on Lake Havel waiting to fly children to Hamburg in November 1948. (*Aeroplane*)

came together to form the North Atlantic Treaty Organisation (NATO), including Canada and the United States. Stalin received the message and on 5 May the siege was lifted. The aircraft had conveyed over one and a half million tons of food and fuel to Berlin, of which the UK had contributed about a quarter.

On 18 November 1948, Buf was posted as Deputy Chief of Staff (Operations/Plans), Allied Air Forces, Central Europe (AAFCE), with headquarters at Fontainebleau, some twenty miles south of Paris. The Commander-in-Chief was General Norstad of the United States Air Force who lived in a splendid house, built in 1814 and given by Louis XVIII to the Duc de Bellune. The camp had been designed and built in a clearing in the Forest of Fontainebleau, and was a tribute to the imaginative thinking of the US Air Force.

When Basil Embry took over the top command in 1953 (two years after Buf left) his guard of honour was composed of British, Canadian, French, American, Belgian and Dutch airmen at a parade of about a thousand. It is not surprising that he found it difficult to devise a scheme for united air warfare in a situation totally different from the war in which they had recently fought. In his autobiography *Mission Completed*, the last two chapters are headed 'Headaches' and 'Frustration'. No doubt that is why Buf has left very little in way of official records of his time there. Embry wrote (and it certainly applied in Buf's time):

> We are in an age of atomic plenty, and this means that both East and West probably have enough weapons available to undertake any major strategic offensive they may decide on ... Why then has there been this consistent reluctance to face realities of the situation? ... The total effect of using, say, a thousand nuclear weapons is so far removed from normal military experience that the mind fails to grasp it unless it can be presented in a forceful and dramatic way. We know that

one thousand bombs of the Hiroshima type are equivalent in energy release to twenty million tons of TNT ... Figures of this sort are hard to comprehend ...

Among the most backward thinkers in this respect are the French and United States armies ... In contrast with their army, the United States Air Force is up-to-date, far-seeing, bold and imaginative in its thinking and this coupled with modern equipment in plenty, high-calibre personnel and splendid morale makes it the most efficient and powerful air force in the world to-day.

Buf certainly worked hard with his international staff devising exercises that were not too much a re-play of 1945 planning. He got on well with the Americans, and one of Carol's godfathers was Major General C.B. Cabell, 'Uncle Cab', who thrilled her with a birthday gift of a bracelet. May 1949 saw the arrival of a new member of the family, a sister for Carol. In June Buf was invited to an International Miltary Meeting at Brussels, though he had to decline an invitation to an Air Demonstration by British Air Forces of Occupation (which had been the Second Tactical Air Force). He accepted an invitation from the Headmaster of his old school, Dean Close at Cheltenham, to speak to the boys about life in the RAF.

Sue enjoyed life at Fontainebleau. There were dances in Paris, in April 1949 the Gala Dance of the Paris Branch of the RAF Association, and in November the Annual Ball of French ex-prisoners of war. There were cocktail parties too, including one with Monty in June. Buf also enjoyed the odd game of squash with a Major Crosby.

But work was strenuous. In July 1950 he prepared a paper on the Higher Control of Strategic Bombers in company with three US observers, and in the following month he was heavily engaged with exercise Trials. His daughter Carol had to badger him to take her for a walk in the forest.

The international sky was growing darker. Operation Plainfare, the Berlin Airlift, took centre stage from June 1948 to May 1949, and when Communist North Korea invaded the South in June 1950 America realised it could not hold back. In December 1950 the NATO Council announced the appointment of Eisenhower as Supreme Allied Commander for Europe, backed by financial assistance with the Organisation for European Economic Cooperation in May 1951. In March 1951 the Headquarters of the US 7th Air Division was set up in England with a major programme to build up RAF airfields for the US Air Force. The strategic bombers were not yet ready and the RAF was forced to 'borrow' seventy Boeing B-29s, which were named 'Washingtons'. These had a range of 2,850 miles at 350mph with a load of 20,000lb.

In January 1951, Buf was appointed Vice-Chief Air Staff to be the Director of Weapons. As such he chaired the Herod Committee, so-called from the initials of 'High Explosives Research Operational Distribution', set up in 1948 to discuss and decide upon all matters relating to the introduction of atomic weapons into the RAF. It comprised all the senior officers responsible for the use and handling of these weapons, including the Commander-in-Chief of Bomber Command and an Air Vice-Marshal from the Ministry of Supply. RAF planning for the introduction of atomic weapons had begun in 1948 when the Second Air Staff Requirements specified that 'the bomb must be designed for use in any part of the world by service personnel who have been given adequate training in maintenance and assembly, and to this end must be made as simple as possible.'

When Penney returned to England from Los Alamos he was invited to design a programme for a British atomic bomb, and in 1950 laboratories were set up at the former RAF airfield at Aldermaston. Several working parties were involved in designing the non-atomic part of Blue Danube (also known as Smallboy), a structure weighing about 3,500lb to enclose the nuclear

of fifty-seven and a half inches in diameter and weighing, with two cylinders, about 6,500lb. To fit into the aircraft's bomb cell, length was limited to twenty-four feet and its diameter to five feet, and it had to be able to be dropped from a height of up to 50,000 feet and at a speed up to 500 knots.

The design work on the casing was done by the Royal Aircraft Establishment at Farnborough, who reported on 26 September 1950 that full-time ballistics trials had been carried out with models dropped from 28,000–35,000 feet from a modified Lincoln. The first dropping trials from a Valiant did not start until November 1954.

During September 1951, the Vice-Chief was able to report confidently to the Secretary of State that the Ministry of Supply development of the atomic bomb was nearing fruition and that active steps were being taken to ensure that the RAF was in a position to accept the new weapons and employ them effectively. As the bomb bays on British aircraft were longer than the American version, a somewhat longer bomb had been designed which would be more efficient ballistically than the American version, and its power greater than that of the (plutonium) bomb dropped on Nagasaki. The policy was to use the new jet medium bombers, initially the B-9 (which became the Valiant) for carrying the bomb – which was likely to be ready before the aircraft. Plans were well advanced for storage of the weapons and the training of personnel needed to handle the weapons from delivery to the RAF to their despatch on an operational mission. A training establishment was to be set up in Bomber Command to start work in about March 1953.

The development of a major new weapon for the RAF was a lengthy, complex and expensive business. By 1945 the Air Staff were clear that Britain needed a nuclear deterrent, and a report of 9 August called for a nuclear fission weapon and new bomber to carry it, relying on height and electronic countermeasures to evade detection. Proposals of 7 November 1946, from which the Vulcan emerged, required a radius of 1,500 nautical miles carrying an atomic bomb or 20,000lb of conventional bombs. On 7 January 1947, Specification B 35/46 outlined a medium bomber cruising at 350 knots at 40,000 feet. On 28 July, Avro were told that their bold delta wing design had been judged the best, even though its development might take longer than the other contestants (one of which became the Vickers Valiant).

On 27 November 1947, the Intention to Proceed was given to Avro's four-engined revolutionary triangular design with two (later four) one-third scale experimental aircraft, the Avro 707, the first of which flew on 4 September 1949. Very important was the bomber's navigation computer providing continuous dead reckoning. In August 1952 (when Buf finished as Director of Weapons), an order was placed for twenty-five Vulcans, expanded by October 1955 to eighty-nine, after the maiden flight of 4 February that year. During the course of its subsequent development (it flew until 1984) its engine-thrust was raised from 6,500lb to 13,000lb from each of its four jet engines. In July 1962, No.617 Squadron received a Blue Steel training bomb which, released at 40,000 feet, would free-fall to 35,000 feet when its own rocket-motor would light, boosting it to Mach 2.3, and when the propellant was used up the bomb would hurtle on to its target. Its research-and-development costs were £60 million, and it was reckoned to be obsolescent when it entered service. In the 1960s, the Americans offered Britain the Polaris submarine-launched nuclear missile instead, and on 30 June 1969, the Royal Navy took the task of nuclear deterrence over from the RAF.

In 1951 a great deal of development was in progress. In addition to the Valiant and Victor bombers, the first jet fighters were coming into service. First was the Gloster Meteor, one of which had the distinction of being the first to destroy a flying bomb on 4 August 1944. The much-improved Mk 8 reached a top speed just short of 600mph, but they were no match for the Russian MiG-15 transonic fighters in Korea. The other early jet fighter was the de Havilland Vampire issued to 247 Squadron in April 1946. In 1949, the FB 5 became a close-support ground-attack fighter-bomber and formed the backbone of the Second Tactical Air Force in Germany. This left the Air Force without an interceptor fighter and the Air Staff decided to introduce the North American Sabre (in its Canadian version) as a stopgap. Some 460 of these were supplied to the RAF, its first swept-wing fighters, with a top speed of 670mph and a range of 2,350 miles with drop tanks. All were flown to England between 8 and 19 December 1952, and the first squadron was formed in May 1953 in Germany.

This was eventually succeeded by the Hawker Hunter, whose first prototype flew on 20 July 1951 (in the middle of Buf's time as Director of Weapons). But it was not until July 1954 that No.43 Squadron received its Hunter F1s, and a good deal of modification was necessary before the F6 entered service in October 1956, with 379 in all being supplied to the RAF, flown by twenty squadrons. Its armament consisted of four 30mm Aden guns and provision for two 1,000lb bombs or sixteen rocket projectiles under the wings.

The first jet bomber to come into service, the English Electric Canberra, had been designed to Specification B 3/45 and was first flown on 13 May 1949. In the Mosquito tradition it was unarmed, relying on its speed to avoid interception. A later Specification, B 5/47, increased the crew from two to three.

This, however, is to look to the future. In December 1950, a month before Buf took up his appointment, Attlee, the Prime Minister, had been having confidential talks with President Truman, including discussion of the atomic bomb. Truman apparently told Attlee that 'he would not consider the use of the bomb without consulting the United Kingdom'. A month or two later the British produced the following

Vulcan with the Blue Steel missile fitted underneath. (*Aeroplane*)

rationalisation: 'The use of these bases in an emergency would be a matter for joint decision by His Majesty's Government and the United States Government in the light of the circumstance prevailing at the time.' Both governments agreed, and there the matter rested.

Modified B-29s of the US Air Force began to arrive in England in mid-1949 but were not atomic-capable until late 1950; exactly when the bombs arrived remains a mystery. There is a suggestion, incapable of confirmation, that a number of bombs, complete with the 'business end', came to be stored in the UK at the same time as the arrival of the aircraft. In 1947, Spaatz and Tedder were the respective Air Force Chiefs of Staff and as far as can be ascertained they acted on their own initiative. Their agreement remained informal and largely undocumented. The situation was not improved by the overnight disappearance of the diplomats Burgess and Maclean in May 1951 and the arrest of Fuchs in February 1952.

By the spring of 1952, plans for the introduction of atomic weapons into the RAF with all their implications for transport, storage, handling, training and location, had been fully laid down. On 29 August 1952, Dr Penney wrote to the Vice-Chief that the programme had been tight, and that it would be optimistic to assume that we should have a completely proven weapon in service before mid-1954. In fact, the first atomic bombs for the RAF were delivered to the Bomber Command Armament School at Wittering on 7 and 14 November 1953 – a historic month for the Force. No.138 Squadron was the first to receive Valiants in January 1955 and six months later it moved to Wittering where it could load up with the Blue Danube Mk 1 atomic bomb. In September, two of these aircraft flew on a proving flight to Singapore, Australia and New Zealand.

Britain was, however, a generation behind the United States and the Soviet Union. In November 1952, the USA carried out an experimental explosion (at Eniwetok Atoll in the Pacific) of a thermonuclear weapon many hundred times more powerful than the atomic bombs used at Nagasaki and Hiroshima, and on 12 August 1953 the Russians successfully tested a thermonuclear device. The first British test-explosion took place in South Australia on 11 October 1956 when a Valiant of No.49 Squadron dropped a Blue Danube from a height of 30,000 feet with the weapon exploding, as planned, at 500 feet. No sooner was this operation completed than the Squadron started preparing for the next, this time with a thermonuclear charge in a Blue Danube at Christmas Island in the middle of the Pacific Ocean on 12 March 1957. Over four months, eleven bombs were dropped, of which three were live nuclear weapons.

But again, this is to look ahead. In March 1950 the last Lancaster left Bomber Command. The Lincoln, its successor, was already five years old, and the V-bombers were not in sight. So the RAF was forced to 'borrow' seventy (later increasing to eighty-eight) cocooned Superfortresses, Boeing B-29s, from the US Air Force. One such aeroplane had dropped the atomic bomb on Japan. It was named the 'Washington' in RAF service and was welcomed by aircrew with its pressurised and heated cabins, but not by the ground staff who were unfamiliar with its construction and found the supply of spare parts difficult. Air exercises in October 1952 in which they attacked British cities demonstrated that they were easy prey to jet night fighters. The era of piston-engined bombers was over, and they were returned, with thanks, to the States in 1954.

In May 1951 the first twin-jet English Electric Canberra was received by No.101 Squadron at Binbrook, originally designed for a crew of three: pilot, navigator/plotter and navigator/bomb aimer. The lesson about navigation had certainly been learnt, but at the cost of signallers, flight engineers and air gunners. With a maximum speed of 570mph at 40,000 feet and a normal range of 2,660 miles it marked a new era in bombing strategy, and in various forms achieved an astonishing record of fifty-five years' active service, retiring in 2007.

Just as Buf's time at the Air Ministry was ending a letter came from the Ministry of Supply, dated 15 August 1952, inviting him to a special session at Porton Down requested by Canadians, 'to exchange views on service policies of respective countries on toxicological warfare generally.' This was another department of weaponry, but one shrouded in secrecy. During the Second World War the German Army developed to an operational level the lethal nerve gases sarin and taban while Britain kept vast stocks of mustard, phosgene and tear gas, but both sides refrained from using them for fear of retaliation. By the end of the war, Britain had stockpiled nearly a quarter of a million 25lb shells and three million aircraft bombs charged with mustard gas.

The post-war cabinet considered the development of a chemical weapon capability paramount, partly as a threat of retaliation to a potential aggressor and partly to enable the development of detection systems and protective clothing. There were two wartime research-and-production sites at Porton Down and Sutton Oak, St Helens, but in 1949 a more isolated research establishment opened at the former RAF site, Portreath in Cornwall, subsequently renamed the Chemical Defence Establishment, Nancekuke. Field trials at Porton Down indicated that sarin was the best course of action, and 20 tons of this chemical were produced between 1951 and 1956 for trials, and the resulting information was shared with Canada and the United States. Such were some of the problems confronting the Director of Weapons.

The year 1952 marked a turning point in the creation of the British nuclear force. Its creation had taken fifteen years and a thousand million pounds; the second period from 1953–1960 saw the production of nuclear and thermonuclear weapons and the V-bomber force. So it is not surprising that in August 1952 Buf was posted to the Headquarters of Bomber Command as Air Officer in Charge of Administration. In January 1953 he was promoted to Air Vice-Marshal.

In 1950, Bomber Command had two Groups (compared with six at the end of the war) containing twenty-three squadrons: No.1 Group with ten squadrons of Lincolns and two of Mosquitos, and No.3 Group with five squadrons of Lincolns, three of Washingtons and three photo-reconnaissance squadrons with a variety of aircraft. By the end of 1955, No.1 Group had grown to twelve squadrons of which ten had Canberras, and No.3 Group had two squadrons of Valiants and thirteen of Canberras, plus two others for photo-reconnaissance. In addition, there were four squadrons of Canberras in the Tactical Air Force in Germany. A vast programme of training and re-training had to be devised to enable this transformation to take place. As Buf had envisaged, Bomber Command set up its own Armament School at Wittering in 1953 so that, by the time the first atomic bombs were delivered there on 7 and 14 November, trained crews were ready to receive and service them.

The first Canberra to be delivered was to No.101 Squadron at Binbrook on 25 May 1951, and by August 1952 it had its full complement. In that year Binbrook became the first all-Canberra base. Selected aircrews were introduced to the mysteries and joys of flying jet-propelled bombers that could fly twice as fast and twice as high as the old Lincolns, and had pressurised cockpits with air conditioning. The Jet Conversion Flight was established at Binbrook with a Canberra and two Meteors, and December 1951 saw the formation of No.231 Operational Conversion Unit at RAF Bassingbourn. The ground crew technicians also had to be initiated into the mysteries of the Rolls-Royce Avon RA 3 jet engine giving 6,500lb thrust. Buf certainly had his hands full administering this Bomber Command, but just to keep his hand in he managed some local flying in a Meteor at Benson, including forty-five minutes solo flying.

In the face of doubts and criticisms of the expensive policy of nuclear deterrence, Lord Tedder made a powerful speech in October 1953:

Despite all the hopes which buoyed people up during the trials and horrors of the late war, the world has been forced to the bitter conclusion that the law of the jungle still prevails; that security without strength is a mirage and that, in fact, weakness invites and indeed provokes aggression.

National strength is not solely in military affairs; it is a complex of moral, political, economic and military factors, and weakness in any one might be fatal in the whole. It cannot be said too often, or emphasised too strongly, that the military strength which the free world has felt it necessary to build up has one prime objective – to prevent another war. It is questionable whether the two world wars, or indeed the Korean war, would ever have happened had it not been for both political and military weakness which misled the aggressor into thinking he could get away with it. Our object is to secure peace not by winning, but by *preventing* another war.

During the last conflict it was the war in the air, unforeseen by many and still not understood by some – which was largely responsible for altering the shape of the war, it became one of areas and it might well be that if there were a war in the future it would be one of continents. [Lord Tedder went on to identify the possible aggressor as Soviet Russia and emphasised that the history of Napoleon and Hitler should be sufficient to illustrate the folly of attempting land invasion of those vast areas.] Only from the air is Russia open to attack. There is still a tendency in this country to regard the war at sea, on land and in the air as separate problems. People forget or ignore the force which in the last war proved to be the one common factor, and did, in fact, unify operations in the three dimensions – the bomber force.

It is forgotten or not known that the bombers played a vital part in limiting the production of submarines, that the waters around Denmark were littered with German shipping sunk by bombers' mines. The end of the *Tirpitz* is forgotten. It is forgotten it was the bombers which were mainly responsible for strangling Rommel's supplies; that the bombers knocked the Luftwaffe out of Sicily and made the entry into Southern Europe possible; that the bombers strangled the communications in Northern Europe, hamstrung the German transport and grounded the Luftwaffe through lack of fuel, making 'Operation Overlord' possible. It is forgotten or not realised that, after the first round of the Battle of Britain had been so gallantly fought by day and night fighters, it was bombers that pushed the air war away from British skies to be fought out and won over Berlin. It is forgotten that the bombers had delayed the V1 and V2 attacks for vital months and reduced them to an unpleasant nuisance. The bombers were the only antidote to the V2.

Lord Tedder said he emphasised all this about the bomber – the offensive component of defence – because he felt it was absolutely essential to remember that purely passive defence with no offensive element was in fact no defence at all. In 1944 the Germans were producing more defensive fighters per month than the total British and American production, but they were, in fact, losing the air war and consequently the whole war.

Lord Tedder then spoke of the new developments in aircraft and weapons, concluding that, in the immediate future, it would be more true than ever that the bomber – and therefore the bomb – would get through. This included the subject of the atomic weapon. 'There are very sincere people,' he said, 'who would ban its manufacture or use.' He believed the armoured knights of old wanted to ban the use of gunpowder. He could understand the Russian proposing that the atomic weapon should be banned, since it was the *only* effective counterweight that the Western powers could wield as a deterrent. He continued:

> There are few people in this country who have more than the vaguest idea as to the fearful potentialities of the atomic weapons now in sight. The development of the atomic weapon has brought the world face to face at last with the ultimate realities of war. I am convinced that this country has a vital part to play in the scientific, technical and political field of the atomic world. If we play our part we can show an example of courage and determination, patience and faith, which will help to inspire the world and give *time* for the fundamental human rights of free speech and thought to spread over the whole world – time for truth to prevail. On this issue I agree with Cromwell: 'Let us trust in God and keep our powder dry'.

A further complication for Buf, though on a lighter note, was the Coronation Review of the RAF by the Queen at Odiham on 15 July 1953 when the fly-past included 640 aircraft, of which 440 were jet propelled.

By way of a change from heavy bombers, on 12 October 1953 Buf was posted to Headquarters of British Forces, Aden, as Air Officer Commanding. This was a surviving link of the old imperial route to the Far East, of which he had had a taste in Egypt. Aden's ancient natural harbour lies in the crater of an extinct volcano which now forms a peninsula joined to the mainland by a low isthmus on which was constructed a major aerodrome, known as Khormaksar (the modern harbour is on the other side of the peninsula). In the nineteenth century, and particularly after the construction of the Suez Canal, Britain became much more interested in the coastal towns of the Red Sea and many treaties were signed with tribal states.

In 1838, Sultan Muhsin Bin Fadl ceded seventy-five square miles including Aden to the British and the next year the East India Company landed Royal Marines at Aden to occupy the territory and stop attacks by pirates against British shipping to India. It was to remain under British control until 1967. It had always been a watering-stop for seamen, and with the advent of steam it became a coaling station as well. When oil was discovered in Arabia its importance for re-fuelling increased and 'Little Aden' was – and still is – dominated by the oil refinery built for British Petroleum, and much housing was built for the workers imported for these projects. In September 1953, a month before Buf was due to depart for Aden, he received a letter from Airwork Ltd with an offer to take out to Aden any personal effects, friends, relatives or domestics in one of their Refinery Dakotas. An invitation to lunch with their Directors was also thrown in. History does not record Buf's answer, though his wife and children did accompany him.

The region with which Buf was concerned was not a nation state, being inhabited by many different Arab tribes divided between numerous factions. The port of Aden had the status of a Crown Colony; beyond that the region became a Protectorate, based on treaties with tribal rulers offering them protection. Beyond that lay the Yemen up to the southern border of the Arabian desert. This became an independent state in 1918 following the Turkish withdrawal, but the Imam refused to accept the frontier agreements and laid claim to the whole of Southern Arabia, though the treaty system was ultimately restored across Aden.

The system, however, fell into decline after the Second World War due to economic development, shifts of population, and the growth of large-scale political movements espousing Arab nationalism, with further interference from the Yemen and from Egypt. So the authority of Aden's sultans, sheiks and emirs was steadily undermined, together with the British power base. Since the opposition to British rule was fundamentally political, military action could only oppose this to a limited degree. It could deal with Yemeni encroachment or tribal dissidence on a small scale, but was irrelevant to the broader revolutionary currents sweeping across southern Arabia in the 1950s and 1960s.

After the First World War, the British Government discovered in Iraq that keeping order was much more cheaply done by air than by land, and so in 1928 the task of defending Aden passed from the War Office to the Air Ministry. The bulk of the British garrison was withdrawn and the RAF's presence was increased from a single flight to a full squadron – No.8 Squadron – which was to operate in conjunction with locally raised troops, the Aden Protectorate Levies. The Yeminis were expelled from Aden at the cost of £8,500 above normal peacetime spending. A Treaty of Friendship was signed in 1933, but raiding across the trade routes remained a problem until the 1960s. In fact, bombing was resorted to very seldom and then only after warning and with property, not people, as targets.

Since the decision of 1928 that Aden and its Protectorates should be controlled predominantly by air power, the commander of the forces based there had always been an RAF officer, and the RAF provided the bulk of administrative services. Unfortunately housing for RAF personnel was very inadequate, with many sleeping on verandas. This, and the general discomfort of the Aden climate, made Khormaksar the most trying RAF station in which to serve. In fact, No.8 Squadron had the remarkable record of being stationed there from February 1927 to May 1967 with one or two detachments away. It

The Air Vice-Marshal at Aden. (Dr Downer)

started with the DH 9As, and when Buf arrived in 1953, it had the jet-engined Vampire FB 9 and in March 1955 it began converting on to the Venom FB 1. With sixteen of these there was also the Aden Communications Squadron of eight Valettas, and in January 1955 its Support Flight of ancient Ansons received modern Pembrokes. In July 1955 a Sycamore Mk 5 helicopter (later increased to four) became available, giving an average of thirty-two aircrews in all. In addition, five squadrons of the RAF Regiment were needed on the ground, and the Aden Protectorate Levies of native Arabs with British officers were very effective. The RAF also built a network of airstrips across the Protectorates, allowing both Government and military pressure to reach remote areas far more easily than before. The flow of intelligence improved considerably with the appointment of specially trained Air Force officers for this purpose. By the mid-1950s Khomaksar had become the busiest station in the RAF.

The year 1954 proved a busy year for Aden's armed forces. There was a recrudescence of sniping at Government forts and a number of raids from across the Yemen border, with a serious raid in May by the Rabizi tribe against the Government fort at Robat. A total of 186 soldiers were sent out, covered by Vampires which also launched three attacks in June with bombs, rockets and machine guns – attacks that continued throughout August and September. In October, the Governor received an unexpected invitation to meet the Imam of the Yemen in Taiz, with whom limited agreement was reached about the cessation of raids across the border.

Buf's responsibilities extended as far south as Kenya. A month after his arrival in Aden he had to 'borrow' Lincolns from No.49 Squadron to operate from Eastleigh from November 1953 until January 1954, with detachments again to Eastleigh and Khormaksar during 1954–5, to help put down the Mau Mau uprising. A detachment of six Lincolns from No.214 Squadron served at Eastleigh from June to December 1954, but heavy bombers were not an ideal way of dealing with terrorists in small nomadic bands often operating in mountainous territory. In April 1954, 8 Squadron sent a detachment of four Vampires to Eastleigh for a ten-day period during which they fired 12,700 rounds of 20mm ammunition and 111 60lb rockets. In October of the following year Buf was recalled to the UK.

After the British withdrawal from Suez, Aden became the pivot of our military power in the Middle East and witnessed an unprecedented build-up of military forces. In 1962 the one thousandth married quarter was opened at Khormaksar; in 1956 there had been fewer than a hundred. Although it qualified as a station for families, conditions were far from comfortable. Buf's wife and children were with him, and Sue had a remarkable function to perform when the Queen paid a ceremonial visit on

Vampire 9s of No.8 Squadron fly past in a neat Vic over Aden. (*Aeroplane*)

HM The Queen at Aden. (Dr Downer)

27 April 1954 on her way to Australia. The Governor of Aden was a bachelor and Sue was called on to play the part of First Lady, which she did with both elegance and pleasure.

This perhaps marked the high point of Aden's colonial history. In 1964 there was a 'bit of trouble up country', which required a brigade of troops from the UK to settle it. Then 1966 saw the beginning of a massive increase in urban terrorism, and 1967 saw the closure of the Suez Canal with strikes in Aden in May closing the harbour to commercial shipping. July saw a mutiny of the armed police, and 29 November was fixed as the final date for withdrawal. Nearly 10,000 families from all the services had been flown home between January and July, and from April to November 24,000 servicemen had been airlifted out, a remarkable achievement for the RAF. So ended 128 years of British rule in Aden.

CHAPTER 23

The Nuclear Scene

In October 1955, Buf was posted to Bomber Command as Senior Air Staff Officer, with responsibility for the operational side of its two groups, and held that post for nearly three years – vital years for that Command.

The whole pattern of attack and defence had been challenged by the German V2 rocket-bombs, and when Germany surrendered the Allies were anxious to lay hands on the engineers who had designed and produced them. Walter Dornberger, one of the main players, gave himself up to the American troops on 2 May 1945, and after a period in custody in England, he emigrated to America in 1947 to become a leading figure in the Bell Aircraft Company. Other German staff were interned in Britain and worked alongside British teams for several years.

After the Berlin Airlift it was clear that the next possible enemy would be Russia, and America worked hard on an Intercontinental Ballistic Missile (ICBM) that would take a nuclear warhead from America to Russia. This resulted in the Thor, but its range was only 2,400km or 1,500 miles, and so it needed a base in Britain. This was agreed to by the Prime Minister, MacMillan, in March 1957, and by 1960 sixty missiles had been stationed across twenty sites.

This posed tremendous questions for the RAF and the British Government. Did it mean the end of the heavy bomber? Was the heavy bomber an alternative carrier for a nuclear missile? Was the heavy bomber too obvious a target for Surface to Air Missiles (SAMs)? Did this, incidentally, mean the end of Fighter Command? In 1955 the Air Council issued an Operational Requirement OR 1139 for a missile that could strike Moscow with a thermonuclear bomb. The contracts were spread over a number of established companies and agreement was reached for these companies to have access to American research. The outcome was the Blue Streak, to be launched from a circular subterranean seven-storey silo that would contain fuel, crew, engineering shops and storage areas. By 1960 the estimated cost had risen to around £450 million.

In 1954, the Air Council issued a requirement for an air-launched propelled controlled missile, and A.V. Roe Ltd won the contract for Blue Steel. It became operational in 1962. After launching from a Vulcan or Victor it would free-fall for some sixty feet when its rocket motor would start and speed the missile up to 1,200mph and a height of nearly 70,000 feet. Its computer would then direct it to its target. This weapon produced many problems and was decommissioned in 1970.

When Buf arrived at Bomber Command in October 1955 it had already received its first Vickers Valiant B Mk 1. In January of that year, an Operational Conversion Unit had been formed at Gaydon to train aircrew for this radically new aeroplane, and in April No.138 Squadron became the first V-bomber Squadron at Gaydon, moving in August to its permanent base at Wittering. Before the end of 1955, two more squadrons had been formed, No.49 at Wittering and No.543 at Wyton. No.49 was charged with the responsibility of developing Britain's airborne nuclear weapons, and one of its aircraft dropped the first atomic bomb on a test site in South Australia in October 1956. No.543 received B (PR) 1s, specially adapted for photo-reconnaissance work.

Amid these startlingly new developments, early in 1956 the Air Council put in hand a study of the future Air Force, which was discussed by the Council in June, and it might well have startled the Air Force, not to mention the general public. The existing plan of 200 V-bombers would be reduced to 100 as Blue Streak came into service, and possibly bombers would eventually be replaced by ballistic missiles. Fighter Command would be reduced from some 500 to 200 aircraft as Surface to Air Missiles were introduced; another fighter after the Lightning and a successor to the V-bombers were envisaged in case the missile programme slipped; the Second Tactical Air Force in Europe was to be cut by two-thirds to some 130 aircraft, all devoted to strike and reconnaissance; and Coastal Command was to shrink from seventy to thirty-six aircraft. Overseas, the Middle East Air Force would remain as it was, but the Far East Air Force would be reduced to a token presence, to be compensated for by a bigger Transport Command. The Air Council assumed that National Service would be abolished, as it was due to finish in 1958.

Following the débacle of Suez in 1956, MacMillan followed Eden as Prime Minister and among his first actions was to appoint Sandys as his Minister of Defence. The annual White Paper was usually published in February, but the Sandys one was delayed until April, mainly because of disagreements about manpower: the Chiefs of Staff had maintained a minimum of 450,000 and Sandys proposed some 380,000, though the Army and the Navy were hardest hit. The Air Force's views on the deterrent concept and its implications were, in fact, similar to those of Sandys, as described in the 1957 White Paper: 'The overriding consideration in all military planning must be to prevent war rather than prepare for it'.

In 1958, Sandys delivered a stern lecture to the NATO Council, that Britain was spending more on defence than any of the European allies, partly because of its commitments for containing Russia outside Europe. 'It is essential,' he said, 'to ensure that our flank in the Middle East and beyond is not turned.' The V-bomber force was to have priority, and it did, despite the protests of the Generals, but Sandys could not defend the front line of 184 aircraft as called for by the Air Council. In August 1957, at a meeting of the Defence Committee, he secured the figure of 144, 102 of which would be Mk 2 Vulcans and Victors. With the development of the much more capable Blue Steel Mk 2 a credible airborne deterrent could be poised well into the 1960s. Its operational efficiency was taken seriously both by Sandys and by Bomber Command, hence the expensive scheme for widely dispersed airfields, overseas as well as home, and the quick reaction procedures which the Command perfected and demonstrated in training and exercises.

A minute from MacMillan to Sandys in August 1957 posed the question, 'What is the threat over the next ten years, the plans for meeting it and the military arguments on which they are based?' – a basic question which started an exhaustive debate. The Air Staff and the Joint Intelligence Committee laid out plans as follows: up to 1960, nearly 300 'Badger' Russian medium bombers backed by a large nuclear stockpile; from 1960 a similar weapon to Blue Steel Mk 1 with missiles to reach Britain; from the mid-1960s a new Soviet strategic bomber with a combat radius of 3,500 miles at Mach 1.7 at a height of 60,000 feet. Against such a monster, the Air Council argued strongly for a substantial force of defence fighters – but that is another story. It was a difficult time for the Air Force, but even more difficult times lay ahead.

Buf's time at Bomber Command from 1955–1958 was a crucial period in its history. In April 1955 the first V-bomber squadron was formed, with Vickers Valiants No.138, first at Gaydon and later at Wittering. No.49 Squadron joined it at Wittering and No.543 Squadron later in 1955, the former for developing airborne nuclear weapons, and the latter for photographic reconnaissance duties. By the end of 1955, three squadrons of Valiants had been formed, followed in 1956 by No.214 in March, No.207 in April and No.148 in July, all at Marham. No.7 followed in November and No.90 in January 1957 at Honington. No.199 was also formed at Honington in the autumn of 1957 for special duties connected with the development of various forms of electronic counter-measure equipment. In September 1955 two aircraft of No.138 Squadron made a proving flight to Singapore, Australia and New Zealand, and the first transatlantic flight took place on 2 September 1956. As early as November 1955, three specially modified aircraft pioneered flight-refuelling trials, using the probe and drogue method that came to be widely adopted.

One of the least happy episodes in the history of Bomber Command was the bombing of Egyptian airfields in the Suez Campaign Operation Musketeer, with the Valiant XD 814 of No.148 Squadron dropping its first bomb on 31 October 1956. Four Valiant Squadrons took part from a base at Luqa in Malta, along with four Canberra Squadrons in Cyprus. One of these, No.10 Squadron, flying from Nicosia, opened the attack by bombing Almaza airfield in Cairo on 26 October. The campaign was a notable failure, leading to the loss of British control of the Suez Canal, the greatly increased hostility of Egypt and the resignation of Eden as Prime Minister. One Canberra pilot was so convinced of the folly of the undertaking that he refused to take-off. He was court-marshalled and dismissed the service.

Bomber Command was ill prepared for this active service, with the Valiants in particular lacking essential equipment. Their bombing system was not yet fully operational; no visual bombsights were fitted; Gee-H could not be used because there were no ground stations and so the crews had to rely on a Doppler system backed up by a periscope sextant; and their aircraft were hastily fitted with T2 bombsights. It is not surprising that only limited damage was done to the targets, which were mainly airfields and barracks. Many useful lessons were learned by the command, calling for some hard thinking about organisation, techniques, equipment and training.

A week after a Valiant dropped Britain's first nuclear bomb at Christmas Island, the Avro Vulcan, second of the RAFs V-bombers, entered service when No.83 Squadron at Waddington received four aircraft on loan from No.230 Operation Conversion Unit on 21 May 1957, receiving its own aircraft in July. In August 1960 it moved to Scampton, ready to receive the Mk B2. Next came No.101 Squadron, formed at Finningley in October 1957, and on 1 May 1958, No.617 Squadron – the 'Dambusters' – re-formed on the Mk 1. These were followed by 44 Squadron in August 1960 and No.50 in August 1961. Altogether there were nine Vulcan Squadrons with eight aircraft each.

83 Squadron Vulcan B2s at Scampton in May 1961. (*Aeroplane*)

One crew from each squadron was at fifteen-minutes' readiness to scramble on its war mission. If political tension increased, the whole V-force would be deployed in groups of two or four aircraft at some fifty airfields throughout Britain, including Scotland and Northern Ireland. The crews would eat, sleep and rest near their aircraft at instant readiness. The Bomber Controller operated from the familiar Bomber Command Headquarters at High Wycombe, with his senior officers' gallery behind him, and his message went out to all V-bombers. At 'Readiness 05' crews would remain in their aircraft for about five hours. At 'Readiness 02' crews on dispersal would start engines and taxi on to the runway for a maximum of about forty-five minutes, with the order to scramble. Aircraft in twos and fours would get airborne, generally in less than two minutes, and in the air each aeroplane had to receive positive clearance to proceed: if they had not received this by the time they had reached 8° east they would automatically turn back. If the Bomber Controller wished to recall the whole force he would send out a Scramble Cancellation Order.

A nuclear attack was an intensely complex business: the route and height of the attack, the avoidance of Soviet Surface To Air Missiles, the finding of the target, the release and guiding of the nuclear missile, and then escape from the nuclear explosion, with aircraft eventually reaching a height of 56,000 feet, and hoping that their home bases still existed. No wonder Bomber Command had to set up its own Bomber School! Buf was at the heart of this vital development.

In August 1958, two weeks after Buf's term expired, the first Douglas Thor Intermediate Range Ballistic Missile Squadron, No.77 in Bomber Command, was formed, and the first missile was handed over on 19 September.

CHAPTER 24

Know Your Enemy

On 1 August 1958, Buf took up the post of Vice-Chief of Air Staff (Intelligence), with the rank of Air Vice-Marshal, and held this for the last three years of his RAF service. The post was a relatively new one, having been created in April 1941, at the end of the 'beam wars'. Before the war the Directorate of Intelligence consisted of a Director, three Deputy Directors, one Assistant Director and a Map Branch. Photographic intelligence was served by a single squadron leader. The total staff of Air Intelligence was some forty officers of whom about half were retired from the Army. At the outbreak of war regular officers were in short supply, and so it was necessary to recruit civilians, who were given a week's training course.

By April 1941 the original Directorate had grown substantially and its Director was upgraded to an Assistant Chief of Air Staff (Intelligence), ACAS (I), of Air Vice-Marshal rank, with three new Directorates each of Air Commodore rank. The new DDI 4 took over responsibility for the study of enemy wireless traffic, their codes, ciphers and call signs, and the production of intelligence from decodes. At the end of the war in Europe there were over 700 members of staff within Air Intelligence, and it is not surprising that the machine did not run altogether smoothly.

The one new vital factor was Ultra, the breaking of the German encoding machine Enigma that was central to the operation of the enemy's army, navy and air force. This decoding, which started to be of use from January 1941, was done at Bletchley Park, the Government Code and Cypher School, and it had to be accompanied by the most rigorous secrecy. No one was allowed to mention the task they were performing, even between husband and wife, and by the end of the war, and for many years after, not one of the more than ten thousand men and women who worked there ever betrayed their secret. This was Churchill's 'goose that laid the golden egg'.

This absolute secrecy posed problems for the dissemination of intelligence derived from the messages. The actual messages had a limited circulation, approved personally by 'C', the head of MI6, Sir Stewart Menzies, mainly to Commanders in the field and heads of departments. Portal received them, but Harris did not. During the spring of 1942 the Air Section of BP came to realise that their daily summaries of operational reporting would have value for the Air Ministry and the home commands, and so a new series of such reports was issued under the name of BMP Reports (from the names of the three principal originators, Bensall, Moyes and Prior). The first was issued on 1 June 1942 to include the first 1,000 bomber raid the previous night. These went daily to a small list of recipients, including Air Intelligence and Fighter, Bomber and Coastal Command. They eventually had over thirty recipients, including the 8th USAAF and the Allied Expeditionary Air Force.

Enigma, however, was not the only source of wireless information. The actual interception of German wireless messages was the responsibility of the RAF Y-Service, with its main station at Cheadle. At the end of 1941 this unit had thirty-two officers and 1,443 staff (most of them women). This station, with one at Kingsdown with thirty-nine officers and 878 staff, intercepted the German low-grade Y traffic which then was dealt with by the RAF Y-Service. Cheadle had compiled an extensive library of call signs and frequencies which, by early 1941, had developed into a comprehensive Order of Battle of the German Air Force. The analysts who achieved this were known as computors (not to be confused with computers – unknown at that time) and from 1 January 1941 they produced a daily report on German air activity. The anomaly about intelligence being produced by a non-intelligence unit was approved by the head of the Air Section at Bletchley Park and eventually, in August 1941, the Air Ministry appointed a senior intelligence officer to the staff at Cheadle, who set about visiting RAF Commands, greatly improving relationships between the producers and consumers of that kind of intelligence.

The treatment of material derived from Enigma was altogether more difficult, owing to extreme security. Hut 3 at Bletchley Park was responsible for the translation and annotation of the high-grade German signals and for reporting the results to home Ministries and overseas Commands. Home Commands were meant to be served by the Air Ministry, but delays were inevitable. Eventually an Air Operational Watch was set up at Bletchley and from October 1943 it was able to send messages with varying degrees of urgency direct to home Commands. Bomber Command had its own Intelligence Officer, Group Captain Paynter, who had been cleared to receive Ultra material, and he visited Bletchley on 24 January 1944 when he was able to suggest improvements

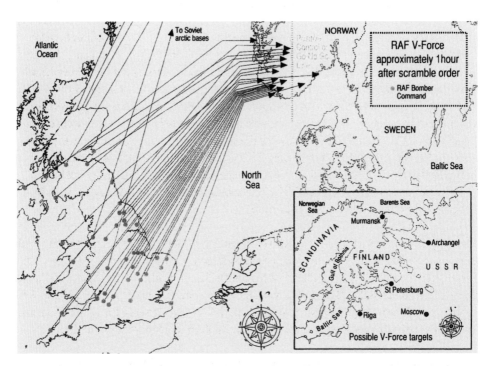

A map of the tracks of the Bombers of V Force approximately one hour after the scramble order. If the bombers had not received a positive message to continue by the time they reached the 'Go/No Go' line they would turn back for home. Map by Maggie Nelson. (*Aeroplane*)

in their reporting. His visit was followed by one from the Head of the Planning Staff from Bomber Command, and it proved an enormous help to the producers of reports to know how raids were actually planned.

The BMP reports were looked on with great favour at Bomber Command and in March 1944 the Bomber Command staff asked if the daily report from Bletchley on the night's raid and the night fighter movements could be delivered more quickly. Thereafter, the maps of the night raids and night-fighter movements were sent by dispatch rider to Harris at Bomber Command for his daily briefing. Further liaison was achieved by the detachment of an officer from Bletchley's Air Section to High Wycombe to provide as much information as possible about the previous night's raids. This necessitated a secure telephone linkage between the officer and the authors of the BMP reports, and it was not possible to obtain vital tactical intelligence more quickly than that, even if it had taken four years to organise.

Eventually, from May 1942, information from Enigma and Y-sources was fused, but for two years the resulting reports went only to the Air Ministry; none went to Bomber Command until June 1944. Some reports dealt with a limited number of subjects in detail, such as the enemy use of fighter assembly points, the measures taken against Mosquito intruders, the delays that happened within the enemy appreciation of emerging bomber tactics on any given night, and the height of flak detonation and the altitude of enemy night fighters over assembly areas and target areas.

In a comprehensive review of the Air Ministry's wartime work, written in 1947, Bottomley, who knew it from the inside better than any other RAF officer, wrote:

> One of the outstanding lessons appears to be the need for a first class comprehensive intelligence organisation on which to base our strategic decisions in the future. In the last war, the most important shortcoming of our intelligence system was in respect of economic, industrial and social intelligence of our enemy. The machinery which existed between the military and other Government Departments, with certain individual authorities which were capable of giving first-class advice, was not really satisfactory. We did not utilise to the full the wealth of specialist technical knowledge we had, certainly in the early stages. This is a matter which I know is now being rectified in a readjustment of our inter-Service and inter-departmental intelligence organisation; but it is a matter which needs most careful and periodic review, in order to meet changing conditions of the future.

The early 1960s was a time of financial stringency and General Templer had been asked to investigate the whole Intelligence Organisation and make recommendations. The Department of ACAS (I) submitted a paper on the functioning and organisation of that department. It started with the observation that intelligence is not an end in itself, but should provide warning of events to be anticipated, the background for policy decisions, and the data on which to base operational plans. Establishing correct priorities is crucial.

The Department's resources are at present (1962) directed towards the following tasks:

(a) To study the Sino-Soviet Bloc air and missile forces and to contribute to joint intelligence studies of the military policy, capabilities and potential of the Sino-Soviet Bloc.

(b) To provide technical intelligence assessments on current and future Soviet air and missile weapons systems with particular reference to nuclear delivery systems, and defence against nuclear delivery systems, and defence against nuclear attack.

(c) To meet the intelligence requirements of the United Kingdom nuclear deterrent by the supply of:

    I.   Detailed intelligence on the equipment, capabilities and deployment of the Soviet air defence system;

    II.   Target materials for pre-planned strategic air strikes;

    III.   Intelligence on the scale and nature of the air and missile threat to the United Kingdom; and by

    IV.   The study of war indicators and the alerting of the deterrent and the Air Defences on receipt of warning of attack.

(d) To maintain intelligence on foreign air forces (other than the U.S. and Commonwealth air forces) with whom the United Kingdom may become involved in limited, cold war or policing activities, as allies or enemies, and to contribute to joint intelligence studies and estimates of threats to British bases or interests overseas.

(e) To provide operational commands at home and overseas with air intelligence (including tactical targeting information as required) for the formulation and support of their operational plans, including overseas reinforcement plans and staging facilities.

(f) To furnish air intelligence as required in support of NATO, CENTO, SEATO.

Another paper deals with the staffing needed for these tasks, with the observation that the Intelligence community is at a disadvantage through having officers of fairly senior level – Squadron Leaders or above – who have not served in the Intelligence business before. Among the duties performed are:

Air ministry and London Staff	99
Group and Command Staff	72
Photo Interpretation	91
Signals Units	51
Station Intelligence	37
Air Attachés	38

Overall there are 443 officers and 1,250 airmen involved in Intelligence. The paper comments that there is sufficient variety of jobs to make an interesting career for officers, and that close association would need to be kept with the General Duties (flying) Branch. Such was the force (and more besides) that Buf commanded.

The 1950s were different because the potential enemy had been an ally in the war and retained overwhelming power on land and in the air. The ambition of Soviet Russia was world domination to be obtained by all possible means, and so the battle was for men's minds as well as their lands. One of the tasks of Buf's department was the monthly circulation of the Air Ministry Secret Intelligence Summary to be studied by all commissioned officers and qualified aircrew, to be guarded with great care and kept under lock and key when not in use. It carried a bold heading, 'Do You Know Your Enemy?' and stated that:

> To know your enemy is a prerequisite for the successful conduct of war. Study of the enemy, his character, motives, aims and methods, is the prime function of Intelligence. Appreciation of the information so gained should be the basis of military philosophy and training. In the past our wars have been conducted against nations and armies; today, we are still prone to confine our intelligence to studying and reporting military potential, organisation and equipment. We miss the point that the real enemy of the Free World is World Communism whose forces and weapons are all of the methods and means used to spread Communism and advance its aims throughout the world.

The summary certainly did not avoid politics and advocated instruction in our own political system as well as that of other countries, so that Communist methods of infiltration could be understood and countered.

Gathering and organising this mass of intelligence was a complex business, but it was concentrated in a Joint Intelligence Committee comprising, in addition to Buf, the Director of Naval Intelligence, the Director of Military Intelligence, the Director of the Joint Intelligence Bureau, the Head of MI6, the Director-General of the Security Service, the Director of Government Communications HQ, and representatives of the Commonwealth and Colonial Offices.

The first responsibility of the Air Intelligence Staff is, according to this Summary:

> To assess and to keep under constant review the size and nature of the air threat to our national security; what the potential enemy and his allies have got and what its capabilities are; where they have got it and what they are likely to do with it. Having found that out, the next job is to feed it into the defence machine – and especially to those responsible for operational policy and planning so that they can decide how the threat is to be met and how the maximum use can be made of the resources available.

The long-range bomber was, for the Soviets, a fairly recent innovation because in the war they had put their trust in massive land forces with close support aircraft. During 1945, however, they began their nuclear programme and on 29 August 1949 achieved their first atomic explosion (detected by a British reconnaissance aeroplane). Atomic bombs needed aircraft to carry them, and their programme was assisted by the gift to them in 1945 of a Rolls-Royce Nene jet engine that they quickly copied and put into production. They were also able to reproduce the Boeing B-29 (code-named Bull) which gave them a medium bomber with a combat radius of 1,700 miles and a bomb load of 10,000lb. By 1958 they were estimated to have 600 of these, but they were being phased out. The Badger, of which they had some 800, was a twin-jet medium bomber, comparable with our 'V' bombers, with a combat radius of 1,500 miles and a 10,000lb bomb load. The new heavy bombers coming into service were the Bison, comparable with the Boeing B-52, with four turbojet engines and a combat radius of 2,900 miles and a 10,000lb bomb load. The Bear, slightly smaller than the Bison, had four turbo-prop engines and a combat radius of 4,200 miles with a similar load. The strength of the two last types was estimated at twenty-five each.

The Soviets, however, had announced a successful firing of an inter-continental ballistic missile, and claimed that:

> The success in designing inter-continental ballistic rockets will make it possible to reach remote areas without resorting to a strategic air force which, at the present time, is vulnerable to up-to-date means of anti-aircraft defence.

The Air Ministry commented: 'Within the next few years the Soviets are likely to have a complete family of guided missiles with a nuclear delivery potential.' The conclusion was:

> The heavy bomber force can be expected to increase, and, with a fully developed flight refuelling force, the Soviets would be able to strike heavily at European and North American targets simultaneously. Thus, until the all-missile age prevails, the Soviet Long Range Air Force will constitute an increasing threat to the West ... It is disturbing that a technically adolescent power should have made such strides to maturity in some twelve years as to be now roughly on a par with the West in missile development and, in fact, to be ahead with some applications in the prestige race.

At least the Air Marshals cannot be accused of preparing for the last war instead of the next one.

At the beginning of 1959 the immediate Soviet threat to the NATO forces in Europe was the 24th Air Army deployed west of Moscow from the Baltic to the Black Sea. It was a predominately fighter force whose aircraft were comparable with their western counterparts, though their air-defence system had some deficiencies. Ground-to-air communications were poor, as was their early warning system. Bomber and transport forces were equipped with out-of-date aircraft, but the very large numbers of aircraft available enabled a great weight of attack. Units were able to change base and operate successfully with smooth efficiency. The article finished with the observation that the crews' patriotisms produced a determined, courageous and ruthless enemy.

A different kind of threat had also emerged with the completion, by 1959, of the Arctic air bases for the Soviet Long-Range Air Force. These would enable a Badger bomber to fly to New York or San Francisco and back and a Bear to reach Mexico, for America was undoubtedly regarded as the major potential enemy. In announcing the alleged successful firing of an inter-continental ballistic missile, the Soviets said: 'The success in designing inter-continental ballistic rockets will make it possible to reach remote areas without resorting to a strategic air force which, at the present time, is vulnerable to up-to-date means of anti-aircraft defence.'

In October 1958 the Summary contained a most perceptive article from a former Air Attaché in Moscow. He wrote:

As we have seen, the Soviets are forging ahead in the further development of ballistic missiles and their present inferiority in nuclear delivery is passing. They are realists and probably content to accept the present state of affairs, confident NATO will not attack them first and sure of their ability to pursue their own political aims without precipitating a third world war. Until their power to destroy absolutely the industrial centres of their potential enemies is an accomplished fact, the Soviet Air Force is a powerful enough weapon to back Soviet foreign policy and to demonstrate the facts both that the West no longer enjoys a monopoly in thermo-nuclear delivery and that the United States in particular is no longer immune from thermo-nuclear attack.

If the Soviet Union is adolescent today one is tempted to speculate on what sort of an adult will emerge in the fullness of time. The pointers are mainly depressing. While implicit belief in the principle of Communism may be lacking for want of spiritual satisfaction or sheer boredom with the incessant flood of propaganda and indoctrination to which they are subjected, the Russian people are growing to accept the policies of their leaders and to believe that, while much of what goes on in the Communist State is right, everything in the West – in the capitalist world – is wrong. To the Soviet citizen capitalism is symbolised by the United States and, encouraged to believe only the worst of life in America, the Russians are developing a violent anti-American complex which is now far more widely and deeply felt than it was even two years ago. Ignorance, misunderstanding and fear of America and the West seem to have obsessed the minds of many Russians, which is exactly what those in power intended to happen.

The NATO Alliance is regarded as an aggressive *bloc*, bent on the destruction of Communism by means of nuclear attack: the re-armament of Western Germany is represented as a deliberate revival of Fascism, also with the object of being set against its historic enemy Communism. The skill with which the political actions and declarations of the West are twisted to support the Soviet propaganda machine is remarkable. The Soviet Press and radio are now able to anticipate a Western political or military move, describe under what circumstances it will happen, ascribe to it the worst possible motives and then, when it does happen, shout 'aggression,' 'scandal,' 'disgrace' with all the confidence of a case proved in advance.

Such seems to be the pattern of the future. But there is one great hope, and that lies in education.

Although general education is pumped full of propaganda and specious arguments in support of world Communism, the thousands of young men and women graduating through the academies and institutes into the learned professions, the sciences and technical services are slowly beginning to fill the intellectual vacuum which existed twenty to thirty years ago. These men and women, no matter what their professional background...– from bacteriology to nuclear physics – have had their minds trained to think, and you cannot confine the thought processes of a trained and active brain. The voice of this new, intelligentsia may not be heard for some time but... when it is it will be too powerful to go unheeded by those in power.

Meanwhile, however, as I draw this report to a close, the *Kolektivs* and workers' organisations of Moscow have once more demonstrated the hold they have over the people. After several days of virulent propaganda directed against American and British action in the Lebanon and Jordan, a mass meeting took place in one of Moscow's squares, at which trained party agitators fanned the crowds to fever pitch and created deliberately and cynically a state of mob-violence which the police were unable to control until ... reinforced with armed troops. The American Embassy witnessed a demonstration of unprecedented violence and most of its windows were broken. The demonstration against the British Embassy was less violent but many of the demonstrators were drunk, and there were ugly elements in the crowd.

Not many days later I and my successor drove my car, bearing its English number plates, freely round Moscow. We mingled with spectators watching the air display and everywhere were smiles, greetings and goodwill. Three days ago we had been manhandled violently in the courtyard of our own Embassy but all that was forgotten.

This is surely the most encouraging contradiction of all, in this strange land. It encourages me to hold to my belief that the Soviet people are slowly making up their own minds what they want, what they like and whom they like, but the adolescence of this country will be a long one.

This is a brilliant piece of 'intelligence', a term which refers to both skill and end product. It has been well defined by one who worked in the famous Hut 3 at Bletchley Park: 'It means reviewing known facts, sorting out significant from insignificant, assessing them severally and jointly, and arriving at a conclusion by the exercise of judgement: part induction, part deduction. Absolute intellectual honesty is essential. The process must not be muddied by emotion or prejudice, nor by a desire to please.' (W. Millward in *Codebreakers*.)

This is an appropriate note on which to finish this account of Buf's service career. He retired on 13 October 1961 with the rank of Air Vice-Marshal with six medal ribbons, of which he said only four had any significance.

Basically an engineer, he was able to supervise the improvement of flares for night raids and went on to fight for the formation of a specialised target-finding force of heavy bombers against formidable opposition. When the Americans entered the war he worked happily with them, and in the invasion of Europe he played a key part in advising on appropriate targets for bombing. After the war, when the whole nature of air warfare had undergone a fundamental charge, he played an important part in the introduction of jet bombers and nuclear missiles. He also served in two of the outposts of empire that were soon to lose that status, and gained a first-hand knowledge of the worldwide political forces at work. His final post concerned the gathering, assessment and distribution of intelligence – basic to any armed force.

Buf was no armchair warrior. He was a skilful and bold pilot and took every opportunity to fly any aeroplane that came his way, from Moths to Whitleys to Spitfires to Lincolns. He was a tough and skilful player of hockey, tennis, squash and golf. He was a gifted leader of men and reckoned that command of a bomber squadron was the best task in the Force. He was a competent poet and painter. He was also a devoted husband and father, which meant more to him than all his other achievements. On retirement he reverted to his boyhood enthusiasm, radio, and for eight years ran his own company, Radionic, making radio construction kits. In 1967, his old county honoured him by appointing him High Sheriff of Radnorshire. He died in 1993, aged eighty-five.

Bibliography

Addison, P. and Crang, J.A., *Firestorm: The Bombing of Dresden, 1945*, Pimlico, 2006
Alanbrooke, Lord, *War Diaries 1939–45*, University of California Press, 2001
Aldrich, R.J., editor, *British Intelligence, Strategy and the Cold War, 1945–51*, Routledge, 1992
Ashton, J.N., *Only Birds and Fools*, Airlife, 2000
Ashworth, C., *RAF Coastal Command*, Patrick Stephens, 1992
Babington Smith, Constance, *Evidence in Camera*, Penguin, 1961
Baker, A., *From Biplane to Spitfire: The Life of A.C.M. Sir Geoffrey Salmond*, Pen and Sword, 2003
Bayley, C., and Harper, T., *Forgotten Wars: The End of Britain's Asian Empire*, Penguin, 2008
Bennett, D., *Pathfinder*, Crécy, (1958) 1998
Bowman, M., *Mosquito Fighter/Fighter Bomber Units of World War 2*, Osprey, 1998
Bowman, M.W., and Cushing, T., *Confounding the Reich: The Operational History of 100 Group (Bomber Support) RAF*, Patrick Stephens, 1996
Bowyer, M.J.F., *The Stirling Story*, Crécy, 2002
Brandon, L., *Night Flyer*, Crécy, (1961) 1999
Brendon, P., *Decline and Fall of the British Empire, 1781–1997*, Jonathan Cape, 2007
Brooks, G., *Hitler's Terror Weapons, from V1 to Vimana*, Leo Cooper, 2002
Cantwell, J.D., *The Second World War: A Guide to Documents in the Public Record Office*, H.M.S.O., 1993
Churchill W.S., *The Second World War* (6 Vols), Cassell (Reprint Soc. Ltd), 1952
Clarke, Robert, *Four Minute Warning: Britain's Cold War*, Tempus, 2005,
Clayton, A., and Russell A., *Dresden: A City Reborn* (2nd edition), Berg, (1999) 2005
Cooper, A.W., *Bombers Over Berlin*, Airlife, (1985) 2003
Cornwell, P. D. *The Battle of France – Then and Now*, Hobbs Cross, 2008
Crosby, F., *Fighter Aircraft of World Wars I and II*, Lorenz, 2004
Darlow, S., *D-Day Bombers: The Veterans' Story*, Grub Street, 2004
Darlow, S., *Sledgehammers for Tintacks: Bomber Command Combats the V1 Menace, 1943–1944*, Grub Street, 2002
Delve, K., *Vickers-Armstrongs Wellington*, Crowood, 1998
Embry, Sir Basil, *Mission Completed*, Methuson, 1957
Flintham, V., and Thomas, A., *Combat Codes*, Airlife, 2003
Furse, A., *Wilfrid Freeman: The Genius Behind Allied Survival and Air Supremacy 1939–1945*, Spellmount, 2000
Gardner, B., 'Tiger Force and Flight Refuelling', *RAF Historical Society Journal*, No.44, 2009
Garrett S.A., *Ethics and Airpower in World War II: The British Bombing of German Cities*, St Martin's Press, New York, 1993
Halley J.J., *Squadrons of the Royal Air Force and Commonwealth 1918–1988*, Air-Britain (Historians) Ltd, 1988
Harris, A., *Bomber Offensive*, Pen and Sword, (1947) 2005
Harris, A.T., *Despatch on War Operations: Preface and Introduction by S. Cox*, Frank Cass, 1995
Hastings, Max, *Bomber Command*, Pan, 1999
Hawkins, N., *The Starvation Blockades: Naval Blockades of WW1*, Leo Cooper, 2002
Hinsley, F.H. et al, *British Intelligence in the Second World War: Its Influence on Strategy and Operations* (4 Vols), H.M.S.O., 1979
Hinsley, F.H. and Stripp A., *Codebreakers: The Inside Story of Bletchley Park*, Oxford University Press, 1993
Hyde, A.M., *British Air Policy Between the Wars*, Heinemann, 1976
Hyde, A.P., *The First Blitz: The German Air Campaign Against Britain 1917–1918*, Leo Cooper, 2002

Lewin, R., *The Other Ultra: Codes, Cyphers and the Defeat of Japan*, Hutchinson, 1982

Jones, R.V., *Most Secret War*, H. Hamilton, 1978

Judt, T.,*A History of Europe Since 1945*, Pimlico, 2007

Knopp, G., *Hitler's Children*, Sutton, 2000

Lake, J., *Blenheim Squadrons of World War 2*, Osprey, 1998

Leaf, E., *Above All Unseen: The RAF's Photographic Reconnaissance Units 1939–1945*, Patrick Stephens, 1997

Maynard, J., *Bennett and the Pathfinders*, Arms and Armour Press, 1996

Meehan, P., *A Strange Enemy People: Gemans Under British Rule, 1945–1959*, Peter Owen, 2001

Middlebrook, Martin, *Nuremberg Raid. 30/31 March 1944*, Penguin, (1973) 1980

Middlebrook, Martin, *The Battle of Hamburg: The Firestorm Raid*, Cassell, (1980) 2000

Middlebrook, Martin, *The Berlin Raids: RAF Bomber Command, Winter 1943–44*, Cassell, (1988) 2002

Middlebrook, Martin, *The Peenemünde Raid, The Night of 17–18 August 1943*, Pen and Sword Aviation, (1982) 2006

Moyes, P.J.R., *Bomber Squadrons of the RAF and Their Aircraft*, MacDonald, 1964

Musgrove, F., *Dresden and the Heavy Bombers*, Pen and Sword, 2005

Neillands R., *The Bomber War, Murray*, (2001) 2004

Nesbit, R.C., *Eyes of the RAF: A History of Photo-Reconnaissance*, Sutton, (1996) 2003

Orange, V., *Slessor: Bomber Champion*, Grub Street, 2006

Orange, V., *Tedder: Quietly in Command*, Cass, (2004) 2006

Overy, Richard, *Bomber Command 1939–45: Reaping the Whirlwind*, Harper Collins, 2000

Owen, R., *Tedder*, Collins, 1952

Price, A., *Battle over the Reich* (2 Vols; 2nd edition), Classic, 2005

Probert, H.A., *Bomber Harris: His Life and Times*, Greenhill Books, 2001

Probert, H.A., *High Commanders of the RAF*, H.M.S.O., 1990

Richards, D., *Portal of Hungerford*, Heinemann, 1977

Richards, D. et al, *Royal Air Force 1939–1945* (3 Vols), H.M.S.O, 1953

Rolfe, M., *Flying into Hell*, Grub Street, (2001) 2005

Scott, S.R., *Mosquito Thunder: No.105 Squadron RAF At War 1942–5*, Sutton, 1999

Sereny, Gitta, *The Healing Wound: Experiences and Reflections on Germany, 1938–2001*, W.W. Norton, New York, 2000

Sharp C.M., and Bowyer M.J.F., *Mosquito*, Faber, (1967) 1971

Slessor, J., *The Central Blue: Recollections and Reflections*, Cassell, 1956

Smith, A. and I., *Mosquito Pathfinder*, Crécy, (2000) 2003

Stubbington, J., *Bletchley Park Air Section: Signals Intelligence Support to Bomber Command*, Minerva Associates, 2007

Taylor, F., *Dresden: Tuesday 13 February 1945*, Bloomsbury, 2004

Taylor, J. and Davidson, M., *Bomber Crew*, Hodder and Stoughton, 2005

Tedder, Lord, *With Prejudice: The War Memoirs of Marshal of the Royal Air Force Lord Tedder*, Cassell, London, 1966

Thetford, Owen, *Aircraft of the Royal Air Force Since 1918* (9th edition), Putnam, (1957) 1995

Thorne, A., *Lancaster At War 4: Pathfinder Squadron*, Ian Allen, London, 1995

Trevenen, James A.G., *The Royal Air Force: The Past 30 Years*, MacDonald and Jane's, 1976

Van der Vat, D., *The Atlantic Campaign*, Hodder and Stoughton, 1988

Wakefield, K., *Pfadfinder: Luftwaffe Pathfinder Operations Over Britain, 1940–44*, Tempus, 1999

Ward, C., *5 Group Bomber Command: An Operational Record*, Pen and Sword, 2007

Watkins, G., *Cracking the Luftwaffe Codes: The Secrets of Bletchley Park*, Greenhill Books, 2006

Webster, C. and Frankland, N., *The Strategic Air Offensive Against Germany 1939–1945* (4 Vols), H.M.S.O., 1961

Wilson, S., *Spitfire*, Aerospace Publications Pty Ltd, 1999

Index